The Historic Architecture of Wales

John B. Hilling

The Historic Architecture of Wales
An Introduction

University of Wales Press
Gwasg Prifysgol Cymru

© Copyright 1975 John B. Hilling

First Edition 1976

Published by
University of Wales Press
6 Gwennyth Street, Cardiff, Wales

Design by Fickling Seaward Partnership
Maps, plans and line drawings by John B. Hilling

Printed in Wales by South Western Printers Limited, Caerphilly

ISBN 0 7083 0626 8

Cyflwynedig

i

Helen

Contents

Appendices

Note: Textural notes and Plates will be found at
the end of each chapter

List of Plates

Note:
Plates 50 to 57 to follow Chapter 7
Plates 58 to 68 to follow Chapter 8
Plates 69 to 75 to follow Chapter 9
Plates 76 to 84 to follow Chapter 10
Plates 85 to 89 to follow Chapter 11

List of Line Drawings in the Text

Preface

Wales has had comparatively few books written about its architecture (other than vernacular architecture) and none, as far as I know, that deal with the subject in a general historic sense from beginning to end, or at least up to the early twentieth century. That is a great pity because it means that there are no other works to compare against this book.

There are, of course, all the books and articles listed in the Bibliography and I have avidly consulted these in my search for information, but that is not quite the same thing for they only deal with certain aspects of architecture in Wales.

It would, however, be entirely misleading if I were to give the impression that this book was written unaided. Indeed nothing could be further from the truth, for nothing can be written in isolation, and it is a pleasure here to acknowledge and thank all the many people who have given me assistance. Valuable help has been given by Mr. Peter Smith, Mr. Douglas Hague and Mr. R. G. Nicol of the Royal Commission on Ancient and Historical Monuments in Wales, by Dr. Douglas Bassett, Mr. D. Morgan Rees and Mr. John M. Lewis of the National Museum of Wales, by Mr. Robin Gwyndaf (Welsh Folk Museum), Mr. Peter Jones (Welsh Arts Council), and Miss Susan Jones. Drawings have been loaned (for copying) by Mr. Philip Allison, Mr. B. Hallwood Lingard, Mr. Alan Miles, Mr. M. T. Pritchard and by the Welsh School of Architecture. I am particularly indebted to Mr. Vernon Hughes who read the complete original draft and made many useful suggestions; to him I owe in large measure the parts dealing with Inigo Jones as well as much information gleaned from his card index of Welsh buildings. The greatest debt is to Professor Dewi-Prys Thomas who, over a long period, has read the various drafts a number of times and has suggested many ammendments and additions most of which have been absorbed into the text, indeed, probably something like a quarter of the text is directly attributable, in one way or another, to Professor Thomas. To both Mr. Hughes and Professor Thomas I am especially grateful, for with their fund of knowledge on Welsh buildings they have been able to give me invaluable information and have also helped me to avoid some of the more serious pitfalls. Nevertheless, as the final arbiter of the contents of the book, I have to take responsibility for any errors and omissions which are bound to occur in its limited length. Finally, I should like to thank Dr. Brinley Jones, the Director of Gwasg y Brifysgol, for his patience and understanding in allowing me so much latitude not only in dealing with the subject matter itself, but also in the general design and format of the book (so capably transferred to detailed design and layout by Mr. Peter Seaward) and, most importantly, for a very generous allocation of illustrations.

John B. Hilling, Llandaf, 1975

Chapter One Introduction

The Architecture of Wales is rooted in a social and cultural environment different from the rest of Britain and Welsh buildings often reflect a completely different historical background. David Bell has written in *The Artist in Wales* that 'the story of Wales — not only the wars and historical events, but the changing and the unchanging character of ordinary people's lives — is written as clearly on the stones and bricks, the stucco and the concrete of its buildings, as in its books.'

Architecture, traditionally 'mother of the arts', has been likened to 'frozen music.' More to the point, it is 'frozen history', for though the people that make history inevitably die and their written records may be irretrievably lost, the buildings in which generations of men and women live, labour and worship, often remain for many centuries. The walls of our buildings ring with voices from the past; the shout of triumph at Raglan, the cry of despair at Castell y Bere, the poetry of love at Ystrad Fflur, the hymn of hope at some Salem and the babble of children in the *tŷ-clom*.

Characteristics of Welsh Architecture

Sir Cyril Fox noted in *The Personality of Britain*, the tendency for 'greater unity of culture in the Lowland Zone, but greater continuity of culture in the Highland Zone.' Wales forms part of the Highland Zone, and her continuity of culture over two millenia is evident in the survival of her language, aptly called by J. R. R. Tolkein, the Senior British Language. Wales is in fact one of the residual areas of Britain, where changes occur less quickly. Traditions and customs are long lasting.

During the Dark Ages and later, the mountainous nature of the country hindered Anglo-Saxon penetration and at the same time helped preserve the independent freedom of the Celtic Church. Consequently, church design was still nourished by Celtic tradition and custom until the medieval period. Continuity of culture meant also that alien concepts were not easily accommodated and the infiltration of non-Welsh ideas into Welsh society from the outside was, therefore, gradual. Thus the last major Romanesque church to be built in Britain was in Wales, at St. Davids. The non-conformist chapel architecture of the nineteenth century in Wales likewise continued with the classical repertoire of design details associated with eighteenth-century churches and chapels in England. Although by the mid-nineteenth century most places of worship in the latter country were conceived in 'Revival Gothic' styles, in Wales this happened much later and only infrequently within the Welsh-speaking denominations.

1. Counties and regions of Wales

One of the main features of Welsh architecture is a difference of kind; that is to say, broadly speaking, Welsh buildings often fall into types of groupings, not exactly paralleled by those in the English lowlands. Usually, there is no hard and fast boundary to the distribution of the groups but within a given area there is more emphasis on one type than on another. Thus there is a marked concentration of megalithic monuments and Iron Age camps in Wales; in England these are largely absent except in the south-western peninsula. On the other hand there was a fairly even distribution of Roman villas and Anglo-Saxon settlements over most parts of south-eastern Britain, but we see only a sparse representation of villas in Wales and Anglo-Saxon work is naturally conspicuous by its absence. Remains of medieval castles are widespread throughout Wales except in the most inhospitable uplands; they are far less frequent in England and Scotland, except in the Marchlands. In England and Scotland again, the parish church is usually the most important feature in the nucleated village. In Wales the church is often small and situated outside the village; its place within the community may be taken by a nineteenth-century nonconformist chapel. The contrast holds good for vernacular buildings as well, at least when comparing their present locations.

A distribution map of the long-house, for instance, would show that this type of farmstead is well represented in most parts of Wales, but very localised elsewhere in Britain, being found now only in a few districts of Cumberland, Devon and Yorkshire and in the Hebridean Islands (fig. 2). Similarly, although box-frame wooden construction was commonly used for timber buildings in widespread areas of northern Europe, it was comparatively rarely used in Wales, its place being taken by the cruck-truss.

Another characteristic feature of Welsh buildings is one of size, particularly when compared with English buildings. Generally, Welsh buildings are smaller in size, simpler in appearance and more straight-forward in construction than those of England. This is not of necessity because the Welsh builder always preferred simplicity (on the contrary, the Celt is naturally flamboyant), but Wales has always been, for historical and geographical reasons, a country under severe pressures, and a relatively poor country with a sparsely distributed population. So the farms and churches of the uplands areas are smaller than those in the rich lowlands east of the English border. Even when considering the castles of Wales, it is immediately apparent that those built by our native Welsh princes are usually smaller than those built by the Norman-French invaders. The native castles were mainly built for defensive purposes, whereas the invaders' castles were built as bases for armies of occupation and fortresses for the military garrisons required to control the conquered territories. In the same way, castles built by the native English, in England, tended to be smaller than those built there by the invading French lords.

2. Distribution of the long-house in Great Britain

Welsh cathedrals are again diminutive when compared with the great cathedrals in England, although all the Welsh ones have extremely long and venerable histories, consequent upon our ancestors being converted to Christianity in Roman and post-Roman times, long before the pagan Saxons, Angles and Jutes coalesced as an English nation.

Physical Background

The architecture of any country is conditioned by the physical environment in which it is set. Buildings are also conditioned by the religious, social, economic and political environments, but these are in one way or another a reflection of the country's topography and situation. The physical environment includes position, relief, climate and structure. Each one of these affects building in some way. Position dictates accessibility to outside influences. Relief, together with drainage, largely controls the siting of individual buildings and of villages and towns. As much of Wales is hilly or mountainous, settlements are generally restricted to the valleys and coastal plains. The Welsh climate, wet though it is in most parts, varies from place to place and affects the type of agriculture and associated farm buildings and also the growth of forests and availability of timber for construction. It also affects the design of roofs. The structure of the rocks is responsible for the type of building stone available. While Wales is mainly a land of stone buildings, the colour and texture of the stone used varies considerably from one area to another. These variations in stone are closely related to the pattern of rocks underlying the soil, as in the presence of slate and the location of brickworks (fig. 3).

In earlier times, when transport was difficult, it was natural to use the most convenient material to hand and thus the rocks themselves contribute in no small way to the character of local buildings. Many of the geologically older rocks, for example, are so hard that 'dressing' and carved decoration is difficult, if not impossible, and the absence of any surface treatment of the stones gives the buildings of some areas an austere but immensely powerful character. The younger rocks on the other hand are usually softer and have well developed planes of weakness so that they can be easily cut and shaped to give a more finished quality. In other places a different appearance may be given by the use of stones that are worn smooth by the action of running water such as the river-washed pebbles used in the cathedral in Llandaf. In marked contrast are certain mountainous districts of Eryri where the readily available building materials were the very large rounded boulders which had been transported across the country during the last Ice Age.

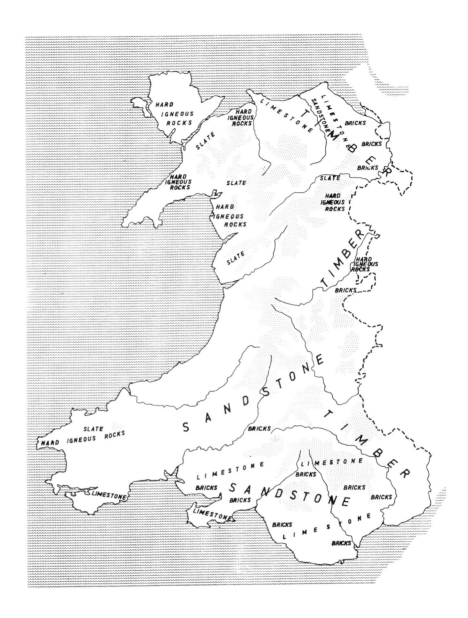

3. Distribution of building materials in Wales

The influence of masonry techniques on architectural character is well brought out by Harold Hughes and H. L. North in their description of some farm buildings, near Beddgelert, in *The Old Cottages of Snowdonia*: 'We note the enormous size of the stones . . . at the base of the walls . . . gradually smaller as the wall rises till, at the top, they are such as one man can easily lift. This is not only a practical arrangement, but gives great scale and dignity to the building. It is quite usual to see the lower courses of a cow-house, about 30 feet long, composed of five or six stones averaging from 5 to 7 feet in length. This, in contrast with the small slates of the roof, gives a wonderful effect of scale, almost Cyclopean . . .'

The colour of buildings also varies with the type of stone used. Thus in the Brecon area the dark red-brown hue of the Old Red Sandstone gives a distinctive warm effect to the buildings there. The commonest types of rock that have been used for buildings are the grits and sandstones which are found in almost all the geological rock formations. Formerly, there were many hundreds of small quarries in Wales from which these materials were extracted, for the stones were more easily worked and could be conveniently trimmed to the required shape and size. They were used both in the isolated farms of rural areas and in the straggling terraces of the mining valleys. Today, however, there are only a few sandstone quarries working outside the coalfields, but stone buildings are still widely distributed throughout most of the country.

Timber buildings, although once quite widespread in distribution, are now almost all confined to the eastern valleys and borderland areas. Up to medieval times most buildings over large parts of Wales — large parts of northern Europe in fact — were constructed of wood. Even the early castles and courts of the Welsh princes as well as the local churches were of timber; consequently most have perished without trace. In the eastern regions timber buildings developed from simple cruck-truss construction into more complicated box-frame structures with walls panelled in wattle and daub, resulting in the 'black and white' houses of Clwyd and northern Powys. In the south-west and north-west the scarcity of timber suitable for building led to the development of dwellings constructed of mud — a kind of everyman's concrete — sometimes with a stiffening frame of timber. Some of these houses, known as *tai clom*, still stand in localized areas of Ceredigion. The survival of the *tŷ-clom* — a type which is comparatively rare in most other regions of Britain — is symptomatic of the thesis mentioned earlier about the continuity of customs in our country.

Paradoxically, thatched roofs were likewise once widespread in Wales. By the end of the nineteenth century thatch had been largely superseded in the more populous districts by the ubiquitous slate which now, in turn, is being replaced by concrete tiles and roofing felt. But even as late as 1903 A. G. Bradley could still write in *Highways and Byways in South Wales,* that 'dropping down into Carmarthenshire and the Towy valley we have passed from a land of slate into a land of thatch . . . (this country), and still more Cardigan, boasts of the quaintest and most picturesque thatched cottages in the world . . . works of art that throw the thatched cottages of Devon and Northamptonshire, the best of their kind known to me in England, hopelessly into the shade. It is the artistic concealment of the chimneys in their braided sheaf of thatch, the billowing nature of the roof comb, and the neat coping of the fringes of gable, eave and comb, which gives the southern Welsh type a distinction unapproached elsewhere . . . today there are thousands scattered' (throughout Dyfed) '. . . whole villages . . . fifty years hence there will probably be none left' — a melancholy prophecy which has been almost fulfilled. However, walls have greater permanence than roofs and often dwellings — even the mud-wall cottages — still stand intact except for their thatched roofs which are now covered with slate, asbestos or corrugated iron!

Brick, first used here by the Romans, appears to have been reintroduced into Wales (probably from the Netherlands) in 1567 by Sir Richard Clough at Bachegraig, Clwyd. Its use in building construction spread very slowly and for a long time brick buildings were virtually confined to comparatively small areas in the north-east and the south-east. Today, in all parts of Wales, brick is the commonest of all walling materials, although even this is now often replaced by other manufactured materials such as concrete, aluminium, asbestos and plastics.

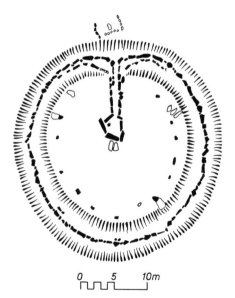

0   5   10m

0   5   10m

4. Pentre Ifan chamber tomb, Dyfed: plan

5. Bryn Celli-ddu chamber tomb, Gwynedd: plan

Chapter Two **Early Remains**

Prehistoric Beginnings

It was probably not until the end of the Palaeolithic period (Old Stone Age), that men began to settle in Wales. They were hunters and food gatherers and lived in caves or very crude shelters. Even during the warmer and wetter Mesolithic period (Middle Stone Age) that followed, man continued to live in much the same way as before. The earliest man-made structures that have survived were later still and consist of tombs dating from the Neolithic period (New Stone Age, 2500 BC to 1800BC). These megalithic chamber-tombs, or *carneddau* (singular: *carnedd*), were mainly built in coastal areas, particularly the south-western and north-western peninsulas and Anglesey, and also along the main river valleys, such as the Usk, Wye and Dee. Each chamber-tomb consisted of an internal burial chamber, or *cromlech*, constructed of tall upright megaliths supporting a massive cap-stone, which was entered through a stone portal and sometimes reached by a passage. The burial chamber was then covered by a large earthen tumulus, a mound either rounded or elongated, and often thirty metres or more in length; this mound has in many cases now disappeared.

There are three main groups of chamber-tombs. The earliest group is probably the 'long carneddau' of the south-east, which share similar characteristics to those found in the Cotswolds of England. One of the largest and best preserved of these is at Tinkinswood near Cardiff. It is rectangular in plan and has a dry-stone kerb wall around the edge of the mound (now gone), and a wedge-shaped forecourt at the eastern end leading into the large burial chamber covered by an enormous capstone one metre thick weighing about 40 tons. Other examples of this type can be seen at nearby St. Lythans and at Parc le Breos in Gower. The second group comprises the 'long carneddau' found in the western peninsulas; these also are rectangular but are distinguished by two curving lines of upright stones forming a semi-circular forecourt. The classic example of a western 'long carnedd' is Pentre-Ifan, near Nevern, of which only the great *cromlech* now survives on the slopes of Carn Ingli (fig. 4 and plate 1). Other good examples are at Trefignath and Presaddfed in Anglesey. The third group comprises the 'round carneddau', again found on the western seaboard. Here the outstanding examples are Bryn Celli Ddu and Barclodiad-y-Gawres in Anglesey (fig. 5). At the centre of the circular mound, each has an irregular burial chamber reached by a long dry-stone passage. At Barclodiad-y-Gawres, impressively sited above the sea, the upright stones of the *cromlech* are decorated with pecked geometric patterns and form one of the most remarkable and mysterious examples of Stone Age art in Britain.

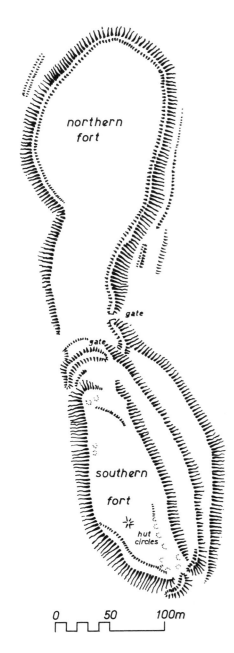

northern
fort

gate

gate

southern

fort

hut
circles

0   50   100m

6.   Pen Dinas hill-fort, Dyfed: plan

We cannot say how many of these megalithic monuments have been destroyed over a period of four millenia. Apart from the extant remains of twenty monuments in Anglesey, for instance, there was evidence at the beginning of the twentieth century of at least another thirty. Even now, throughout Wales, there are still over a hundred and forty of these great memorials to forgotten tribal leaders.

The Bronze Age which followed is again characterised by its burial mounds. These, however, are structurally and visually less interesting than those of the preceding period, being very little more than grass-covered hummocks containing individual graves. Historically, the most famous is Bedd Branwen, again in Anglesey[1]. The Bronze Age peoples also built numerous stone circles, but the purpose for which these were erected has been lost in the mists of antiquity. They were possibly used as tribal meeting places as well as for religious and ritualistic ceremonies. Stone circles in Wales are small when compared with the gigantic size of Stonehenge, which was of course, built by peoples of the same ethnic culture. Nevertheless, there is a strong link between the Welsh circles and the Wiltshire monument for the enigmatic 'blue stones' of Stonehenge were quarried on the sacred mountain of Preseli in Dyfed, an area steeped in Welsh mythology, and then transported to the plain of Sarum. The best known stone circle in Wales itself is Y Meini Hirion situated on the lofty mountain overlooking the sea at Penmaen-mawr in Gwynedd. It consists of 30 stones spaced at irregular intervals. Another well-known stone circle with monoliths varying between 1.4 and 3.3 metres high can be seen embedded in the circular churchyard wall at Ysbyty Cynfyn above the Rheidol gorge, not very far from Aberystwyth.

The period known as the Iron Age is denoted by the migration of Celtic peoples from central Europe into Britain. The first Celtic settlement in Wales took place about 400 BC, after which successive waves spreading westwards into the country brought with them their art, language and customs. By the time the Roman legions landed in Britain the continental Celts had lost their independence and had become assimilated within the Roman Empire. With the invasion and the resulting collapse of native resistance in what is now England, some of the Celtic leaders retreated to the comparative safety of the Welsh hills there to mount their last-ditch battles against the might of Rome. The territory we now know as Wales thus became one of the last refuges of Celtic culture in Europe.

The Celts of Wales appear to have lived mainly in fortified hill-top villages necessitated as much by growing inter-tribal strife as by Roman aggression. Many hundreds — over 500 — of these hill-forts, strongly defended by earthen banks and ditches or by stone walls, came into being all over Wales and the Marches. Most of the forts are over an acre in extent but some, particularly on the eastern borderland,

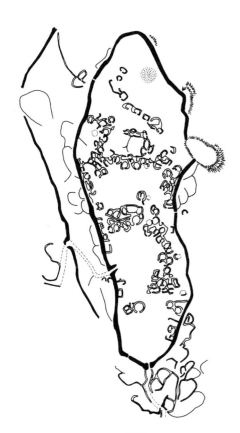

are very large and cover anything from 20 to over 60 acres.

The commonest hill-forts are of the bank-and-ditch type. At first the forts were normally surrounded by a single bank-and-ditch, but when it became necessary to strengthen the defences further banks and ditches were added outside.

On Pen Dinas, dominating the Ystwyth and Rheidol rivers where they enter the sea, there are two separate forts joined together by connecting banks (plate 2). The earlier fort on the northern summit of the ridge consisted of an oval enclosure with a single bank and ditch. This was abandoned in favour of a much stronger fort built with multiple ramparts on the southern peak; finally, the two forts were joined together by constructing two parallel earthen banks across the saddle of the ridge (fig. 6).

The stone-walled hill-forts are largely confined to the north-west. Tre'r Ceiri (i.e. *Town of the Giants),* in the Llŷn peninsula, is a remarkable example of a Celtic town surrounded by a massive stone rampart in places nearly five metres thick (fig. 7). Dramatically crowning one of the three peaks of Yr Eifl, 490 metres high and often shrouded in mist, it contains the remains of 150 stone dwellings, mostly circular with passage entrances, up to 8 metres in diameter, arrayed across the ridge in bands. There are two strongly defended entrances to Tre'r Ceiri, one of which also gave access to cattle enclosures protected by a parallel and separate wall on the western side, high above the sea. The most impressive encampment of the sort in the south is Garn Goch, four kilometres from Llangadog in the Tywi Valley. This fort is of unusual length — 700 metres long and 1600 metres in circuit — and its massive ramparts (still 6 metres high in places) must have taken many decades to complete.

Some hill-forts had an extra means of defence in the form of *chevaux de frise* comprising groups of sharply pointed stones set upright into the ground immediately outside the entrance to the camp. The best known example is at Pen-y-gaer near Dolgarrog, which had the formidable *chevaux de frise* in addition to the normal surrounding rampart wall and four successive lines of banks and ditches. The few hill-forts where *chevaux de frise* have been incorporated suggest that their inclusion may have been influenced by Ibero-Celtic refugees for, apart from Wales, the only other country in Europe where this unusual form of defence appears to have been used was Spain.

7.   Tre'r Ceiri hill-fort, Gwynedd: plan

Roman Interlude

The last wave of Iron Age people to arrive in Wales were a Celtic tribe known as the Belgae. They came in the early years of the first century AD and brought with them our first coinage system. Shortly afterwards, in AD43, the Romans invaded Britain for a second time. This operation was a complete success and within three years virtually the whole of southern Britain, up to the River Severn, had been conquered and was under Roman occupation. Some Belgic tribes retreated westwards and it was one of their princes, known as Caradog (Latinised *Caratacus*), who organised the Silures and Ordivices of southern and mid-Wales and led them in their thirty-year struggle against the Roman legions. It was not until the year 75, after a number of vain attempts, that the Romans were able to reduce the two tribes into submission. The final subjugation of Wales was completed in AD78 when the Venedotae of Gwynedd were routed (though not until a Roman cavalry regiment had been exterminated) and the island of Mona (Anglesey) occupied. Thus Wales became part of the Roman Empire. An era commenced which lasted for three centuries until, in 383, Magnus Maximus (Macsen Wledig in Welsh) denuded the country of troops in his bid to usurp the imperial throne.

The Roman occupation of Wales was essentially military in character, as might be expected, and numerous forts were erected all over the country at regular intervals of one day's march.

The Romans brought with them a standardised building technique, totally different from anything that had existed in Britain hitherto, partly derived from the Greek post-and-beam tradition and partly from the Etruscan system of arches and vaults. The Greeks' development of post-and-beam construction had culminated in perfected types known as 'orders'. The Romans introduced not only the Doric, Ionic and Corinthian orders of the Greeks, but also added two of their own invention, the Tuscan and Composite.

If the architectural forms introduced by the Romans were different, so also were their types of buildings. Instead of organically irregular hill-forts and circular dwellings the Romans laid out geometrically planned forts and towns on Mediterranean lines, and built forums, baths, aqueducts, temples and amphitheatres as well as domestic villas. Roman buildings were constructed of timber and shaped stone or brick faced with stucco, while their low roofs were covered with clay tiles; their concrete floors were sometimes finished with mosaic tiles. The extent to which the Romans succeeded in adapting their Mediterranean architecture (particularly their traditional low roof pitches) to British conditions is a matter of conjecture. They must have had trouble with the high and sometimes continuous

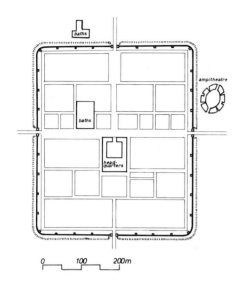

rainfall of Wales, and it may be well argued that when they left in the late 4th century the native British (proto-Welsh), saw little point in perpetuating some of the more idiosyncratic peculiarities of an architecture evolved to suit a climate much warmer and drier than theirs. In the event, as became clear after the Roman departure, there would be little time left for building, let alone architecture.

The military occupation was controlled from two very large legionary fortresses at the north-eastern and south-eastern corners of Wales, Deva (Chester) and Isca (Caerleon), each about fifty acres in extent. Over the years much of Roman Isca has been excavated by archaeologists. The permanent base for the Second Augusta Legion for two centuries, this fortress, rectangular in plan with rounded corners, was defended by a stone rampart with gateways at the centre of each wall and fortified towers placed at regular intervals (fig. 8). The enclosure was divided into two unequal parts by the main street, the *via principalis*, 7.6 metres wide, along which were placed the main buildings such as headquarters, corn granaries, treasury and hospital. The remainder of the area within the walls was rigidly packed with long, narrow barrack blocks arranged in pairs, each of which accommodated a company of 100 men commanded by a centurion. At Caerleon the foundations of one of these barrack blocks has been preserved.

Beyond each of the fortresses lay a small *vicus* (civil settlement), where the soldiers' families and the traders lived and where the shops and temples were located. At both Deva and Isca there was also a great oval-shaped amphitheatre built mainly as a training ground for soldiers, but used also for sports and public displays; fully excavated, that at Isca now forms one of the most impressive monuments of Roman Britain (plate 3). The arena, open to the sky, was encircled by an earthen bank which was originally buttressed with stone walls on the outside and terraced inside with tiered seating for some 6000 spectators. If the first Christians known by name in Wales, Julius and Aaron, were in fact sacrificed at Caerleon at the threshold of the 4th century as reported, they were probably martyred in this amphitheatre.

The auxiliary forts, scattered all over Wales, were smaller versions of the legionary fortresses and varied in size from about four to eight acres (fig.9). The excavated remains of two of these can be seen at Brecon (Y Gaer) and at Caernarfon (Segontium) (plate 4). Outside the fort of Segontium, there was also a small temple dedicated to Mithras. Cardiff Castle was built within the walls of one of the later forts and sections of original Roman masonry can still be clearly seen there, as well as a realistic reconstruction of the northern Roman gateway on its originial foundations.

The two legionary fortresses and the auxiliary forts were linked to each other by a

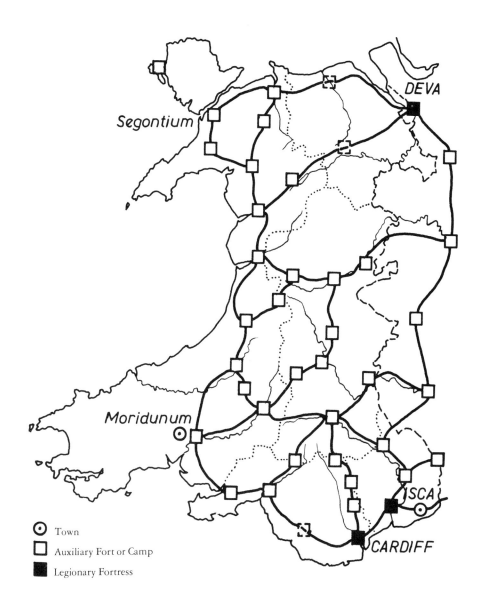

DEVA

Segontium

Moridunum

ISCA

CARDIFF

⊙ Town

□ Auxiliary Fort or Camp

■ Legionary Fortress

9. Distribution of Roman Forts and the Roman
Road Network in Wales

13

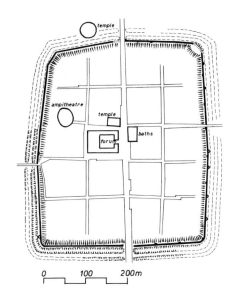

0   100   200m

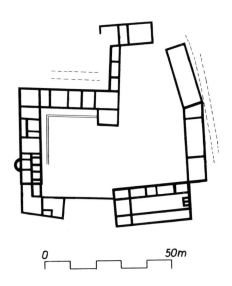

0   50m

10.   Roman town, Caer-went, Gwent: plan

11.   Roman villa, Llantwit Major, Glamorgan: plan

complete network of roads in order that troops could move quickly to any trouble spot. The roads were the first planned system of communication in Wales and, although the topography did not allow tracks as straight as Roman roads in the flat lowlands of eastern Britain, they usually had hard paved surfaces and avoided very steep gradients.

The only civil town designed as such by the Romans in Wales was Venta Silurum at Caer-went, in Gwent , built to replace the Silurian tribal centre at nearby Llanmelin. Planned in a manner similar to the forts, it was enclosed by a defensive wall, much of which still stands, and was divided into smaller sections by a main street running from east to west and by secondary streets running from north to south (fig. 10 and plate 5). At the centre of the town there was a *forum* (market place) and an aisled *basilica* (assembly hall). Nearby there was a temple and public baths and a small amphitheatre. Apparently there was also a small Christian church at Caer-went, built (probably at the end of the fifth century) on the remains of the Roman baths. There was also a considerable Roman settlement at Moridunum (Carmarthen); until recently this was thought to have been more of an adjunct to the auxiliary fort than an independent town community, but excavations may indicate a greater civil importance than was previously realised.

Roman villas are comparatively few in most parts of Wales. They were most numerous in the fertile coastal areas of the south, particularly in the Vale of Glamorgan, but others are known to have existed in the Usk and Tywi Valleys and in Anglesey. The finer houses with decorated wall plaster and mosaic floors were centrally heated by a hypocaust system under the floors which also provided warm water for the bath-houses. The finest villa excavated so far is at Llantwit Major; the extent and complexity of its outbuildings, which included baths, workshops, stables and barns, suggest that this was the centre of a rich estate (fig. 11). The floors of the house were covered in elaborate mosaic and the walls decorated while the stone for the columns was specially imported.

By the end of the fourth century the many forts, the town at Caer-went and the villas all appear to have fallen into partial disuse. Roman methods of buildings and sanitation became less viable and were gradually forgotten as marauding pirates constantly pillaged the coastlands. The indigenous tribes reverted to less settled ways of living but this was no reversion to barbarism. The Celts had been and were, after all, as expert as any Romans in the creation of artifacts as a comparison of native craftsmanship with Roman work in Britain clearly shows. It is, indeed, difficult to believe that everything was forgotten once the Romans left, for the Celts were themselves intensely Romano-British.[2] Moreover, while the Celtic inhabitants of Wales were pagan when the Romans came it is probable that the Romano-

British nobility at least were largely Christian when the invaders — by now serving a Christian empire — departed.

Celtic Survival

In the two centuries following the collapse of Rome Wales experienced, in the most extreme form, a cultural shock from which it took some time to recover. The causes of this cultural shock are plain but they are worth recording here as they go a long way to explaining why, for architecture, this period was a 'dark age.'

As part of the Roman empire Wales, along with the rest of Roman Britain, had become officially Christian by edict of the emperor Constantine the Great in the fourth century. By the early fifth century, following the withdrawal of troops by Maximus and Stilicho, Rome could no longer protect her province and despairingly a Christian Celtic Britain was accorded autonomous status within the fragmenting empire. At impossible odds the Romano-Briton now stood alone facing the assaults, from the south, east, north and north-west, of five invading pagan nations — Jutes, Angles, Saxons, Picts and Scots. Amazingly, even with continual reinforcements from the continent, it nevertheless took the three Germanic nations (of the five mentioned) over two hundred years to press westwards from the North Sea and the English Channel to the present frontiers of Wales, erasing during their long drawn out and exceptionally violent campaigns (often against each other) practically all trace of Christianity, Roman standards and the British language in the area occupied, henceforth to be called Angl-land. In this virtually continuous two-century long war of attrition there were many British successes such as Arthur's epic victory at 'Mount Badon' in 518 and famous reverses such as Catraeth (Catterick) about 590[3]; but in the final phase the British suffered two major defeats at the very gates of Wales, at Dyrham north of Bath in 577 and at Chester in 616.[4] With these two catastrophies the Cymry of Wales were isolated and cut off from their kin in the south-west and the north of Britain.

It seemed, all that was left of the Roman-British heritage in terms of religion, culture and language was now crammed into Wales plus a small area called by the invaders 'West Wales' (Cornwall) and a rapidly disappearing British outpost on the Scottish border known as Rheged. After their victories at Dyrham and Chester the Saxons repeatedly attempted to push further west. Repeatedly thrown back, they never succeeded in making permanent inroads beyond the present Welsh frontier. The Welsh defence was at once tragic and heroic. It was also decisive and in the 'dark ages' following the Roman withdrawal Wales achieved the unique distinction of being the only part of the western Roman empire which succeeded in standing firm and of not being overrun by Rome's destroyers.

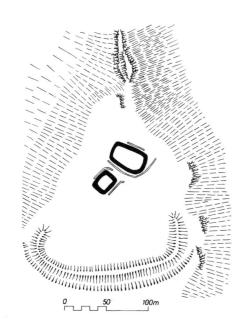

0   50   100m

The cultural result of concentrating so many energies on the defence of the last citadel of the British homeland was the sacrifice of material standards on the one hand and the development of extraordinary spiritual standards on the other. The rich fund of creativity latent in the Celtic imagination was sublimated in matters of the mind; a faith which stressed that 'The Kingdom of God is within one' also reinforced, in centuries of continuous battle for Welsh survival, the unimportance of temporal things — including visual architecture. The Welsh saints forged a spiritual church of sublime power; the Welsh language evolved as a kind of aural architecture of unsurpassed magnificence.

The fortress of Wales was defended as a number of separate kingdoms. In the north-west, Cunedda, a Romano-British prince who migrated from Strathclyde at the beginning of the fifth century, established order and helped to drive out Irish settlers who had occupied parts of Anglesey and Arfon. He founded the first of the great dynasties that continued to rule over much of Wales for more than eight centuries until the Edwardian conquest. Thus the leading power in Wales from the fifth to the ninth century was Gwynedd in the north-west, whose princes were directly descended from Maelgwn Gwynedd, the great grandson of Cunedda. By the mid-ninth century the ruler of Gwynedd, Rhodri the Great, had the whole of Wales apart from Morgannwg, under his domination. Before the middle of the tenth century most of Wales was united under the rule of Hywel Dda, grandson of Rhodri the Great and fourteenth in direct descent from Cunedda. In order to consolidate his kingdoms Hywel Dda codified the customs of different parts of Wales into a single and comprehensive legal system, an astonishing system which in some important respects was more advanced than anything in Europe; some of its principles have only been adopted in English law during the present century.

By the eighth century Mercia had become the dominant kingdom in England and there followed a period of intermittent strife between the Teutonic Mercians and the Celtic Welsh. Eventually, a compromise was agreed between them and the great earth embankment known as Clawdd Offa or Offa's Dyke (after the King of Mercia) was built, from Prestatyn in the north to the mouth of the Wye in the south, as an agreed frontier and barrier between the Anglo-Saxon east and the Celtic west. Although embattled and isolated from its neighbours on all sides, Wales continued to be influenced by their cultures. Thus, in building, ideas were borrowed both from pagan England to the east and from Christian Ireland to the west. Nevertheless, during the Dark Ages, a main and most important link was maintained with Gaul and Europe; a kind of life-line with civilisation.

During this traumatic Celtic period there was comparatively little organised commerce; towns could not develop. The people lived in small villages or isolated

12.   Dinas Powys hill-fort, Glamorgan: plan

16

0   10   20m

farmsteads. Apart from the *llys* of a local noble or prince the buildings were invariably small and in most parts of Wales were usually made of perishable materials. Occasionally a Roman fort may have been re-occupied as an easily defended *llys;* the Iron Age hill-forts were certainly re-used for that purpose. One such hill-fort was Dinas Powys, near Cardiff, which was occupied during the fifth and sixth centuries. Discoveries of wine jars and continental pottery there show that trade was still being pursued between Wales and the Mediterranean lands. The arrangement of drainage gullies within the enclosure of the camp at Dinas Powys suggests that the *llys* included two rectangular buildings with rounded corners and hipped roofs set at right angles to each other (fig. 12). Similar sites in Gwynedd are sometimes associated with princely families. Thus Dinas Emrys is traditionally linked with Ambrosius, a fifth-century ruler, Garn Boduan was the residence of the sons of Owain Gwynedd and Plas Cadnant is supposed to have been the home of the mother of Rhodri the Great.

In the north remains of enclosed farmsteads show both Roman and Irish influence. Pant y Saer, in Anglesey, is a good example of the type of enclosed settlement found throughout the north-west. The enclosing wall, 2.5 metres thick, is oval in plan and resembles an Irish *rath* (fig. 13). Inside there are two circular dwellings one of which contains a raised stone bench used for sleeping and sitting. Not far away are the remains of Din Llugwy, a fourth-century chieftain's farmstead or *llys* which shows the effect of Roman influence superimposed on the native tradition. Here the enclosing walls are straight, forming a pentagonal court around which were placed six rectangular dry-stone buildings (fig. 14). In addition, there are also two circular dwellings built in the traditional Celtic manner (plate 6).

In Gwynedd, where stone was easily available, the remains of numerous circular huts are still visible on the hillsides. Excavated examples prove to have been occupied during the latter part of the Roman period and they may well have continued in use long after. Often the huts were grouped inside an enclosure in a similar manner to the hut circles at Tre'r Ceiri hill-fort. The circular huts presumably had thatched roofs supported on central poles while upright stone slabs probably marked the positions of beds and seats. Many of the enclosed hut groups, such as those on Holyhead Island, are still known as 'Cytiau Gwyddelod' (Irishmen's Huts) or 'Muriau'r Gwyddelod' (Walls of the Irishmen), a reference to the tradition (unsupported, however, by archaeological evidence) that these were the settlements of the Goidels or Irish who were driven out by the Brythonic Celts during the fifth century.[5]

0   10   20m

13.   Pant y Saer farmstead, Gwynedd: plan

14.   Din Llugwy farmstead, Gwynedd: plan

When we come to the later Celtic or early Welsh period remains of secular buildings are virtually non-existent and it is necessary to rely almost entirely upon literary

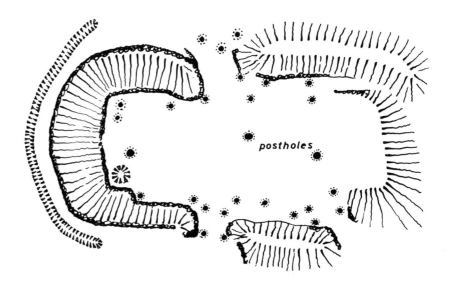

posttholes

original ground level

15. Platform house, Gelli-gaer Common,
Glamorgan: elevation, plan and section

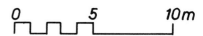

evidence. Our climate and the wars (particularly the later deprivations inflicted by Normans) have wiped out pages of our history. Fortunately, the Welsh laws compiled by Hywel Dda in the tenth century shed invaluable light on the way in which buildings were arranged and constructed. The laws specifically stipulate nine buildings for the king, thus suggesting that the royal *llys* comprised a collection of separate structures surrounding the main hall. The nine buildings were the great hall, chambers, kitchens, chapel, barn, kiln-house, privy, stables and dog-kennels. The hall itself was, according to the Laws, constructed with six columns to support the roof and may therefore have been built with two parallel rows of timber posts or crucks, three on each side, to form a central living area and side aisles for sleeping as in the aisled-halls found in Ireland. Effectively, the Laws of Hywel Dda incorporated the first known building regulations of Britain. They include some stringent fire regulations, e.g. in a township no smithy could be erected within nine paces of adjoining buildings, and because of the hazard of its forge, strict conditions were laid down specifying the use of non-combustible roofing materials, and which materials were illegal.[6]

A distinctive form of early house type is known as a 'platform house' because of the way in which it was built outwards on an artificially levelled platform across the sloping hillside. Remains excavated at Gelli-gaer Common, Glamorgan, show that these homesteads were rectangular buildings constructed of timber or stone with a pitched roof carried on a central ridge pole which may have been supported on timber columns (fig. 15). In the north-west the structures were sometimes grouped side by side on a levelled platform as was apparently the case with Llys Bradwen, the home of a seventh century *pendefig* (i.e. noble), Ednywain ap Bradwen, sited on the lower slopes of Cadair Idris above Arthog. The remains of platform houses are in all cases so scanty, however, that accurate dating is extremely difficult. Examples of varying sizes have been discovered in many parts of Wales and over a wide range of altitudes. While some of these sites may represent very early homesteads dating from the latter part of the Celtic period, others could equally well be examples of the farmer's *hafod* (temporary summer-house) built in the late Middle Ages but still within a native constructional tradition.

Early Christian

After the Roman departure in the early fifth century, Christianity was effectively consolidated in Wales by men like St. Cadog, St. Illtud and St. David. Welsh Christianity at that time was, however, primarily monastic and as already explained the emphasis was on the meaning and philosophy of the religion rather than with its external appearance. A spartan asceticism combined with the rapidity of the

religion's consolidation meant that at first it had little positive influence on the decorative arts. Intercourse in the post-Roman period with an England overrun by pagan tribes was negligible and for a long time Ireland was the most important source of inspiration although, paradoxically, the conversion of Ireland to Christianity appears to have been partly the result of missions from Romano-British Wales.

Celtic art within Wales had miraculously survived the Roman occupation and was later able to continue its development largely unimpeded by Anglo-Saxon influences. When eventually the church did patronise the arts the traditional curvilinear and elaborately inter-laced forms of the Celts were used both for illuminated manuscripts and for their superb memorial stone.[7] Monuments in the form of simple inscribed stones, cross-decorated stones, and carved stone crosses have survived in abundance, particularly in the western peninsulas of Llŷn and Pembroke and in Anglesey and Glamorgan. Though in general not so sculpturally accomplished as the best Irish crosses, the great number of Welsh monuments with their wealth of inscriptions both in Latin and in Ogham script make them important records of the history of early Wales and the Early Christian church. The earliest decorated stones, from about the seventh century, were roughly incised with a cross on crude slabs.[8] Later the cross was set in its own frame. Finally, during the ninth century and afterwards, carved stone crosses (of which 69 have survived), were ornamented with intricate curvilinear and rectilinear patterns accompanied by complex designs of inter-laced plait-work. Late crosses in Wales, such as those at Penally (early 10th cent.), Nevern (late 10th cent.) and Carew (early 11th cent.) differ in type from the well-known Irish high crosses which in general are highly naturalistic in design (fig. 16). The Welsh crosses, together with those found in south-western England and south-western Scotland, belong to a different school of sculpture. They are more conventional in design being basically intricate variations on a limited number of patterns. Nevertheless, it can be argued that the stylised technique used on the Welsh crosses called for a higher degree of craftsmanship than that required for the Irish crosses. As Nora Chadwick has written 'the art which could repeat the same design with an unerring hand over the entire surface argues an astonishing control over the tools. A single false step, a slip of the tool, and the entire cross would have been ruined. But we do not find false cuts. The whole is of an almost mechanical perfection, and must have been the result of endless practice.'[9]

Unfortunately the remarkable beauty of the illuminated manuscripts and the stone crosses is not evident in the meagre architectural remains for as in Ireland the spirit of the country was alien to the conception of material power and splendour. In church building, the influence of Celtic art seems to have been comparatively

16.   Early Christian Cross, Penally, Dyfed

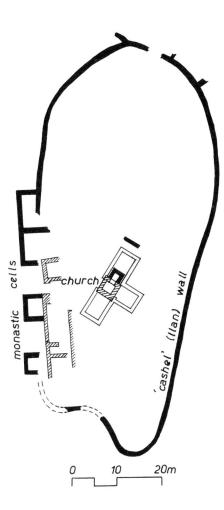

church

monastic cells

'cashel' (llan) wall

0   10   20m

17. Ynys Seiriol Celtic monastery, Gwynedd: plan showing earliest parts (probably 7th century) in black

slight. No doubt this apparent lack of influence can be partially explained by the dearth of large buildings constructed in stone as well as by the monastic form of the Church. Yet despite such drawbacks certain decorative features of Celtic art survived the long centuries to be used again in buildings of the early Middle Ages as will be seen in the next chapter (fig. 24).

In the more basic elements of site and layout the asceticism of the early church was more influential. A large proportion of the churches that exist to this day in Wales — although rebuilt in later centuries — were originally founded in these Early Christian times, and this may account for their often isolated positions in far valleys and on remote moorlands. The circular or oval boundary walls of the *llan* in which many of them still stand testify to their great antiquity, for when Augustine (first archbishop of Canterbury, 601) arrived in Kent from France to convert the still heathen English, many of the cells and churches which have given the Welsh nearly six hundred 'Llan' place names had already been long established.[10] Conclusive proof of this is the fact that those British peoples with Welsh leaders who emigrated to Brittany (Armorica) from Devon and 'West Wales', as a result of the Saxon invasions, in the fifth century established there a large number of 'Tre' and 'Lan' place-names, the Breton *lan* corresponding to the Welsh Christian *llan*. Obviously the word must have existed in Wales before the emigration. No other parts of the Christian world are as thickly covered as Wales and its early colony, Brittany, with the holy names of their Early Christian origins.

Generally the sites selected by the saints for their first churches were new ones but occasionally existing Roman camp sites, such as Caerhun, near Conwy, or even older sites, such as the Bronze Age circle at Ysbyty Cynfyn, were chosen. Other examples of an Early Christian circular *llan* are to be seen at Llangelynin in the Conwy valley, Llanelltud near Dolgellau and Pennant Melangell in the Berwyn Mountains. Llanilltud, near Brecon, is a typical isolated site and although the church here is a nineteenth-century rebuilding, the boundary wall of the ancient *llan* is an almost perfect circle raised above the level of the surrounding moorland. Even more isolated is St. Cwyfan's Church near Aberffro. Here the tiny church (rebuilt in the 12th century) was sited in the centre of a little circular island (only 30 metres across), the edges of which mark the position of the *llan* wall.

Eschewing worldliness and material comfort, the earliest monastic cells were simple in the extreme. They appear to have been, without exception, very small rectangular structures of stone or timber. Thus at Rhos (near Llandudno), St. Trillo's chapel was a mere 2.5 metres wide by 3.5 metres long with a vaulted roof of large stone pebbles. St. Beuno's chapel at Clynnog Fawr was 3 metres by 5.5 metres and St. Patrick's chapel at Whitesands Bay on the Pembroke coast was 4 metres

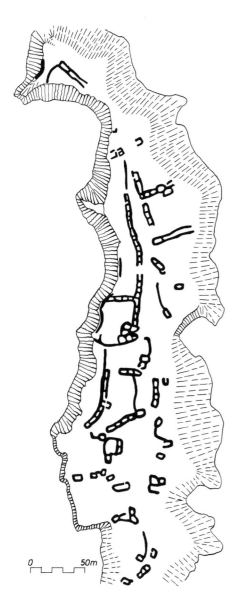

0   50m

18.   Gateholm settlement, Dyfed: plan

square. Windows and doorways were probably square headed, for the arch was avoided wherever possible in early buildings. Even in later buildings lintels were often used over openings in preference to arches. The semi-circular apse was unknown.

The best example of an early monastic settlement — pre-dating even the famous Iona, St. Columba's first Christian base in Scotland — is on Ynys Seiriol, a small island off the east coast of Anglesey. Very little now remains of the original chapel ascribed to St. Seiriol (*fl.*500—550) except the foundations of three walls, but fortunately, the height of the walls and the lines of the roof of the earliest building have been left imprinted on the face of a later tower, showing that the oratory was originally 1.5 metres square internally and had a high barrel vaulted ceiling with a sharply pointed roof. The remains of the chapel stand within a large oval-shaped *llan* surrounded by a dry-stone wall (fig.17). Grouped along the northern side of the *llan* are traces of masonry walls forming small rectangular cells which were once the living quarters of the monks. The general layout of St. Seiriol's monastery bears a striking resemblance to that of the better-known Nendrum, a seventh-century island settlement off the coast of Ulster. In both cases the church is at the centre of a roughly oval enclosure with the monks' cells along the perimeter. Another island settlement which may possibly be of monastic origin is Gateholm near the St. Bride's peninsula in Dyfed (fig. 18). It has an unusual layout consisting of long irregular chains of stone-walled cells or compartments, hidden by undergrowth, occupying virtually the whole extent of the island.[11]

There are no extant examples of complete buildings belonging to the Celtic monasteries. There are, however, a number of holy wells traditionally associated with the early saints and although these have usually been reconstructed or rebuilt a number of times they may offer a clue to the constructional methods and appearance of the Celtic chapels. Many of these wells, such as Ffynnon Feuno at Clynnog, Ffynnon Gybi at Llangybi and St. Seiriol's Well at Penmon (all in Gwynedd), were rebuilt in the eighteenth century although they may have been in continuous use since the sixth century. One of the best preserved is the Maen-du Well, Brecon, which was repaired or reconstructed (according to a datestone by the entrance) in 1754 (fig. 19). Of its history we know very little but its small size, its primitive dry-stone walling, its built-up stone roof and its general similarity to the remains of the original monastery chapel on Ynys Seiriol all suggest a pre-medieval (or at least an early medieval) building, the constructional details of which were preserved in the eighteenth century reconstruction.

Gradually, between the early seventh and the early eighth century, the Celtic Churches of Ireland, Scotland and Northumbria accepted the supremacy of the

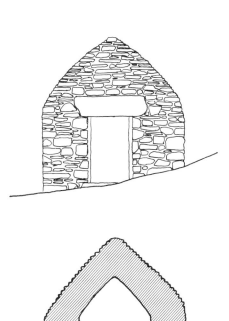

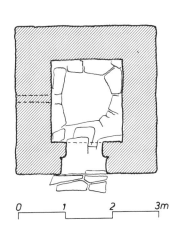

19. Maen-du well, Brecon, Powys: plan, section and elevation

Roman Church. Significantly, the Welsh church did not fully submit to external authority until very much later. Many centuries had elapsed since Rome had left the Romano-Britons to the mercy of the Saxon and Jutes. After a long span of independence of a Holy City that had capitulated to Goth and Vandal, the Welsh were in no mood for a *détente*. In any case, the Roman and Welsh Churches had in the meantime followed very different paths.

Bangor capitulated first in 768, but the churches of Deheubarth, Powys and Llandaf remained doggedly independent of Rome until well into the ninth century. Meanwhile the more important of the early Christian monasteries emerged as *clas* or 'mother' churches. Each was run by a *clas* of canons, under an abbot, thus retaining their collegiate organisation. Thirty-four *clas* churches are known to have existed, among them Ynys Seiriol and Clynnog Fawr, as well as major centres of scholarship and learning such as Llanilltud Fawr (Llantwit Major) and Llancarfan both in the Vale of Glamorgan, and Llanbadarn Fawr near Aberystwyth together with the later cathedral churches of St. David's, Bangor and St. Asaph. Very little is known about the buildings of these *clas* churches but in some cases they must have been very extensive. The monastic college of Llanilltud Fawr, for instance, is reputed to have had seven halls and several hundred pupils. No remains of Illtud's monastery have been found for it probably comprised small individual wooden cells clustered around the larger timber halls and church. Their superstructures have perished but their foundations still lie under houses near the present church. The remarkable collection of memorial stones and carved Celtic wheel-crosses now in St. Illtud's Church, but originally in the churchyard, bear moving testimony to the renown of this important and ancient centre of Welsh Christianity.

It seems more than a coincidence — in 'cultural continuity' terms — that the monastery should actually have been founded and developed within the estate of the largest Romano-British villa discovered in Wales, a villa which had achieved its richest phase during and after the reign of the Christian emperor Constantine the Great. It was at places like Llanilltud Fawr that the flame of Christianity was kept alight in Britain during the dark age when the rest of the island, apart from the Celtic west, was overwhelmed by pagan barbarism. It was at Llanilltud too that, according to local tradition, the young Patrick lived and studied for a time, before his abduction by sea raiders to Ireland, where, with the help of missionaries from Brittany he rekindled the flame of Christianity.

NOTES TO CHAPTER 2

[1] Branwen, according to legend the daughter of Llyr, is one of the central characters in the collection of Welsh sagas known as the *Mabinogion*.

[2] Specifically in terms of architecture and building, it is significant that the Welsh language — the only living language directly evolved from the British tongue — still retains many of the Latin roots by which it was so greatly enriched. Thus many Welsh building terms are closely related to the Latin originals. See 'Glossary of Welsh Architectural Terms', p.206

[3] The earliest extant Welsh poem, *Y Gododdin,* dating from the sixth century, vividly describes in heroic verse the Battle of Catraeth where 300 mounted British commandos were cut down by several thousand Anglian infantry. The poem was written by Aneirin, the sole British survivor of the battle.

[4] At the Battle of Chester, according to a later report from as respected a scribe as Bede himself, at least a thousand unarmed Welsh monks from the nearby monastery of Bangor Is-coed (who were supporting the British troops with their prayers and the Cross of Christ) were massacred by the Saxons. The Monastery itself was completely destroyed by Aethelfrith of Northumbria and never rebuilt.

[5] A similar type of multicellular enclosure has survived in use to this day in the form of large stone-built sheepfolds, containing numerous irregular shaped compartments, found in Eryri. These sheepfolds apparently date from the eighteenth century.

[6] In the event of fire spreading to adjoining premises, the laws also laid down the amount of compensation payable to neighbours.

[7] Very little of the illuminated manuscripts produced in Wales has survived. Noteworthy amongst these, however, is a manuscript written at Tyddewi (St. David's) in the late eleventh-century which is now preserved in Corpus Christi College, Cambridge; written by John, the son of Sulien, Bishop of Tyddewi, it is illuminated in the Irish tradition in green, black, yellow and red.

[8] The earliest dateable monument with a cross on it is a memorial stone in Llangadwaladr Church (Anglesey) to King Cadfan of Gwynedd, who died c.625. Other inscribed stones without crosses are dateable from the mid-sixth century.

[9] Nora Chadwick, *The Celts* (Harmondsworth, 1970), p. 254.

[10] The second element in the 'Llan' name is nearly always the name of the saint who either founded the church himself or launched a cult whose followers dedicated the church in his honour, e.g. Llanilltud, the *llan* of Illtud; only occasionally is the second element descriptive, e.g. Llandaf, the *llan* on the (River) Taf.

[11] Alternatively, Gateholm might have been an Iron Age town similar to Tre'r Ceiri in the north, but defended by the sea instead of massive walls.

1.   Pentre Ifan chamber tomb, Dyfed. The
     Neolithic *cromlech*.

25

2.   Pen Dinas Iron Age hill-fort, Dyfed.

3.   Roman Amphitheatre at Caerleon,
     Gwent. c.AD 80.

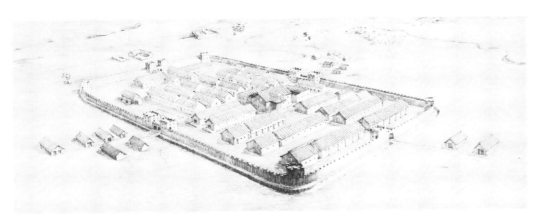

4. Segontium Roman Fort, Caernarfon,
   Gwynedd. Drawing by Paul Jenkins
   showing the fort about AD 250, with the
   Temple of Mithras in the foreground.
5. Roman town walls of Venta Silurum,
   Caer-went, Gwent.

6. Din Llugwy farmstead, Llanallgo,
   Gwynedd. 4th. century.

Chapter 3
The Middle Ages I ~ Religious

Although sections of the Church in Wales recognised the Papal authority of Rome in certain matters as far back as the eighth century it remained in general independent of the Anglo-Saxon church. It is not surprising that the Welsh Church was far closer to the Celtic Churches of Ireland and Scotland in its organisation. The Normans, when they arrived, were determined to alter the situation. They eventually succeeded in obtaining the allegiance of the Welsh Church to Canterbury, but not without strong opposition from the Welsh princes who, understandably, preferred their spiritual welfare to be in the care of Welsh rather than foreign bishops.

The *clas* or 'mother' churches, formerly the most characteristic institution of the pre-Norman church in Wales, were gradually squeezed out of existence. A few became cathedrals or were taken over by the foreign monastic orders that arrived with the Normans; others became 'collegiate' churches or degenerated into simple parish churches while the rest were suppressed and their possessions transferred to monasteries in England.

The Normans attempted to replace the loose-knit organisation of the native church with a continental pattern of hierarchical ecclesiastical government, firstly establishing four Welsh dioceses and then sub-dividing these into parishes. The process was extremely slow, for much of the country was sparsely inhabited, and in the areas remaining under native rule (particularly northern Wales) large parts were still unregimented by the time of the Edwardian Conquest in the late thirteenth century.

Similarly, church buildings in the politically independent parts of Wales were less directly influenced by the new Norman attitudes in architecture than were those in the lordships under semi-permanent Anglo-Norman domination in the lowland south. How far this was the consequence of St. David's tradition of asceticism and of using native craftsmen inured to their own methods or how far it was due to straitened economy, together with the more intractable nature of the materials of the north, is difficult to say. Whatever the reason, the result was two differing versions of architecture — Celtic Romanesque and Norman Romanesque — one being spartan, conservative and robust, while the other was more experimental and given to fashionable change. Both, however, made use of the semi-circular arch, a typical feature of Roman architecture from which the term 'Romanesque' is derived.

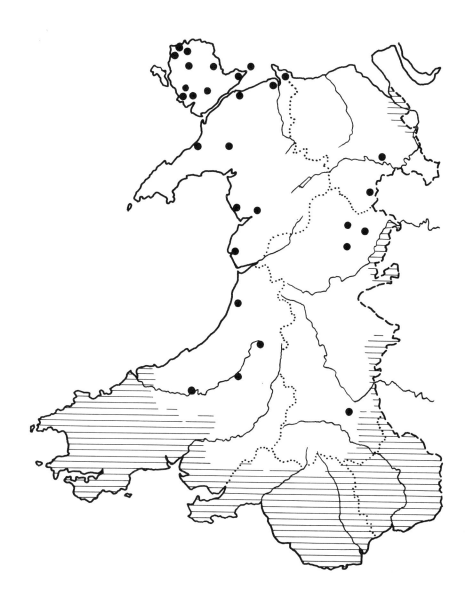

20. Distribution of Churches with Celtic-Romanesque features. Territory under Anglo-Norman domination in 1267 is shaded. See Appendix D for list of churches

Celtic Romanesque

During the twelfth century Early Christian ideas continued to influence the design of churches in those parts of Wales not under Norman domination; only gradually were Norman design concepts — derived in turn from the Romanesque architecture of Western Europe — hesitatingly introduced into the native buildings (fig. 20). The Celtic type of square-ended chancel was, however, persistently retained in nearly all churches.

The lesser churches of the medieval period have few distinguishing features in layout apart from their rectangular stubbiness. Usually they comprised a simple nave and chancel, both of which were short in relation to their width. Aisles were not required for the small churches serving the scattered communities of upland Wales. Towers were also rare before the fifteenth century; a simple bell-cote on the west gable sufficed. There was little architectural ornament or carved detail on these lesser churches and doorways were often constructed without dressed stone.

In the larger *clas* churches continental influence did lead to the adoption of a cruciform plan as a standard layout in most cases, but the plan was adapted to suit the traditionally austere needs of Welsh ritual; the churches were therefore smaller in size and less elaborate in layout than those of an England which, by the twelfth century, was thoroughly under the control of Norman clergy and French architects. The more important churches of Wales were characterised by a short aisled-nave, simple transepts and a square-ended chancel in which was accommodated the small *clas* or community of canons (plate 7). The greater Norman-French churches of England during this period, on the other hand, had extremely long aisled-naves, numerous altars and chapels and often an apsidal-ended chancel.

The twelfth-century priory church at Penmon (built six centuries after its founding) in Anglesey, and the late thirteenth-century rebuilding at Llan-ddew, near Brecon, are examples of the smaller *clas* churches. The striking similarity of these two churches, separated by a considerable time and distance, illustrates the continuity of cultural tradition which persisted, in the case of Llan-ddew, even after the Edwardian conquest. Both buildings have short unaisled-naves and stubby transepts and in each case the squat central tower rests on corner piers which intrude well into the interior with a sculptural effect. The basic formal similarity between Penmon and Llan-ddew is belied, however, by the extreme contrast of their settings, the former being an exposed peninsula barely protected from east and northerly sea-winds, while the latter nestles in a verdant tributary valley of the Usk.[1]

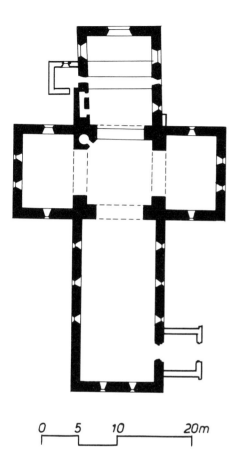

0 5 10   20m

An excellent example of one of the larger and more important *clas* churches is St. Padarn's, Llanbadarn Fawr, near Aberystwyth originally founded in the sixth century. Here the building has survived almost unchanged since the beginning of the thirteenth century. Cruciform in plan, it is a massive but simple structure with a large, chunky tower (fig. 21 plate 8). Inside, the stark white walls of the nave and the few lancet windows at high level give the church an atmosphere of austere dignity in keeping with its early origins. The churches at Llanddewibrefi and Llandysul, in the Teifi Valley, are markedly similar in style and layout to Llanbadarn Fawr, so much so in fact, as to allow the suggestion that they were all built by the same school of masons who were 'highly original and capable of producing by the simplest means a remarkable effect, Roman in its grandeur.'[2] Evidence of the ancient foundation of Llanddewibrefi is afforded by no fewer than five Celtic crosses there and an early eighth century memorial stone recording the murder of Idnert, abbot of the *clas* at Llanbadarn Fawr.[3]

The architectural details of the smaller native churches are usually very simple; they are modest and show few traces of alien influence. Where a more ambitious architectural expression was required, Norman forms were selectively borrowed and adapted to suit the materials at hand. Eventually, in the thirteenth century, all superfluous ornament was discarded in favour of a restrained form of Early Gothic. Mouldings were reduced to a minimum and decoration was reserved for a few special areas. This conscious restraint of architectural detail is found in a number of churches but is most memorable in the plain pointed arches of the tower crossing at Llanbadarn Fawr, the chancel arch at Llangristiolus, Anglesey, the elegant trio of tall lancet windows at the east end of St. Mary's, Beddgelert and the extraordinarily pure lancet windows of St. Mary's, Llanaber in Meirionnydd.

Although so sparingly used, the sculptural decoration was often quite rich, combining as it did the newer Romanesque style together with the flat, almost two-dimensional, curvilinear and naturalistic forms of traditional Celtic work. The early twelfth-century arch of the south door at Penmon clearly illustrates the meeting of the styles. Here the semi-circular inner panel has low-relief sculpture and interlace patterns of Celtic origin surrounded by a crude Romanesque outer band. The chancel arch at Penmon, built a generation later, shows a more emphatic Romanesque influence in the outer bands of chevron and chequerwork patterns surrounding a thin inner band of low-relief decoration. At Aberffro in Anglesey the situation is reversed. Here the chancel arch has a Romanesque inner band of deeply moulded chevron-work and a Celtic outer band of naturalistic, but flat, intertwined foliage and beak-heads.

21.   St. Padarn's Church, Llanbadarn Fawr, Dyfed: plan

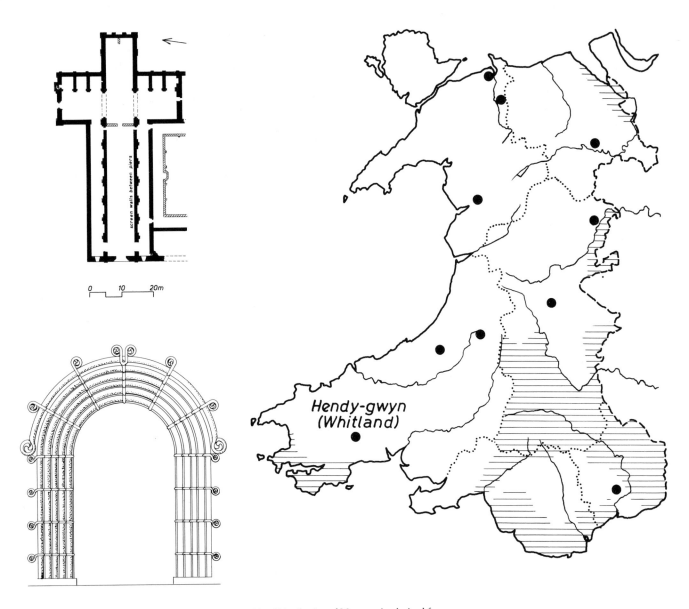

23. Ystrad Fflur (Strata Florida) Abbey, Dyfed: plan

24. Celtic-Romanesque arch, Ystrad Fflur (Strata Florida) Abbey, Dyfed

22. Distribution of Monasteries derived from Hendy-gwyn (Whitland) Abbey. Territory under Norman domination at the time of the Lord Rhys (c.1155) is shaded. See Appendix E for list of monasteries.

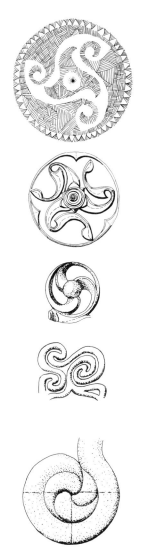

25. Examples of Triskel decoration: (a) 2nd cent. bronze shield plaque from Tal-y-llyn, (b) 2nd cent. bronze plate from Moel Hiraddug, (c) ornament on Early Iron Age (1st cent.) Tankard from Trawsfynydd, (d) detail of 9th cent. Early Christian Cross from Penally, (e) detail of scroll (late 12th or early 13th cent.) from arch at Ystrad Fflur (Strata Florida) Abbey.

Apart from the *clas* and similar churches there were also the churches belonging to the regular monastic orders of continental origin. Of all the new orders the Cistercian (launched at Citeaux, France, in 1098) with its ascetic ideals and severe rule, seems to have fitted in best with the native tradition. Although often warmly supported by the Welsh princes, the Cistercians were strictly organised according to a standard pattern and in the layout of their churches they held rigidly to the continental formula of a long nave. Their monasteries, particularly those founded from Whitland, were built in the thinly inhabited countryside (where they held great sheep farming estates), away from centres of population, and thus today the ruins of many of them have a striking appearance in harmony with the grand and desolate scenery in which they were situated (fig. 22). In the Cistercian abbeys of Aberconwy, and also of Cymer near Dolgellau and Glyn-y-groes (Valle Crucis) near Llangollen, enrichment appears to have been limited to foliate carvings on the pier capitals. At Ystrad Fflur (Strata Florida) in the Teifi Valley, the capitals of the nave arcade were similarly decorated with restrained foliate carving.

But Ystrad Fflur is in a class of its own, symbolising its position at the summit of native church architecture and its prestige as an important medieval centre of Welsh culture and learning.[4] Although originally established under temporary Norman patronage it was entirely rebuilt on a new site between 1184 and 1235 by the Lord Rhys of Deheubarth when the Welsh nobility had regained their local territories. The layout of the ruined abbey is generally in accordance with the normal Cistercian pattern except for its unusual solid screen walls (fig. 23). The feature that makes the architecture of Ystrad Fflur exceptional, however, is the archway of the great west door which has, fortunately, survived intact (plate 9). This is the most ornamental part of the church and seems to imply that the native instinct for embellishment was here stronger than Cistercian constraint, which normally eschewed all forms of ostentation including even bell-towers. The arch of the west door comprises five bands of roll mouldings which are swept round the semi-circular door opening and down the sides without any capitals or accent at the springing; a sixth outer roll ends at the springing in spiral scrolls enclosing three-legged triskel motifs. The six rolls are 'bound' together by bold stone straps ending in similar scrolls but incorporating four-legged swirls. Although Romanesque inspiration may be detected in the stepping-back of each roll, the design of the scrolls themselves is purely Celtic and forms a direct link over a long millenium with the art of the pre-Roman Iron Age in Wales (figs. 24 and 25).

Norman Romanesque

Norman architecture first appeared in Britain about 1050 with the rebuilding of Westminster Abbey from designs based on the French abbey of Jumieges in Normandy. Being designed by French architects, the earliest English cathedrals — large and austere in style — were directly inspired by the cathedrals of Normandy. From about 1090 onwards a new series of cathedrals, which included Durham and Gloucester, was started. In these cathedrals the architecture had become more massive as well as more decorative. Thus by the time that Norman Romanesque architecture arrived in Wales in the early twelfth century the style was already well developed.[5] During the course of the century the Normans, having established their southern lordships set about rebuilding churches throughout their new territories. Starting first with the cathedral at Llandaf in 1120 they moved westwards — erecting churches on the way in a tremendous burst of building activity — to the furthest limit of Dyfed where, in 1180 they built the most remarkable cathedral of all at Tyddewi (St. David's).

The earliest Norman church in Wales favoured the continental type of plan with a semi-circular apse at the east end. Both Bangor and Llandaf cathedrals as well as the priory church at Usk were first built with apses. At Llandaf the presbytery arch which originally led into the apse can still be seen. For an extant example of Romanesque apse it is necessary to go only a short way across the present English border, to Kilpeck (a church originally of Celtic foundation) in Herefordshire.

Gradually the Normans abandoned the apse idea and adopted instead the Celtic form of a square-ended chancel. The nave and chancel were, however, usually more elongated than in the native churches. In the more important Norman churches accommodation was increased by lengthening the nave still further, or by increasing the width by the addition of side-aisles or by adding transepts to form a cruciform layout. The cruciform plan became normal for most of the larger churches. It was used in the original Norman churches at Llandaf, St. David's, Bangor and at Tintern Abbey, although in all these examples the original layout was superseded by later additions and rebuilding.

The development of medieval church architecture in Wales was strongly influenced by the establishment of new monasteries, the majority of which were founded in the twelfth century. They were based on continental institutions so that in their organisation and planning they were entirely different from the Celtic monasteries of the Early Christians, which by then were several centuries old and had largely out-lived their usefulness. The earliest monastery to be founded by the Normans in Wales was at Chepstow, about 1070; this belonged to the Benedictine Order who

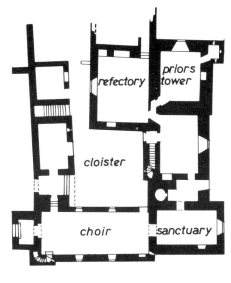

refectory

priors
tower

cloister

choir

sanctuary

0   5   10m

26. Caldy Priory, Dyfed: plan

altogether built eight monasteries. The Augustinian Canons, who arrived at Llanthony in 1103, established six monasteries. The largest and most influential group was the Cistercian Order; they built fifteen monasteries and nunneries throughout Wales. The earliest of these, such as Abbey Dore, Tintern, Basingwerk, Margam and Neath, were Norman foundations introduced from their establishments in England. The majority of the Cistercian monasteries, however, were endowed by the Welsh princes and were derived from Whitland in Dyfed, which had in turn been founded from the continent (fig. 22).

The most important building in the medieval monastery was of course the church which, except in the smallest communities, was usually cruciform in plan and had small chapels attached to the transepts. The monastic buildings included a dormitory block and refectory and were generally arranged around a courtyard, called the cloister garth, to one side (nearly always the south side) of the church. This standard plan can be seen clearly at the small priory on Caldy Island, off the coast near Tenby, which has the most complete group of monastic buildings in Wales, although in this case the church is only a two-cell building comprising a nave and sanctuary (fig. 26). In a very large monastery, such as Tintern, the layout was much more ambitious (fig. 27). Here there are two open courts — most unusually on the north side for drainage reasons. One cloister was reserved exclusively for lay brothers and contacts with the outside world, while the other was related to a hospital which was protectively sited away from any noise. At Tintern there was also a separate group of buildings for the abbot consisting of a large hall, living area and private chapel.

Apart from the church itself the most important element in a monastery was the chapter house. It was here that the monks assembled each morning to listen to the reading of a Chapter of the Rule and where most of the day-to-day business of the monastery took place. In Cistercian monasteries the earlier chapter houses were normally square or rectangular in shape and modest in size (fig.28). However, the Cistercians bestowed a certain distinction on two of their Welsh houses, for only at Margam and Abbey Dore did they later (in the thirteenth century) adapt a polygonal plan for the chapter house, both being twelve-sided.[6] The Margam Chapter house is 15 metres in diameter and has a central column supporting elaborate vaulting. Even in ruins it is a most elegant structure.

The Benedictine priory church of Ewenni in Glamorgan is our finest remaining example of an early Norman church in Wales. Founded by the first Norman lord of Ogmore, William de Londres, it comprises a long nave dating from the early twelfth-century and a presbytery and transepts added a few decades later, all of which are massively constructed and impressively fortress-like in appearance.

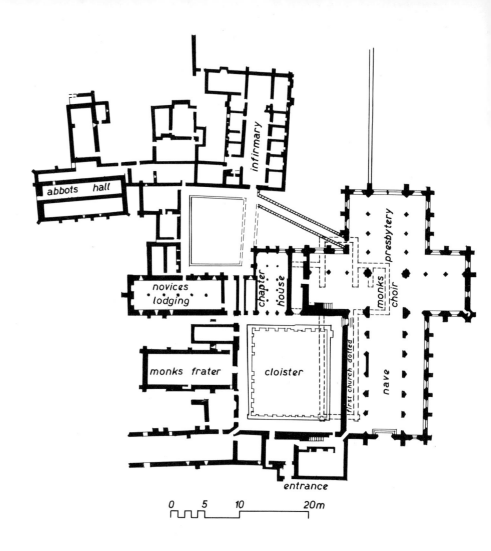

infirmary

abbots hall

presbytery

novices
lodging

chapter
house

monks
choir

monks frater

cloister

first church dotted

nave

entrance

0   5   10   20m

27.   Tintern Abbey, Gwent: plan

St Dogmaels

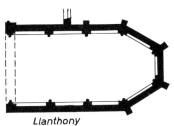

Llanthony

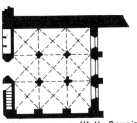

Glyn-y-groes (Valle Crucis)

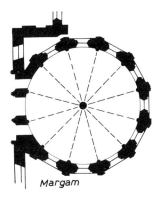

Margam

28. Comparative plans of Chapter Houses

Inside, there is very little of the incised decoration so typical of some later Norman churches. Even the huge drum piers inserted at the end of the twelfth century, when an aisle was added, are quite plain except for moulded bases and reeded capitals. The arches of the tower crossing are severely square-cut and undecorated while the presbytery has a simple barrel vault ceiling sub-divided by moulded ribs. Ewenni Priory is remarkably unspoilt — an example of Norman attitudes at their most powerful.

Another important factor in the layout of churches is the siting of the tower. As a general rule there was only one tower and this was placed at the west end of the nave or, as with some of the tapering towers found in South Pembrokeshire, alongside the nave. In the larger cruciform churches a central tower was placed at the crossing of the nave and transepts, as at Ewenni Priory. In England many of the cathedrals had a pair of subsidiary towers at the west end of the nave as well as a central tower, but in Wales there is only one Norman example of this type of tower arrangement. This is the Augustinian Priory at Llanthony situated in the remote and still arcadian Vale of Ewyas in the Black Mountains of Gwent.[7] The earliest part of the priory had been under construction between 1108 and 1134 and was soon followed by the central tower with its narrow round-headed openings. The twin-western towers were built at the beginning of the thirteenth century, but by then the transition to Gothic had started and so pointed panels occur alongside the round-headed openings in these later towers (plate 10).

Perhaps the most characteristic features of Romanesque work are the use of semi-circular arches for all openings and the way in which mouldings are emphatically decorated (fig. 29). Often these two features are seen together, for usually the doorways and chancel arches were given the greater enrichment. Decoration, however, was used sparingly at first and consisted of simple geometric patterns. These were developed into rich mouldings which were often deeply cut; the most common were the chevron, lozenge and cable patterns. Llandaf Cathedral, although rebuilt many times, still contains excellent Romanesque arches. The finest is the splendid twelfth-century presbytery arch which consists of four concentric bands of zig-zag ornamentation and carved roundels. The north doorway at Llandaf has two bands of lozenge enrichment and the south doorway has three decorated bands. At Chepstow priory-church the fine west door has no less than five richly decorated bands stepped back in plan towards the centre. In the greater English and continental cathedrals the arcades dividing the nave from the aisles were vertically sub-divided into three parts comprising the main arcade at the lowest level, the 'triforium' fronting onto the main gallery at aisle roof level and finally the 'clerestory' at the top of the wall. In the earlier churches these were simple arched openings cut out of the wall but later the arches became wider, forming continuous

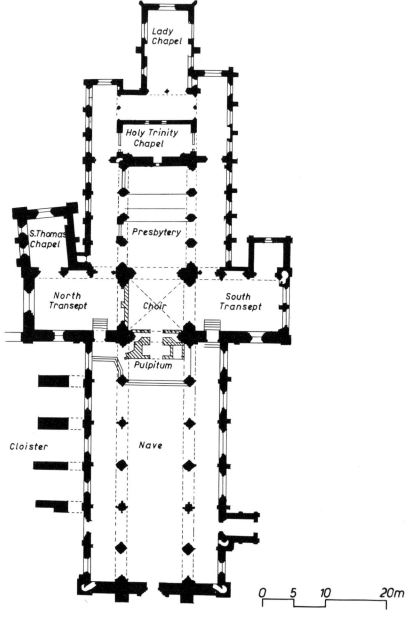

Lady
Chapel

Holy Trinity
Chapel

Presbytery

S.Thomas
Chapel

North
Transept

Choir

South
Transept

Pulpitum

Cloister

Nave

0   5   10   20m

29. Norman-Romanesque arch, Llandaf
Cathedral, Cardiff

30. St. David's Cathedral, Dyfed: plan

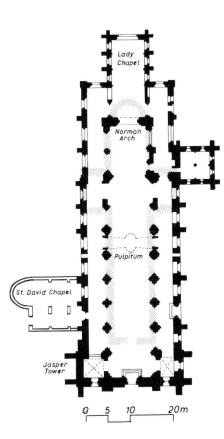

arcades separated only by piers, and the lower main arcade became dominant in size. The final stage of this development is strikingly illustrated in the nave arcades of St. David's Cathedral, the last major Romanesque church to be built in Britain.

The valley of Glyn Rhosyn by the village known in English as St. David's but in Welsh as Tyddewi ('The House of David'), was a place of renowned sanctity ever since Wales' patron saint established his first spartan cell there in the sixth century and made it 'the principal seat of Christianity in all the West'. It was not untypical of the Normans, a race as devout as they were ruthless, to have a special reverence for a shrine so well known to them before they left France. Significantly, soon after the Normans arrived blood-stained in this far promontory, the Pope (in 1120) raised its international status to that of a unique place of pilgrimage — two journeys to Saint David's being made equal to one to St. Peter's in Rome itself. The cathedral the Normans built — and the one which we see today — was possibly the fourth church to occupy this historic spot (fig. 30 and plate 11).

The nave, of six bays, was built by Bishop Peter de Leia in the closing years of the twelfth century (1180–1193) and is remarkable for both its originality and its rich decoration (plate 12). The piers are alternately circular and octagonal in cross-section and have superimposed shafts with stiff-leaved capitals. The main arcade has decorated arches of semi-circular shape springing from the shafts and occupies half the total height of the nave. Above this are the small pointed arches of the triforium inter-woven between the highly decorated arches and pilasters of the tall clerestory which has two bays to every one of the main arcade. The unusually rich effect is continued into the slightly later choir, but with transitional pointed arcade arches, and culminates at the east end in one of the most impressive groups of transitional lancet windows in Britain. The lancets are only slightly pointed so that, seen from a distance, they appear almost semi-circular; they are flanked by profusely decorated mouldings of quite exceptional delicacy. Below this group of lancet windows, behind the high altar, the bones of Dewi Sant rest in a casket.

Early and Middle Gothic

At the end of the twelfth century St. David's Cathedral was still being built in an enthusiastically Romanesque manner. By then the lighter Gothic style had already arrived in eastern Wales at Llandaf, the cathedral being enlarged from 1170 onwards by adding new aisles onto the Norman nave (fig. 31). Then the nave itself was lengthened and rebuilt with graceful arcades of pointed arches of similar design to those at Wells Cathedral in Somerset, the first major Gothic building in western England.[8]

The most obvious visual difference of course between Romanesque and Gothic is that Romanesque arches and openings were all semi-circular while the Gothic were pointed. Yet, essentially, the genesis of Gothic architecture was not the result of an aesthetic urge. The Gothic system was an organic structural system which had been evolved in northern France in order to answer the problem of building larger and higher buildings with adequate lighting. It was a rational system in which the weight and thrust of the roof was transferred down to the ground via a skeleton frame of vaulting ribs, columns and buttresses, all in equilibrium. The external wall thus became mere infill panels, no longer structural, which could be filled completely with glass if required. The key to the whole system was the use of pointed arches of different spans, but of similar height so that rectangular vaults could be constructed without impairing their stability. Early Gothic builders in Britain tended to ignore the structural possibilities of the system, using instead the pointed arches and the vaulting shafts as superficial forms of decoration. This is particularly true of Welsh churches where stone vaulting was rarely used.

The general lightness and refinement, together with the emphasis on the vertical that is associated with early Gothic architecture is immediately apparent in the nave of the Cathedral at Llandaf although in fact it never had any stone roof vaulting. The piers are octagonal in cross-section with recessed grooves on the angled faces so that in elevation they appear as a series of vertical lines, and this preoccupation with verticality is emphasised by clusters of shafts that extend up to the roof. The aisle walls on the other hand continue merely as thick screens with window openings cut into them.

The parish churches at Llanidloes in northern Powys and Haverfordwest in Dyfed also have fine early thirteenth-century nave arcades. The five-bay arcades in St. Idloes's church have superbly executed foliated capitals to the pier shafts. The arcades originally formed part of the vast nave of Abbey Cwm-hir some way to the south, but were removed to their present home in 1542 after the dissolution of the monasteries.[9] At St. Mary's, Haverfordwest, the piers are completely surrounded by clusters of shafts which have capitals carved with conventional foliage, animals and grotesque heads.

At Llandaf the vertical emphasis seen in the nave is also evident on the west front (built 1220) with its three tall lancet windows (plate 13). St. John's Cathedral, Brecon, has an equally fine array of lancet windows at the east end of the choir. Here the windows are deeply recessed and have been carefully arranged to fill the full width of the gable and ascend in height to the tallest lancet in the centre. The side walls of the choir are also filled with lancet windows in groups of three to correspond with the vaulting bays above.

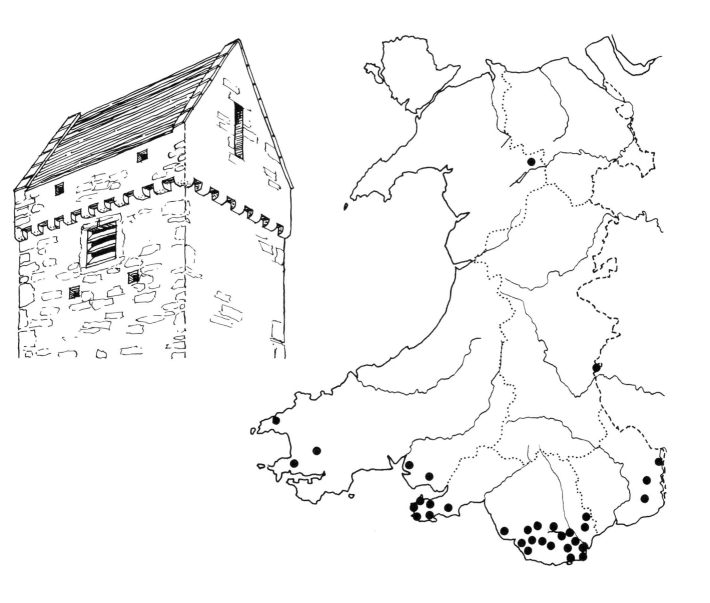

32. Distribution of Churches with Saddleback Towers (including some towers demolished in the nineteenth century). See Appendix F for list of churches.

41

From individual lancet windows the next step was to group them together in closer pairs or triplets under a single dripstone hood and then to pierce the blank space between the window heads with additional small circular or foliated lights, thus forming 'plate tracery'. The choir at St. Mary's, Haverfordwest, has a fine example of plate tracery of three lancets with, in between, cinquefoil lights.

Windows in the fourteenth century became yet more elaborate. The whole of the space between the lancet windows' heads was glazed and sub-divided with curved tracery bars in place of the solid stone plate. On the whole there are few good churches of this period but Tintern Abbey (rebuilt 1270-1320), is a notable exception (plate 14). Although roofless these last four centuries, the architectural character of the windows has been largely preserved. The abbey has a great west window of seven lights with geometric tracery of trefoils and circles and the remains of an even more magnificent eight-light window, 8 metres wide and almost 20 metres high, occupying the whole of the eastern presbytery wall. At both Llandaf and St. David's the aisle-walls of the cathedrals were rebuilt during this period with windows of curvilinear tracery containing sinuous S-shaped bars.

Church roofs were normally constructed in wood, using framed trusses. Shaped braces were sometimes added under the rafters and tie-beams, the spaces in between being panelled with wood or plaster to form a curved ceiling. This type of roof, known as a waggon roof, can be seen in churches in many parts of Wales, but is most commonly found in the eastern districts where wood was much more plentiful.

Towers were often added to churches in the early and middle Gothic periods to serve as lookouts or refuges in times of trouble. Like the Norman towers they were usually stout and defensive in character. One of the best examples of this fortress-like type is the tower at Brecon Cathedral, a tough and forbidding structure with very small openings and an embattled parapet. Occasionally, towers were built away from the church on a slight hill nearby, as at Llandaf and Henllan near Denbigh, so that they could be seen (and the bells heard) more clearly from a distance. Early spires were apparently rare in Wales although many of the seventeenth-century ones of the south-east may have replaced medieval spires.

In the southern coastal areas, particularly the Vale of Glamorgan and Gower, towers were built with saddleback, or pitched-roofs, giving them a very distinctive triangular shape (fig. 32 and plate 15). Another type of tower with regional characteristics is the timber lantern-belfry found in remote churches in the eastern borderlands and along the Severn Valley in Powys (fig. 33). The oldest examples are built over the roof and supported on timber frames standing on the floor of the

33. Distribution of Churches with Timber Lantern-belfries (including vestigal remains and some belfries demolished in the nineteenth century). Note the similarity to the distribution of half-timbered houses shown on fig. 58. See Appendix G for list of churches.

nave. They probably represent a constructional technique that derives from the time when the churches of the area were built entirely of wood. The church of Llantilio Crossenny, Gwent, had its wooden belfry supported on four timber posts, each 18 metres long within the stone-built central tower.[10] Later, the timber lantern-belfries were built on top of low stone towers at the end of the nave as at the old parish church of Newtown in Powys and at Skenfrith in Gwent.

When stone vaulting was used it was usually in a basic form as in some of the churches of South Pembrokeshire. These have plain barrel-vaults slightly pointed at the apex. More sophisticated stone vaulting was reserved for the greater churches, but even then it was only sparingly used. The small chapter house at Llandaf has one of the few early examples. The roof of the fourteenth-century chapel of St. Thomas in St. David's Cathedral is a later and better example which contains some elaborately carved stone bosses at the meeting points of the vaulting ribs. The vaulted and ribbed fourteenth-century chapter house at Glyn y Groes (Valle Crucis), Llangollen, is also complete.

It is not only the quality of the vaulting which should give one cause to pause in the chapter house of Glyn y Groes, embowered like Tintern in a valley of dramatic beauty. Here is a classic example of the relationship in Wales between man, his history and his architecture. Founded in 1201 as the last Cistercian monastery in Wales by Madog ap Gruffydd, Prince of Powys, Glyn y Groes was in northern Wales second in prestige only to the great monastery of Aberconwy in Conwy.[11] Madog, an ally and cousin of Llywelyn Fawr (Llywelyn I or 'the Great'), was at his death in 1236 interred here in the chancel of his abbey. The abbots of the abbey were great patrons of poetry and the voices of famous poets such as Iolo Goch in the fourteenth century and Guto'r Glyn in the fifteenth century were often heard in these vaulted walls. Both poets are buried at Glyn y Groes. Another voice which echoed from these walls was that of Owain Glyndŵr, Prince of Wales. The chapter house was newly built when he saw it first, and it was proper that he should walk often under its pointed doorway, for he was the great-great-great-grandson of the abbey's founder. Minute compared with the chapter houses of the great English cathedrals this square, becolumned, quoined and vaulted room at Glyn y Groes nevertheless has a special place in the history of Wales.

Late Gothic

The economic decline and poverty experienced throughout northern Europe for much of the fourteenth century, as a result of desperately poor harvests and widespread plague, continued into the fifteenth century. In Wales, agricultural

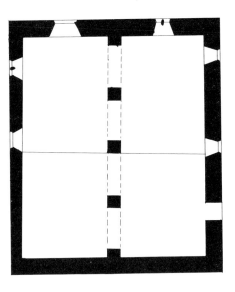

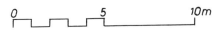

34. St. Rhychwyn's Church, Llanrhychwyn, Gwynedd: plan

depression, continual poverty and hatred of oppressive officialdom nurtured the seeds of national rebellion which culminated, during the first decade of the fifteenth century in the Glyndŵr War of Independence. The war of liberation was warmly supported by scholars and dissatisfied Welsh churchmen everywhere; Cistercian monks and Dominican friars were particularly ardent in their support of Owain Glyndŵr, for an important part of his aim was ensuring a national Welsh church independent of Canterbury and the establishment of two Welsh universities. The scorched-earth tactics of the patriots and the eventual recovery of power by the English forces only resulted, however, in a trail of devastated and ruined churches, throughout the length and breadth of the country.

Economic recovery was at first slow but after the middle of the fifteenth century the pace quickened, enabling many churches to be not only repaired, but also improved and enlarged.

A comparatively common way of enlarging a church was to add a wide aisle to one side of the nave, thus doubling the size of the building and giving it the appearance of a double-aisle church. In the more prosperous valleys, the extension often took place in the fifteenth century while in the more mountainous parts enlargement tended to be later. Llanrhychwyn parish church (traditionally known as Llywelyn's Church after Llywelyn ap Iorwerth), in Dyffryn Conwy, is a typical double-aisle church of the simpler kind (fig. 34). It was first lengthened in the fifteenth century by the addition of a chancel and then further enlarged by the addition of an aisle in the early sixteenth century to give it an almost square plan. The more splendid, and earlier, double-aisle churches are mostly in Clwyd, particularly Dyffryn Clwyd where there are good examples at Denbigh (Whitchurch), Llanefydd, Llangynhafal and Llanrhaiadr. The prevailing popularity of the cult of the Virgin Mary in the fifteenth century is a possible explanation for the deliberate duality of churches in a number of cases. Thus, for instance, at Llanefydd and Llansilan (both in Clwyd), and Llanfynydd (in Dyfed), the chancel of the new aisle was dedicated to St. Mary.

The rectilinear manner of late Gothic known as Perpendicular was employed for new church building everywhere; as in England it provided Wales with a golden age in church architecture. With the Perpendicular style the structural potentialities of the Gothic system were at last realised. Windows became wider and often occupy almost the whole width of the wall panel between the buttresses which in consequence became larger and more pronounced. Even relatively undistinguished churches would sometimes have excellent windows, as at Llanrhaeadr Dyffryn Clwyd near Denbigh, where there is a very fine Jesse Window dating from 1533. There was also a tendency to heighten the aisle and nave arcades although arches themselves became depressed and broader. This flattening of arches is one of the most distinctive features of Perpendicular architecture and in the windows it was emphasised by continuing the vertical mullions straight through to the underside of the arch, giving a gridiron effect.

Of Perpendicular churches in Wales, the best known group is that built by Margaret Beaufort, the second wife of Lord Stanley of Derby, in Clwyd. They are situated within a few miles of each other at Wrexham, Gresford, Holt, Mold, Northop and Holywell (St. Winifred's Chapel), and have become well enough known to be included amongst the so-called 'Seven Wonders of Wales'.[12]

St. Giles's Church, Wrexham, is the finest of the group. Its six-bay nave belongs to an earlier church but was rebuilt after a fire in 1463 with a new flat timber panelled roof, its master-mason or architect being John Hart. At the same time an octagonal chancel was added at the east end. The interior is lit by five-light windows to the aisles with clerestory windows above the nave arcades. At the west end there is a superb five stage tower (added 1506), 41.5 metres high, with octagonal turrets at each corner and 29 statues in ogee-arched recesses (plate 16). Gresford Church is very similar to that of Wrexham and is notable for a splendid seven-light east window, a lofty timber roof with carved beams and panels and some richly carved oak screens. This tower is in three stages, the lower one of which belongs to the fourteenth century and the two upper stages to the early sixteenth century; it is crowned by an embattled parapet enriched alternately with pinnacles and sculptured figures. Holt, Mold and Northop have similarly fine churches with well-proportioned towers although they are somewhat overshadowed by the magnificence of Wrexham and Gresford. The delicious St. Winifred's Chapel at Holywell is a most elegant little building, and has an exceptionally fine undercroft incorporating a star-shaped pool. Above the pool there is a fan-vaulted ceiling with a central boss carved with details of the life of the martyred St. Winifred, a local saint.

In the north-west the outstanding churches of the late Gothic period are at Clynnog Fawr in Arfon and at Holyhead and Llaneilian in Anglesey. Outwardly much plainer than the 'Stanley' churches they were each rebuilt within a few years of each other at the end of the fifteenth century or the beginning of the sixteenth, possibly by the same masons. The wealthy collegiate church of St. Beuno at Clynnog Fawr is especially good (plate 17). The Welsh Saint, Beuno, was deeply revered and his importance, and the love of the faithful for him, is reflected in this building. Nobly proportioned on the outside, and light and austere inside, his church has a fine tower with diminishing storeys, large windows with precisely organised tracery, and a good hammerbeam roof. St. Cybi's Church within the walls of the Roman fort at Holyhead was another collegiate establishment. The present building (much

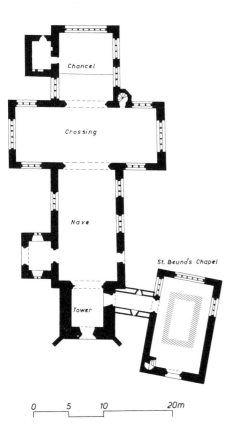

35. St. Beuno's Church, Clynnog Fawr, Gwynedd: plan showing foundations of Early Christian church shaded

restored by Sir Gilbert Scott in the nineteenth century), has a cruciform layout with high ceilinged aisles separated from the nave by wide four-centred arches. Externally, the walls and tower are battlemented while on the south porch and the parapet of the south transept there are elaborate late Gothic carvings. Llaneilian's church is only partly a rebuilding. The spacious and well-lit nave, complete with battlemented parapets, is of the late fifteenth century but the stumpy tower attached to the west end and its curious pyramidical spire date from the twelfth century. Inside there is a good rood-screen. On the south side of each of these three interesting churches, there is a small detached *capel-y-bedd*, the mausoleum of the saint, built on the site of the original sixth or seventh-century foundation. In the case of Clynnog Fawr and Llaneilian the chapels of Beuno and Eilian are connected to the main building by short stone passages (fig.35).

The crocketted and pinnacled towers found in the south-east are based on a type originating in Somerset. St. John's Church, Cardiff, has a particularly handsome example completed in 1473 by the same John Hart reputed to have built the tower of Wrexham parish church. The tower at Cardiff, in three stages with two graceful ogee arches at the base and a large window over the entrance, is elaborately crowned at the top by an exquisite embattled parapet with lantern pinnacles and delicate open stone-work at each of the four corners (plate 18). The Jasper Tower at Llandaf Cathedral — also in three stages — is similarly crowned with elaborately decorated pinnacles and open stonework parapet. St. Woolos, Newport, and the 'fenland' churches of Peterstone, St. Brides and Mathern, are other churches in this area with good Perpendicular towers.

A feature of many late churches was the finely executed timber ceilings. St. Peters, Rhuthin, has a superb flat panelled roof over the north aisle containing 480 panels in black oak, each carved with its own special design. Llangollen parish church displays a particularly well carved opentruss roof with angels on the hammerbeams. A similarly carved hammerbeam roof, at Cilcain, also in Clwyd, probably originated in nearby Basingwerk Abbey. At Old Radnor, in Powys, the lonely but very large and impressive Late Decorated church has an oak-panelled roof heavily moulded and decorated with shields and bosses.[13] St. Mary's, Tenby, and St. Mary's, Haverfordwest, in Dyfed, both have excellent panelled roofs. At Tenby, the carved bosses (169 in all), are skilfully carved with humorous designs. The most impressive of all the roofs, however, are those at St. David's Cathedral. In the choir the flat timber ceiling is supported on five great beams, each elaborately carved, and each of the four bays thus formed is divided into twelve main panels (which are further sub divided into four smaller panels) with decorated bosses at the intersections. Over the nave there is an amazing oriental-looking roof with huge decorated wooden pendants supported on magnificently carved and fretted beams, the sixteenth-century timber equivalent of stone fan-vaulting of which there is also a fine example in the Trinity Chapel at St. David's.[14]

Perhaps the most remarkable feature of late medieval churches in Wales, however, is the *croglen* or rood-screen. Excellent examples have survived in isolated places away from the heavy hands of the iconoclastic reformers. How many, we wonder, were gutted and destroyed in later centuries? These examples of Welsh craftsmanship remain, to remind us of a lost heritage. In some cases, the rood-screens and rood-lofts are traditionally supposed to have come from nearby monastic houses, e.g. Llanrwst from Aberconwy, Llanegryn (near Tywyn) from Cymer, and Llananno (near Llandrindod) from Abbey Cwm-hir. The most impressive examples have the *croglen* placed under a loft, the whole construction forming a division between nave and chancel. The soffit and parapet of the loft together with the supporting beam were most intricately carved and decorated while the face of the structure was sometimes constructed with numerous recesses for carved statues. The screens and lofts appear to have been carved by local craftsmen so that each region has its own distinctive characteristics. Thus screens in the Severn Valley area are bold and rich while those hidden away in the Black Mountains are generally more restrained and delicate, as at Llanfillo and Patrisio. The rood-loft at Patrisio, based on a simple repetitive pattern, has the different charm and slender grace of lace-work (plate 19). But the screens at Llananno in the heart of Powys and Llangwm Uchaf in Gwent, are exuberant with an unbridled abundance of intricate detail.

One cannot but sense that the Welsh craftsman responsible for such complex and embroidered works of art — lineally descended as they were from Celtic forebears who similarly, in their bronze and iron work before the Romans came, achieved such magical intricacy, and descended also from the carvers of the profusely sculptured crosses of the Early Christian period — were working in an age-old ethnic tradition. In the marvellously original interpretations of a limited range of themes, a sculptured Celtic cross and the medieval Welsh carpentry of a *croglen* can be seen to be not just isolated phenomena but part of a wider cultural field that included sound as well as vision. Our innate tendencies in the arts — when historical conditions allow a kind of flourishing — are exactly mirrored in the uniquely complex sound patterns of alliteration and assonance in Welsh poetry throughout the centuries. A *cywydd* by Dafydd ap Gwilym (contemporary of Chaucer) is the aural equivalent of Celtic interlaced work, and of a late rood-screen. It is no accident that the senior British language — Welsh — should be in structural terms probably the most architectonic of all living European languages. And it is no coincidence that (as Glanmor Williams has written) 'the poets of Wales ranked carpenters alongside themselves as artists, and it was no mean tribute to the mastery of the woodworkers over their medium that the bards were fond of likening their own use of words to the carpenters' carving of wood.'[15]

NOTES TO CHAPTER 3

[1] Giraldus Cambrensis, Archdeacon of Brecon in 1175, waxed eloquent (in his *Itinerary through Wales*) in praise of Llan-ddew where he had obtained, he said 'in these temperate regions . . . a place of dignity . . . a small residence, well adapted to literary pursuits, and to the contemplation of eternity.'

[2] Sir Cyril Fox, *Archaeologia Cambrensis,* vol. 86 Cardiff, 1931).

[3] Llanddewibrefi is a particularly sacred spot and reputedly witnessed a famous miracle in the early sixth century when the patron saint was preaching there at a synod. According to Giraldus Cambrensis 'David was reluctantly raised to the archbishopric by the unanimous consent and election of the whole assembly, who by loud acclamations testified their admiration . . .'

[4] Much of the famous *Brut y Tywysogion* ('Chronicle of the Princes'), was written at Ystrad Fflur. By the thirteenth century Ystrad Fflur had become the national sanctuary and during that century no less than nine of the minor Welsh princes were buried there. Dafydd ap Gwilym, perhaps the greatest of all Welsh medieval poets, is also reputed to have been buried in the grounds of the monastery.

[5] In England the earliest Romanesque architecture is known as Anglo-Saxon and pre-dates the Norman conquest. Anglo-Saxon buildings appear to have had little impact on the architecture of Wales except in a few churches in the extreme south-east such as St. Peter's, Cogan (near Penarth), which still retains some herring-bone masonry in its walls.

[6] Margam and Abbey Dore have a further uniqueness; the first is the only Cistercian church in Britain with a nave still consecrated as a permanent place of worship and the second is the only Cistercian church with its choir still in use. Abbey Dore, like all the churches in the Ewyas district of Herefordshire, remained within the Diocese of St. David's until the beginning of the twentieth century. The name 'Dore' is a derivation of the Welsh *dŵr* (water).

[7] Giraldus Cambrensis, writing in 1188 when the chancel, transepts and centre crossing had been completed, commented that the church . . . 'is covered with lead and constructed of wrought Parian stone (the local Red Sandstone) . . . and with these the church is beautifully built.' He also considered the situation of Llanthony 'truly calculated for religion, and more adapted to canonical discipline than all the monasteries of the British isle.'

[8] Earlier churches in similar style had been built at Canterbury and by Cistercian monks in northern England.

[9] The nave of Abbey Cwm-hir measured 73 metres by 21 metres and was the largest in Wales.

[10] The timber posts remain but the belfry was replaced in 1709 by a spire.

[11] Aberconwy was almost completely destroyed by the troops of Edward I and all its priceless chronicles of the Welsh princes burnt.

[12] The Seven Wonders of Wales in the rhyme are: 'Pistyll Rhaeadr and Wrexham Steeple', Snowdon's mountain, without its people: Overton yew trees, St. Winifred's well, Llangollen Bridge and Gresford Bells'.

[13] The justifiable main claim to fame of Old Radnor is two unique treasures; the transitional Gothic Renaissance organ casing of about 1500, considered to be the oldest in the British Isles, and the truly remarkable font — obese and megalithic — of unknown antiquity, but doubtless once used as a pagan cult-stone.

[14] The nave roof of the cathedral is a very special case for there appears to be no parallel elsewhere. It was erected between 1495 and 1508 to replace the original high-pitched roof and in constructing it the builders had to incorporate massive tie-beams to contend with sagging arches and deflecting walls.

[15] Glanmor Williams, *The Welsh Church from Conquest to Reformation* (Cardiff, 1962).

7. Penmon Priory, Anglesey, Gwynedd. 12th century.

8. St. Padarn's Church, Llanbadarn Fawr, Dyfed. Early 13th century.

50

9.   Ystrad Fflur (Strata Florida) Abbey, Dyfed. Thw West Doorway.

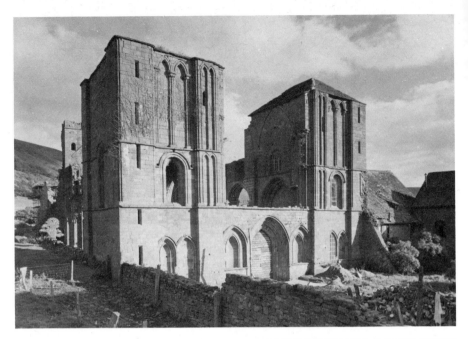

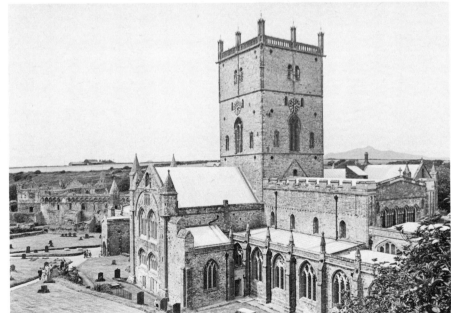

10. Llanthony Priory, Gwent. Early 13th century west front.

11. St. David's Cathedral, Dyfed. 12th to 15th centuries. Bishop's Palace in the background.

12. St. David's Cathedral, Dyfed. Interior showing 12th century Nave arcades and early 16th century Nave ceiling.

13. Llandaf Cathedral, Cardiff. The west front showing early 13th century lancet windows in the centre, 15th century (Perpendicular) Jasper Tower on left and 19th century Prichard Tower on right.

14. Tintern Abbey, Gwent. Late 13th century
    to early 14th century.
15. St. Mary's Church, Caerau, near Cardiff.
    The western tower has a 'saddleback' roof
    typical of many coastal churches in
    Glamorgan.

54

16. St. Giles' Church, Wrexham, Clwyd.
'Perpendicular' tower added in 1506.

17. St. Beuno's Church, Clynnog Fawr,
    Gwynedd. Late 15th century or early 16th
    century.
18. St. John's Church, Cardiff. 'Perpendicular'
    tower added in 1473.

19. Roodscreen and roodloft at Patrisio
Church, near Crickhowell, Powys.

Chapter 4
The Middle Ages II ~ Secular

The greatest architectural heritage of Wales is its many castles. It is a land of castles, earth and stone, numbering hundreds and located in all parts, but most densely in the southern lowlands and along the narrow coastal belt of the north. Their remains, often on dramatic sites, make them striking and melancholy reminders of a turbulent past. The range of castles covers almost all types from small twelfth-century earthen mottes to massive and complex stone structures, covering many acres, built as late as the mid-fifteenth century. Thus it is possible to follow in Wales the complete development of castle building from modest beginnings to some which may be counted amongst the most splendid fortresses of Europe.

The chief reason for the profusion of castles stems from the very different reactions of Wales and of England to the French (i.e. Norman) invasion. It will be remembered that the Romano-British ancestors of these same princes had, between the departure of the Roman legions in 410 and the Battle of Chester in 616, desperately withstood the advance across Britain of the foreign invaders of that time, Angles, Saxons, and Jutes; after over two hundred years of rearguard action they had at last stopped the invaders on the very borders of Wales. Now, in contrast to the swift overthrow of Harold's England following the Norman *coup de grace* at Hastings in the autumn of 1066,[1] it took the same invaders, again, over two hundred years to achieve the subjugation of Wales itself, a conquest somewhat uncertainly achieved even by 1284.

The remains of something like six hundred early castles may be seen today in Wales and the Welsh Marches as the testimony of these two hard fought centuries[2] (fig. 36). They symbolise on the one hand the persistent pressure of the invaders, and on the other, the determined opposition and tenacity of the Welsh princes in the defence of their country.

The Castles of the Normans

Soon after the collapse of the English state in 1066 the Norman conquerors were probing the frontiers of Wales with their forces. While Gwent succumbed fairly quickly (it had previously been raided and wasted by Harold not long before his death), over twenty years were to elapse before the southern coastal areas, as far as Pembroke, were overrun and the land shared out amongst Norman free-booters. The Welsh, refusing to capitulate, withdrew to the safety of the hills.

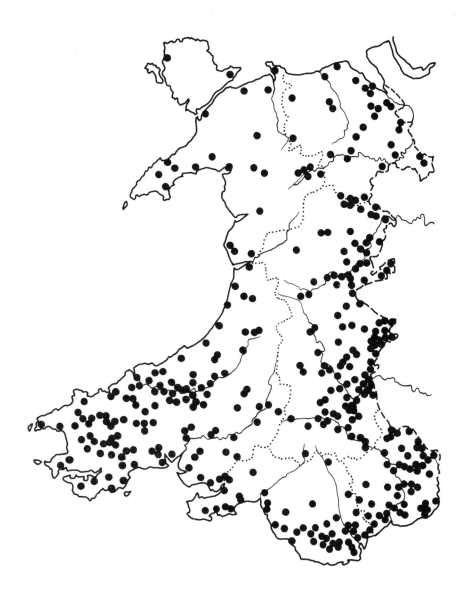

36. Distribution of Castles (mainly Timber and
Earthwork) in the 11th and 12th centuries (after
A.H.A.Hogg and D.J.C.King)

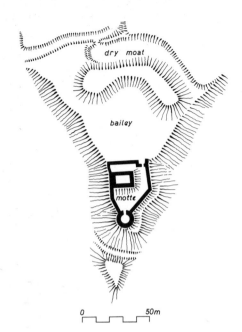

dry moat

bailey

motte

0   50m

37.   Motte-and-bailey castle, Ystradfellte,
Powys: plan

As the invaders penetrated further along the perimeter of the country, they erected castles to defend their newly won territories from the incursions of their former owners.

Apart from the notable exception of Chepstow, the earliest of the Norman castles were of earth and timber and of these the commonest type was that now known as a motte-and-bailey (fig. 37). The motte (*tomen* or *twmpath* in Welsh), a flat-topped earthen mound in the shape of a truncated cone, was surmounted by a circular stockade of timber and a wooden keep-tower. The mound itself was encircled by a ditch, the excavation of which provided the material for the mound. Normally, there was also an outer courtyard or bailey adjoining the motte, to accommodate the horses and supplies; this was defended by an earthen bank carrying another stockade. In addition to the motte-and-bailey type there were various forms of ring-work castles. In the simplest form the motte was omitted altogether, the keep being placed on the flat ground within a circular earthen bank; sometimes the keep and bailey were merged into a single defensive structure.

An excellent example of an early Norman motte, a very large one, still encircled by its moat, was that built about 1090 by Robert Fitzhamon at Cardiff Castle. Other good examples exist at Morganstown (near Cardiff), at Crug Eryr (near New Radnor) and Montgomery (Hen Domen) in Powys, at Rhuddlan (Twt Hill) and at Sycharth and Castell yr Adwy in Clwyd (plate 20).

The more important of the motte-and-bailey castles were later rebuilt in stone (fig. 38). The keep was nearly always the first part to be replaced though not of necessity on the top of the motte. Usually entered at first-floor level from an external staircase, it contained a great hall and the private apartments of the lord. After completing a new keep the bailey defences would be reconstructed as a stone curtain-wall and finally a square or twin-towered gateway was sometimes added to the curtain-wall to defend the main approach to the castle.

The earliest stone keeps were square or rectangular in plan and massive in construction. The three-storey keep at Ogmore (built by Guillame de Londres in 1120) is one of the earliest examples although now in a very ruined state. The main hall on the first floor — now open to the sky — is of peculiar interest because the remarkable hooded fireplace still to be seen there is probably the oldest in Wales. The original earthen ramparts surrounding the castle were retained and used as a base for a curtain-wall erected in the early thirteenth century. At Coity, also in the Vale of Glamorgan, the new keep and curtain-wall were built together inside the original moat at the end of the twelfth century. The keep is somewhat smaller than that at Ogmore, although the walls are of great thickness, and it is unlikely that it

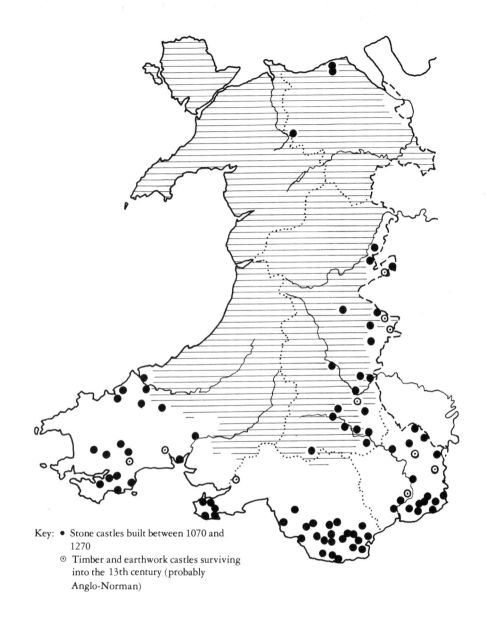

Key: • Stone castles built between 1070 and
1270
⊙ Timber and earthwork castles surviving
into the 13th century (probably
Anglo-Norman)

38. Distribution of Early Stone Castles
(Foreign). Territory subject to Llewelyn ap
Gruffydd in 1267 is shaded. See Appendix H for
list of castles

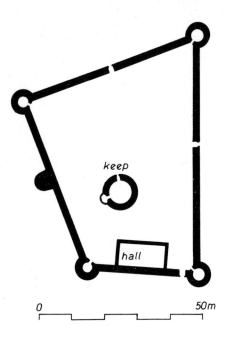

keep

hall

0   50m

was intended for permanent residence. In the thirteenth century a handsome three-storey round tower was projected from the curtain wall, to provide cross-fire, while in the following century the castle was further strengthened by additional gatehouses and curtain-walls enclosing the outer ward or bailey.

In most cases where motte-and-bailey castles were rebuilt in stone the original motte was re-used as the site of the new keep. When this happened it was usual to replace the timber stockade on top of the motte either with a square tower or a more advanced form of redoubt, known as a shell-keep, either polygonal or circular in plan. One of the finest and best preserved examples of a shell-keep stands within the remains of the Roman fort at Cardiff, where in the thirteenth century, the Normans replaced the earlier keep with a twelve-sided masonry curtain-wall on top of Fitzhamon's earlier motte (fig. 109 and plate 21). Cardiff was one of the most important fortresses in southern Wales, for it was from this base that the conquering lords attempted to control the rich and fertile lands of the Vale of Glamorgan. In order to further strengthen the castle the huge earthen rampart of the castle was raised over the remains of the Roman wall to form a large rectangular bailey and the original outer ditch was deepened. Nevertheless, precautions on this scale had not been sufficient to prevent a famous feat in 1158 when Ifor Bach of Senghennydd with a few followers scaled the walls of the old keep at dead of night and kidnapped the castle's lord, the Earl of Gloucester, together with his Countess and son and held them in the hills until his political demands were met. Two-and-a-half centuries later, in 1404, Owain Glyndŵr took the castle by storm and burnt the Norman township of Cardiff.

The castle of Tretower, in the lovely Usk Valley near Crickhowell, is an interesting if unusual example of the development of Norman military architecture. There at the end of the eleventh century a typical motte-and-bailey castle was built to block and control the pass over the Black Mountains. The large bailey was triangular in plan and at one corner there was a small earthen mound surmounted by its wooden keep-tower. In all the subsequent rebuilding this basic layout was retained and can still be clearly seen. At some time during the middle of the twelfth century, the wooden keep was replaced by a stone polygonal shell-keep incorporating the hall and domestic rooms. Within a few decades however, the castle was overwhelmed and gutted by the Welsh during one of their interminable counter-offensives. This probably occurred either in the campaign of Rhys ap Gruffydd of Deheubarth in 1197 or in the great sweep southwards of Llywelyn Fawr (the Great) himself in 1216. On its restoration to Norman hands, it seems to have been decided not to repair the much damaged shell-keep; the defence system was reinforced instead by a great round tower, three storeys high, slotted into the very narrow confines of the keep. It would appear that this policy was unique for there seems to be no other

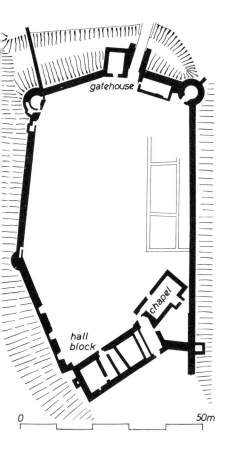

instance of a large round tower being built actually inside and independent of an earlier square or polygonal keep. It was during these last building operations, in all probability that the bailey stockade (presumably destroyed in the Welsh attacks) was replaced by a stone perimeter wall.

The round towers, such as the one at Tretower, newly introduced in the thirteenth century were a considerable improvement on the earlier angular towers, the corners of which were vulnerable to attack by battering rams. Circular towers on the other hand offered a smooth surface all around and stones could not therefore be so easily dislodged. The most impressive example of the round type is the monumental Great Keep at Pembroke Castle, built probably about 1210 by William Marshal (plate 30). Five storeys high with six-metre thick walls and originally covered by a stone dome, it stands independent of any other structure in the centre of the courtyard. Its colossal scale is emphasised by a complete absence of surface relief apart from two slight set-backs dividing the tower into three stages.[3] Skenfrith Castle, in Gwent, is altogether smaller and simpler in scale than Pembroke, but nevertheless, illustrates the use of rounded towers perfectly. Here, the isolated keep-tower is circular, as are all the towers at the corners of the quadrangular curtain wall (fig. 39).

Many keeps were not built as separate and isolated structures but were incorporated into the fabric of the outer curtain-wall. White Castle and Caldicot Castle (both in Gwent) are examples of this type of 'ring-castle.' At the former the keep is rectangular in plan and built parallel with the curtain-wall, but at Caldicot the keep was erected at one corner of the courtyard as a formidable round tower on top of the original motte. At Manorbier, in Dyfed, the keep-tower has been replaced by a large hall-block (dating from the twelfth century) which closes the gap between the curtain walls at one end of the inner ward (fig. 40). The arrangement of ring-castles varies considerably. Caldicot and Manorbier are irregular in plan and so is Penrice in the Gower; White Castle is oval-shaped, Grosmont (also in Gwent) is semi-circular, while Castell Coch at Tongwynlais near Cardiff (possibly of Welsh, not Norman, foundation) was built to a triangular layout with large round towers at each of the three corners.

Amongst the most striking of all the early castles, however, is that at Chepstow alongside the river Wye which here forms the dramatic frontier between Wales and England. The shape of its spectacular site, between the high limestone cliffs of the Wye on one side and a deep ravine on the other, strictly controlled the layout of the castle, which consequently has an irregular plan of extraordinary length divided by cross-walls into four separate courtyards or baileys; the earliest part is the

40. Manorbier Castle, Dyfed: plan

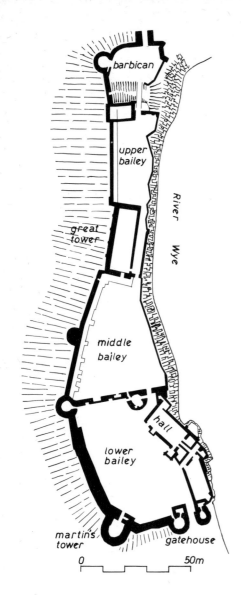

rectangular keep in the centre of the castle, where the site is narrowest. This was the first of the Norman castles to be started on the Welsh side of Offa's Dyke (between 1067 and 1072, simultaneous with their first Welsh monastery here) and because of its strategic importance, it was constructed in stone. From Chepstow the Normans pushed westwards along the southern coastal strip building castles as they went, and reached the Tywi estuary in Dyfed by 1112. For almost two centuries this plus the Pembroke promontory (which had been seized separately from the north by the Earl of Shrewsbury) was virtually the limit of permanent Norman occupation.[4]

Even Gwent was not at first easily held as the constant rebuilding and enlargement of Chepstow Castle testifies. The alterations and additions carried out there, mostly during the middle years of the thirteenth century, eventually covered the whole of the long narrow ridge (fig. 41). The final result was a magnificent array of rectangular and circular towers, perched on the edge of the precipitous cliffs overlooking the Wye, all linked by lofty curtain walls and comparable in general effect with the great Edwardian castles built later in northern Wales (plate 22).

Cestyll Cymru — The Castles of the Welsh Princes

Altogether there are about two dozen stone castles which are known to be of Welsh origin (fig. 42). Apart from two early outposts north of Cardiff, they all lie within the territory which was subject to Llywelyn ap Gruffydd (Llywelyn II) — the last independent Prince of Wales — and were mostly built in the thirteenth century.[5] Before his death the Normans had succeeded in northern Wales in building only a few castles and these were mostly sited in the valleys near the eastern border. The Welsh fortresses, on the other hand, were sited in most parts of northern and central Wales, with heavier concentrations in Eryri and the Vale of Tywi. About half still have quite considerable remains; the rest show only featureless fragments, for eventual destruction by victorious Normans was sometimes exceptionally thorough, as was to be expected.

More than a third of the native castles were sited in Gwynedd, in the mountainous north-western part of the country. One of the largest and earliest of these was Castell Degannwy, near Conwy. It occupied an ancient fortified site straddling two volcanic outcrops overlooking the sea on both sides. A double line of defence joined the two hills, the larger of which carried a small bailey with three round towers and the other one a large D-shaped tower. Being so closely associated with the royal house of Wales, Degannwy was virtually blotted out by Edward I as the final affirmation of his triumph and consequently little now remains of this once important royal *castell*.

41. Chepstow Castle, Gwent: plan

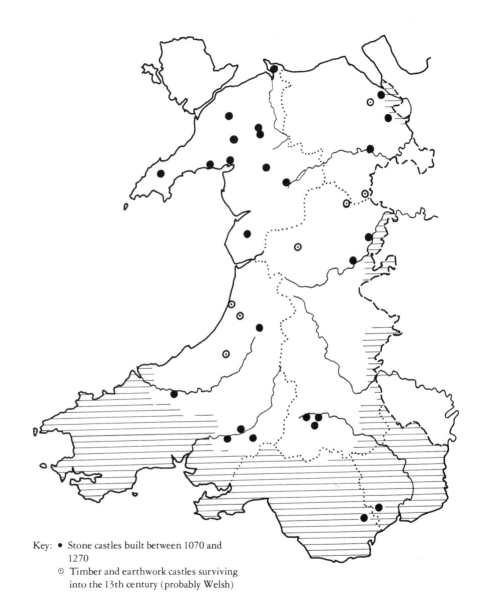

Key: • Stone castles built between 1070 and
        1270
      ⊙ Timber and earthwork castles surviving
        into the 13th century (probably Welsh)

42.   Distribution of Early Stone Castles (Welsh).
Territory under Anglo-Norman domination in
1267 is shaded. See Appendix H for list of castles

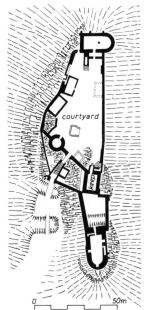

43. Castell Dolwyddelan, Gwynedd: plan

44. Castell y Bere, Gwynedd: plan

The *cestyll* at Dinas Emrys, Dolwyddelan and Dolbadarn all crown rocky outcrops guarding important valleys leading into the heart of Eryri, the last stronghold of the Welsh princes. Castell Dinas Emrys, near Beddgelert, was built on the site of a Dark Age camp and had a square tower of which there are now only scant remains. Castell Dolwyddelan, the royal manor of Nantconwy, is traditionally the birthplace of Llywelyn the Great (Llywelyn I). The tall rectangular keep probably dates from his time, about 1170, and now stands as a lonely sentinel in the rugged landscape. The ruined west tower, built later but also rectangular, together with the angular curtain wall, may date from the end of his reign (fig. 43). Only sixteen kilometres away another of his strongholds, Castell Dolbadarn, stands at the foot of Yr Wyddfa (Snowdon), in romantic surroundings by the edge of Llyn Peris. Its most important feature is the large round tower attributed to Llywelyn the Great (plate 23). Of the rest of the castle only fragments of the curtain wall and two rectangular towers are now left. The history of this *castell* is obscure but traditionally it is the place where Llywelyn ap Gruffydd imprisoned his brother, Owain Goch, for more than twenty years.

Castell Cricieth, in the Llŷn peninsular, is situated on a rocky spur overlooking the sea. Although captured and partly rebuilt by Edward I, the major features of the castle are the work of the Welsh princes. The polygonal inner ward with its massive twin-towered gateway was built by Llywelyn the Great. The *castell* is still well preserved, mainly no doubt as a result of Edward I's renovations. The outer ward, irregular in plan to fit the site, with two large rectangular towers at the angles, is thought to have been built by Llywelyn ap Gruffydd in the mid-thirteenth century.

Further south, among the mountains of Meirionnydd, there were four Welsh castles. Only one of these — Castell y Bere, lying at the foot of Cadair Idris — has any significant remains. Even here the remains are not very extensive, despite the fact that Edward I later repaired it for his own use. The high quality of the carved stonework at Bere shows, however, that it was one of the most richly ornamented as well as one of the largest of the native castles. Built by Llywelyn the Great as his headquarters in the early thirteenth century (c.1221), it must have been, in its heyday, a very impressive structure. The fortress was built on an isolated rocky outcrop, with a precipitous south face, high above the Afon Dysynni and 'must have presented the ideal picture of an eagle's nest dominating its valley.'[6] A triangular barbican, built across the rocks and overlooked by a round tower, defends the entrance behind which is a large courtyard with the residential quarters and, on the highest point, a rectangular keep (fig. 44). The castle was further defended by formidable D-shaped towers soaring above the cliffs at either end of the site. As in so many of the Welsh castles the ground plan at Bere is directly related to the ground itself and hugs the contours, emphasising the topography of the hill (plate

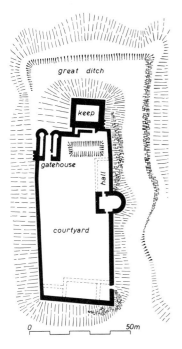

great ditch

keep

gatehouse

hall

courtyard

0   50m

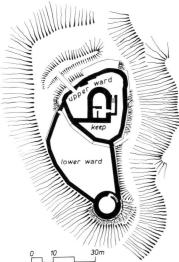

upper ward

keep

lower ward

0   10   30m

45.   Castell Dinas Brân, Clwyd: plan
46.   Castell Ewloe, Clwyd: plan

24). Is there not here an echo of the organic attitudes of the earlier Celts as expressed by the sinuous lines of banks and ditches which defended their hill-forts, and the sensuous interweaving of their decorative art?

In Powys there were five native stone castles, but only two in the north-east show anything other than the barest of remains. Castell Dinas Brân was built in the mid-thirteenth century on the crest of the mountain overlooking Llangollen and the Dee far below. The ruins show that it comprised a large rectangular ward containing a large square keep at one end and a typically Welsh apsidal tower on one of the long sides overlooking a formidable rock-cut ditch (fig. 45). The apparently simple plan was remarkably well fitted to the towering site and provided at the same time the basis for an opulent residence as well as an enormously powerful fortress.[7] Castell Ewloe, near the mouth of the Dee, is more complete than Dinas Brân and appears to have been built at two different periods. The older part, in the form of a large apsidal tower, was almost certainly built by Llewelyn the Great as a forward base to fend off the Earls of Chester (fig. 46). Surrounding the keep are the curtain walls of the upper ward built above a precipitous rock face. This ward, together with the lower ward and the circular tower beyond, was built in the mid-thirteenth century by Llywelyn ap Gruffydd. The original Welsh castle of Powys itself (or Castell Coch as it is known in Welsh), near Welshpool, has been completely obscured by later building. Also Welsh in origin was the curious castle at Caergwrle, built about 1277 by Dafydd ap Gruffydd with English help as a redoubt from which to launch attacks both against his brother, Llywelyn II, and the English barons.

The Tywi valley, in southern Wales, was the main stronghold of Dyfed and here there was a trio of native castles near Llandeilo. Castell Dinefwr is historically the most important of the three and is comparable with Castell y Bere in the north. For centuries Dinefwr had been the southern capital, the seat of Rhodri Mawr (the Great) himself in the latter part of the ninth century, and during the late twelfth-century it became the headquarters of Rhys ap Gruffydd (the Lord Rhys). The existing remains of the *castell*, overlooking the Tywi, comprise a large thirteenth-century round keep-tower surrounded by an angular curtain-wall which still stands more or less intact and may date from the late twelfth-century.

Dryslwyn, a few kilometres away, was built on top of a steep hill also near the banks of the Tywi. The remains are now mere fragments of the original large *castell* which consisted of three curtain walls with a hall and chapel in the inner ward. The citadel of Carreg Cennen stands at the very edge of a 100 metre precipice and is one of the most romantically impressive castle sites in the whole of Wales. While most of the original Welsh structure has been obscured by later additions, built at the end of the thirteenth century, the character of Castell Carreg Cennen — megalithic

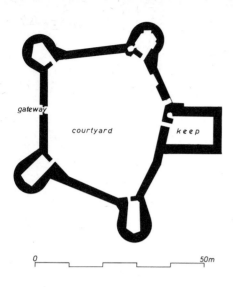

gateway

courtyard

keep

0   50m

and defiant — is still as intensively Cymric and Celtic as its name. Here is the classic example of the *castell* designed as a fortified 'last stand', the last refuge for the men of Ystrad Tywi if both Dinefwr and Dryslwyn fell.

Further east, in the upper Usk valley, there were possibly three castles belonging to the Welsh princes. Castell Pont-senni (Sennybridge) and Castell Camlais, on Mynydd Illtud, alone have any remains. Camlais is a near perfect example of a high conical mound encircled by a deep ditch, but the round stone tower which once stood on the summit of the mound has almost disappeared.

Of the two native castles north of Cardiff, only Castell Morgraig has extensive remains and these, although excavated in 1903, are now again largely overgrown. It was probably built by one of the Welsh Lords of Senghennydd, on the steep slopes of Caerphilly Mountain, to defend the valleys to the north against the Norman lord of Glamorgan. It appears never to have been occupied, however, which suggests that the Welsh were forced to withdraw from the site before completing the work. The interesting plan of Morgraig shows that it was pentagonal in shape, with round towers at four of the corners and a rectangular keep at the fifth (fig. 47). The well-carved stonework, found during excavations, indicates that it would have been a fortress of some architectural pretentions if history had allowed its completion.

Edwardian and Later Castles

Throughout the twelfth and thirteenth centuries there was almost constant warfare between the Welsh and the Anglo-Normans. The territories owing allegiance to the Welsh rulers fluctuated with the strength or weakness of individual princes. By the middle of the thirteenth century Llywelyn ap Gruffydd, Prince of Gwynedd, seemed all-powerful. Following a series of victories by Llywelyn the Treaty of Montgomery was concluded in 1267 and Llywelyn was confirmed as Prince of Wales. At its greatest extent, as a consequence of this treaty, the area under Llywelyn's rule expanded to include all the counties of modern Wales except Glamorgan, Gwent and the extreme south-west corner of Dyfed. The treaty, however, was little more than an armistice and did not ensure a lasting settlement. Between 1273 and 1277 disputes arose between Llywelyn and the new English king, Edward I, sparked off by the prince's right to erect a castle within his own domain at Dolforwyn in the Severn valley, close to the English border. The eventual outcome was the first War of Independence, which ended in 1277 in partial defeat for Llywelyn when famine forced his surrender. This was followed by the second War of Independence (1282-83) which was even more disastrous. Llywelyn ap Gruffydd — the last of the princes in continuous line of descent from Cunedda Wledig, founder of the royal dynasties

47.   Castell Morgraig, Glamorgan: plan

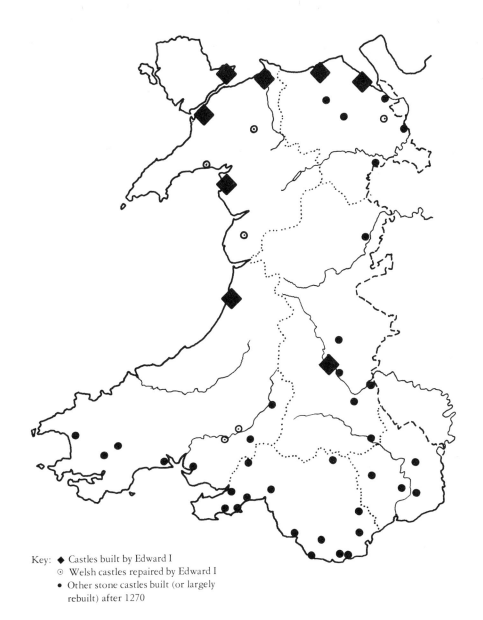

Key: ◆ Castles built by Edward I
      ⊙ Welsh castles repaired by Edward I
      ● Other stone castles built (or largely
         rebuilt) after 1270

48. Distribution of Edwardian and Late Stone
Castles. See Appendix I for list of castles.

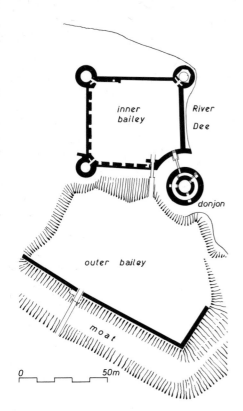

in Wales during the fifth century — was assasinated near Builth on 11 December, 1282.

In order to retain control of his newly-won lands Edward I immediately started to build vast new fortresses for his army of occupation all along the coast of northern Wales, at intervals of 20 to 30 kilometres, from Flint to Aberystwyth (fig. 48). These were a new and much more formidable type of castle than the earlier Norman ones and were planned where possible with near-impregnable concentric wards, i.e. an inner ward with a high curtain-wall surrounded by an outer ward with a lower curtain-wall which sometimes also served as a retaining wall, as at Harlech. The outmoded keep was dispensed with, its place being taken by a more aggressively planned defence structure based on a system of massive twin-towered gatehouses and massive circular towers (or polygonal towers in the case of Caernarfon) attached to massive curtain-walls. The chief architect and designer of the castles, mentioned many times in contemporary documents, was James of St. Georges-d'Espéranche whom Edward had borrowed from his cousin Count Philip of Savoy.[8] Immensely strong though the Savoyard's castles were, two of them — Aberystwyth and Harlech — were overwhelmed by Owain Glyndŵr's massed forces in 1404 during the third War of Independence.

Flint castle, one of Edward's original quartet of fortresses, was not of the concentric type.[9] Begun in 1277 it was arranged according to a most unusual plan consisting of a rectangular court enclosed by lofty walls with strong drum towers projecting from three of the corners, but with a much larger round *donjon* or keep-tower in place of the fourth corner, separated from the rest of the castle by a circular moat.[10] (fig. 49).

Edward's second castle, built alongside the Clwyd at Rhuddlan between 1277 and 1282, was his first of a concentric type, but of deceptively simple plan. The inner ward is lozenge-shaped with single round towers at two opposite corners and paired round gatehouse-towers at the other two corners. The outer ward is more irregular in shape and is protected by a low curtain-wall surrounded by a moat fed from the adjacent river. In order to ensure that the castle would be provisioned in the event of a siege the Afon Clwyd was canalised and deepened at great expense, to make it navigable for sea-going ships. It was from Rhuddlan in 1284 that Edward I issued his *Statute of Wales* proclaiming the conquered lands as a private principality of the king. Aberystwyth castle, on the west coast, was built about the same time as Rhuddlan and was similar in layout except that it had only one twin-towered gatehouse.

The largest castles built by Edward were at Conwy and Caernarfon. The former was started in 1283, within a few weeks of the defeat of the Welsh armies. In the

49.   Flint Castle, Clwyd: plan

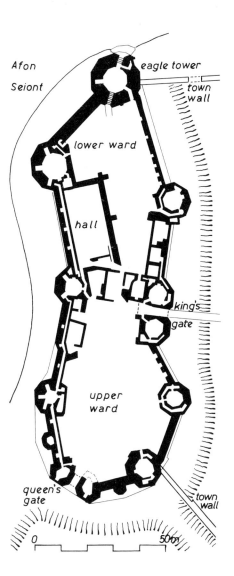

50. Caernarfon Castle, Gwynedd: plan

summer of 1283 ditching was also started at Caernarfon. Because of their elongated rocky sites, both castles were built with a single curtain-wall and could not therefore be concentric in form. Conwy castle has eight bold circular towers and is subdivided into an upper and lower ward by a cross-wall. Whereas Conwy is massive and rounded Caernarfon castle is massive and angular, tall, and aesthetically more pleasing. It is even more irregular in plan, but was similarly divided into two wards and was protected by colossal curtain walls and eleven immense towers (including two twin-towered gatehouses), polygonal in plan, and two smaller towers (fig. 50). The main towers at Caernarfon are topped by long octagonal turrets and the connecting curtain-walls are threaded with internal shooting galleries in a complicated arrangement at various levels. The formidable strength of the castle is nowhere more apparent than in the main entrance, the King's Gate, which was approached by a drawbridge and protected by five gates and six portcullises with arrow-loops between the divisions and 'murder holes' in the vaulting above. The architectural treatment throughout is highly sophisticated for a military structure, with finely coursed masonry in different coloured bands and subtle offsets to the walls and towers (plate 25). No expense was spared in building this spectacular citadel, for it was intended to be seen as the status symbol of the conqueror, palace of an Anglo-Norman 'Prince of Wales' and the administrative headquarters of his new principality. Altogether it took almost half a century to build (and even then it was never completely finished) and cost at least £20,000 or something like five or six million pounds in terms of today's money.

The lavishness with which the castle at Caernarfon was built did little to cow the Welsh into abject submission, however, as is shown by the violence of their insurrection of September 1294 led by Madog ap Llywelyn. In the rising the town was overwhelmed and occupied, the walls thrown down and the castle burnt. For six months the great castle built to overawe the Welsh was in the hands of the Welsh. In the summer of 1295 Edward had to start again from the bare lower walls.

Strategically Caernarfon was, along with the great castles at Conwy and Harlech, part of the military scheme 'to embrace and grip the intractable heart of northern Wales.'[11] Tactically, Caernarfon was a special case. The extravagant nature of its design, and the way the building progressed after Madog's rebellion, suggests that it was not only a source of great pride to Edward I, but it may also have been a peculiar attempt at ameliorating the wounded pride of the Welsh. Why else should the timber Great Hall of Llywelyn ap Gruffydd have been removed in 1316 from the prince's former residence and re-erected within the walls of the castle a few years after Madog (a cousin of the prince) had captured and burnt it? Even more telling perhaps is the fact that the castle was erected almost within a stone's throw of the Roman fort of Segontium, a place traditionally associated with Constantine and Helen his mother, wife of the emperor Magnus Maximus.[12]

One of the Welsh names for Caernarfon was Caer Cystennin (i.e. Fort of Constantine), and this, incidentally, was also (and still is) the Welsh name for Constantinople. The capture of one of the chief places of the Welsh princes — the *Constantinople* of Wales — was therefore of great symbolic importance and this is reflected in the concept of the castle which Edward I commissioned, the angular towers of which were designed to be almost identical in appearance (even to the alternating bands of stone) with the towers of the mighty town walls of the other Constantinople on the Bosporus.[13] The latter had been conquered by the Crusaders in 1204. It is probable, therefore, that the system of curtain-walls and numerous projecting towers which had encircled Constantinople since the fifth century was the original prototype for the great concentric castles (e.g. Krak des Chevaliers) built by the Crusaders in Syria and the Holy Land, a system which in turn was adopted by Richard Coeur de Lion in France and by Edward I in Wales. It is significant, however, that of all Edward's castles only Caernarfon was actually built with polygonal towers (despite the obvious military disadvantage of angular corners) in likeness to the original towers of Constantinople itself.

Caernarfon's distinctive treatment was not confined to a quotation from Imperial Constantinople; it was, for instance, royal policy that decreed the castle as the birthplace, in April 1284, of Edward of Caernarfon (later to be King Edward II) — the first royal child born in Wales since the death of Llywelyn ap Gruffydd. It was this Edward who, in 1317, had three sculptured Roman eagles placed on the topmost turrets of the principle tower — known since then as the Eagle Tower. The tribute to Roman Segontium (which can be clearly seen from the tower) is obvious, but, ironically, the eagle was also the symbol of Owain the Great, King of Gwynedd in the twelfth century and great-great-grandfather of the last Llywelyn.

For Edward's fully developed concentric castles we must turn to Harlech and Beaumaris. Both are superb examples of this type. Harlech, started in 1283, is splendidly situated high above the sea on a steep cliff with a dry-moat cut into the rock on the landward side (plate 26). The castle has a strikingly regular plan consisting of a quadrangle with massive round towers at the four corners linked by high curtain-walls and a majestic gatehouse in the centre of the eastern side, all enclosed by lower walls. Nevertheless, despite Harlech's great strength the castle was successfully beseiged and captured in 1404 a century after its building, by Owain Glyndŵr and was used — until 1409 — as one of the chief administrative centres of independent Wales.

The last of the castles to be built by Edward I in Wales was Beaumaris.[14] Started at the beginning of 1295, as a counteraction to Madog's capture of Caernarfon the previous autumn, it is still almost intact. It lies on a flat site near the Anglesey shore

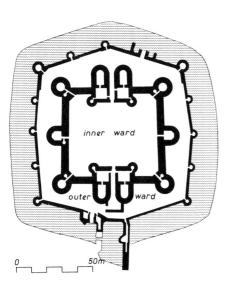

inner ward

outer ward

0   50m

51. Beaumaris Castle, Gwynedd: plan

and is perfectly symmetrical in layout (fig. 51). There is a square inner ward with two twin-towered gatehouses as well as corner and mid-wall towers and surrounding this is an octagonal outer ward with a dozen small round towers. The whole castle was then encircled by a broad wet moat with a dock for shipping, near the entrance, directly connected to the sea. In design and layout Beaumaris is a masterpiece of medieval planning, the epitome of the concentric ideal, with every part covered by cross-fire from the towers. Though overshadowed by Caernarfon and Harlech in sheer grandeur and drama, it is perhaps today the most attractive of all Edward's castles (plate 27).

The most complex and awesome of all the conentric castles, however, was Caerphilly in southern Wales. Admired as the 'greatest castle in the British Isles' by the late H. J. O'Neil (former Chief Inspector of Ancient Monuments) it is also one of the more remarkable fortresses of Europe (plate 28). It was built not by the king but by a Norman baron, Gilbert de Clare, as a redoubt to withstand the threat of Llywelyn ap Gruffydd.

It was, in fact, started in 1271 — a decade before the Edwardian concentric castles of the north — and therefore represents the earliest of the great concentric castles. Covering an area of 30 acres, the castle we see today is the largest medieval fortress in Britain after Windsor, and is, possibly, the largest concentric castle ever built. The central, and apparently the earliest portion is typically concentric in form with a rectangular inner ward incorporating round corner towers and two twin-towered gatehouses, as later in Beaumaris, and an outer ward (fig. 52). This is built on a low-lying spur the neck of which was cut off in two places by moats to form a bastioned redoubt or 'Hornwork' to protect the western side of the inner castle. To the north and south two large artificial lakes were formed, completely enveloping the inner castle and hornwork, converting them into fortified islands. The water in the lakes was held back by a long dam on the eastern side which was later developed into a strongly fortified barrage wall of a type unique in Europe, nearly 300 metres in length, with the main gatehouse in the centre approached by two drawbridges. Finally, another enormous moat was cut to protect the outer face of the barrage! Such was the measure of the Norman lord's fear of the Welsh. The Great Hall at Caerphilly has fortunately been preserved, although the roof, floor and windows have been refurbished. It is a structure of some architectural distinction with graceful ogee-pointed windows and rich interior mouldings.

Other powerful castles were built, re-built or extended by the Marcher lords during the time of Edward I in Clwyd and Dyfed.[15] In addition, many other smaller castles were built during the thirteenth century in various parts of Wales (fig. 48).

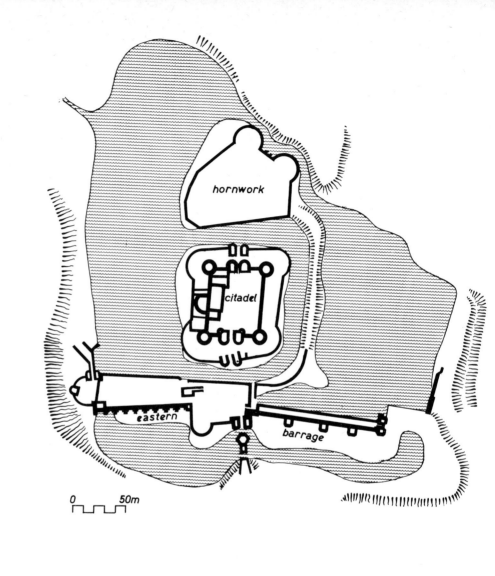

hornwork

citadel

eastern

barrage

0   50m

52.   Caerphilly Castle, Glamorgan: plan

Fortified Palaces and Houses.

One rather special group of castles that must be mentioned comprises the fortified palaces of the bishops. The Bishop's Castle at Llandaf, built about 1280 or a few years earlier, has a medium-size quadrangular courtyard with the remains of a grim twin-towered gateway at one corner and ruins of smaller towers at two of the others. As Edward Freeman wrote in 1850, 'the remains have nothing distinctively episcopal about them; they might as well have been the stronghold of any Norman robber, the lair of the wolf of the fold, rather than its shepherd.' Although ostensibly an ecclesiastical palace it may well have served a more military purpose and formed part of a joint system of defence for the lords of Glamorgan, of whom the bishop (in his lay capacity of lord of the manor of Llandaf) was one. Certainly many of the constructional details at the Bishop's castle are very similar to those at Caerphilly and it is possible that they were both built by the same masons. In 1402 the fortified palace of the 'wolf' of Llandaf was thoroughly sacked by Owain Glyndŵr and its appearance today is virtually as he left it.

The Bishop of St. David's palaces at St. David's and Lamphey were much more extravagant than Llandaf both in size and in architectural treatment. The palace of St. David's, although ruined, is a particularly magnificent building, without equal in Britain (plate 29). Its three imposing wings enclose a square courtyard with the chief apartments built at first-floor level over vaulted undercrofts. The great hall, added by Bishop Henry de Gower in the early fourteenth century, has tall traceried windows and an elegant rose-window at the east end. But the most notable feature of the palace is the beautiful arcaded parapet with which Bishop de Gower embellished the exterior of the great hall and added to the existing east wing. The arcading is veneered with a chequerwork pattern of coloured stones, giving the building an exotic charm in rich contrast to the austere exterior of the nearby cathedral and the grey, rugged landscape of the windswept peninsula. Similar arcaded parapets were also used by de Gower at his other palace, Lamphey, and at Swansea Castle.

The final phase of castle building in Wales relates to the fortified manor houses of the late medieval period. Generally these were large houses meant for embattled living rather than strongholds for garrisons of soldiers. Occasionally, a motte-and-bailey site was re-used, as in the case of Owain Glyndŵr's *llys* at Sycharth. Although burnt by the English in 1403 we know from Iolo Goch's descriptive poem (composed about 1390) that Llys Sycharth included a large cruck-built timber hall set on top of the motte *mewn eurgylch dwfr mewn argae* (in a fine circle of water within an embankment) and that there was a bridge across the moat and lesser buildings in the bailey.

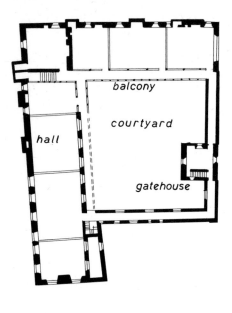

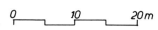

0   10   20m

The siting of Glyndŵr's *llys* was unusual, however, being chosen probably for psychological rather than defence reasons. More often an old castle would be completely superseded by a new building. Tretower Court, for instance, was mainly built in the fifteenth century to replace the Norman castle nearby.[16] Here the main part of this charming stone and timber-framed house comprises two wings on adjacent sides of an attractive courtyard with a large stone-built gatehouse on the entrance side. The gatehouse was linked to the rest of the house by a wall-walk at first floor level, on one side, and by a cantilevered timber balcony on the other (fig.53).

In the north the best known example of a fortified house is Gwydir Castle, near Llanrwst. Started by John ap Maredudd in the sixteenth century, as a four-storey quasi-military mansion, Gwydir was added to and rebuilt over a long period up to the eighteenth century, largely with materials brought from nearby Maenan Abbey. Unfortunately, much of it was gutted by fire at the beginning of the present century, and very little of this picturesque building, with its mullioned windows and choice mouldings, now remains as originally built.

With the building of Raglan Castle in Gwent, on an altogether grander scale than either Tretower or Gwydir, the long era of castle-building in Wales comes to a magnificent end. Originally a Norman motte-and-bailey castle, it was entirely re-built in the mid-fifteenth century to withstand not arrows but cannon-fire(plate 30). Started probably by Sir William ap Thomas, the main lines of the grandiloquent design and layout were conceived by his son, William Herbert, the first Earl of Pembroke. The final fruition of Raglan comprised a large double-courted building with sumptuous apartments on the perimeter and a great hall, 20 metres long, in the centre, between the two courtyards. The art treasures of the family were housed in a palatial gallery, almost 40 metres long, on the first floor. In addition, there was a remarkable Great Tower — hexagonal in plan and built on the site of the original motte — traditionally known as the Yellow Tower of Gwent. The Great Tower, four or five storeys in height, was isolated by a wide and deep moat so that it could be held independently of the rest of the castle in the event of siege. Even these precautions were considered insufficient and further defences in the form of an apron wall with gun-turrets were added around the base of the tower. Additions were also made to the remainder of the castle in the late sixteenth and early seventeenth centuries. The finale of this splendid place came with the surrender of Raglan in 1646 after a two month seige at the end of the first Civil War. The Great Tower which had survived the gun-fire of the seige almost unscathed, was then partly destroyed by Cromwell's mines so that it should never again threaten the peace of Parliament.

Medieval Town Planning.

Apart from Caer-went and Moridunum (Carmarthen) in the Roman period, urban life was not a normal feature of pre-Norman Wales. The native settlement pattern was characterised by isolated farmsteads for the economy of the country was entirely rural. Very small nucleated settlements did, nevertheless, develop at centres of local government — the *maerdrefi* or 'royal' villages — and in the bond-hamlets of serfs who cultivated the royal lands. Occasionally, these pre-urban nuclei appear to have developed into small-scale urban settlements by the medieval period as at Lampeter, Nefyn, Tywyn and Pwllheli. By and large, though, the *maerdrefi* had relatively little influence on the subsequent growth of urban centres.

An urban economy did not develop in Wales until after the Norman conquest; even then it was largely a matter of creating fortified artificial boroughs for new settlers who were introduced under the protective wing of their Norman masters. Towns were founded in the shadow of the castles as much for political as for economic reasons. The Norman lords encouraged their subjects to live near the castle so as to provide a reserve of men capable of defending the lord's territory. In return, charters were bestowed on the towns which gave the burgesses rights to hold fairs and markets. These, and other privilages allowed the settlers, were unavailable to the Welsh living outside the walls.

Most of the towns existing in Wales prior to the Industrial Revolution were founded in this way (fig. 54). The charters of the early towns were largely based on those of Breteuil, a small town in northern France. The 'Laws of Breteuil' were noted for the liberality of the privileges granted to its citizens and these were first adopted in Britain for the new French borough at Hereford, from where it spread to many places in southern Wales, including Cardiff.

In planning the new towns, provision was made for plots of land of standard sizes for the burgesses as well as centrally placed plots for a church and a market. For defensive purposes the settlement was attached to the lord's castle and enclosed by a ditch and strong walls with gatehouses where the roads entered the town. The internal layout of streets was largely fortuitous and depended on the topography of the site. Thus there is no standard layout pattern in the Norman boroughs; each one is different.

With later growth the Norman core became redeveloped with newer buildings, but in many towns, the medieval layout has survived more or less intact. Cowbridge and Llanidloes were based on a cruciform plan with gateways at the centre of each of the four walls. At Cardiff, the western boundary of which was formed by a curving river,

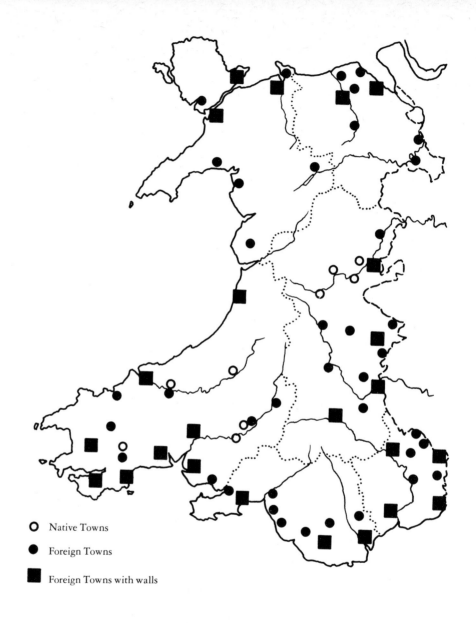

O Native Towns

● Foreign Towns

■ Foreign Towns with walls

54. Distribution of Planted Towns in the
Middle Ages. See Appendix J for list of towns.

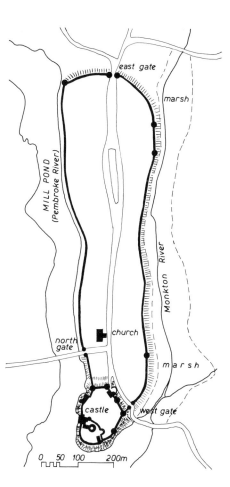

the streets still retain the original T-shaped plan. Both Welshpool and Pembroke have linear plans, but whereas Welshpool's main street follows the river valley, at Pembroke it is aligned along a ridge of high ground between two parallel rivers (fig. 55 and plate 31). Carmarthen, Brecon and Montgomery have irregular block plans within tightly restraining town walls. In Brecon it is the parish church which dominates the town so unusually rather than the castle; the latter is separated from the town by a deep narrow valley. Finally, among these examples there is Tenby, sited on a rocky promontory jutting out into the sea, with a rather vaguely gridded street layout within a severely rectilinear town wall.

Most of the early medieval boroughs have now lost their town walls either as a result of decay or because of nineteenth century expansion. The remains of town walls and their gateways may still be seen in southern Wales however, at Chepstow, Cowbridge, Tenby and Pembroke. A most unusual type of gateway is the fortified gatehouse standing astride the Monnow Bridge at Monmouth (plate 32). Though the Monnow Bridge has since been widened the imposing gatehouse still stands as it was built in 1272.

Out of more than eighty boroughs in medieval Wales, less than a dozen were of native origin and few of these were destined to become fully fledged towns. Some were established in Dyfed in the late thirteenth-century by the Bishop of St. David's and Dinefwr may have been a Welsh borough before nearby Llandeilo was created by the Normans. In the Severn valley Llywelyn ap Gruffydd endeavoured to set up a new town and market in 1273 alongside his castle of Dolforwyn. Because of its nearness to Montgomery and the threat it posed to the English borough's trade, its development was prevented by Edward I. Less than a decade later other boroughs were established across Mid-Wales by the princes of Powys at Caersws, Llanidloes, Newtown and probably also at Machynlleth. Their regular street layouts indicate that the planning of these Welsh new towns had been strongly influenced by Norman precept. In the north Llywelyn's own royal seat at Aberffro, in Anglesey, also seems to have attracted a civil settlement around it, but the ending of native rule in the late thirteenth-century, probably destroyed any future that the town may have had.

The really outstanding examples of medieval urban planning in Wales are the chain of *bastide* towns that Edward I established in the north, along with his castles, at Flint, Rhuddlan, Conwy, Caernarfon, Harlech and Beaumaris in the latter part of the thirteenth century. Like the Norman towns of the south they were naturally based on French models. Whereas the *bastide* towns of south-west France rarely had a castle (and thus provided little security except against small-scale attacks), the Welsh examples were designed to withstand all-out organised warfare, for the

55.   Pembroke, Dyfed: plan of town and castle

Anglo-Normans were constantly alert to the danger of Welsh insurrection. Each town was surrounded by a strong defensive wall with projecting towers, all guarded at one end by the castle. Internally, the layout of each town was based on a gridiron system of rectilinear plots and straight streets. At Caernarfon, for instance, the plots or 'burgages' each measured 24 metres by 18 metres while at Beaumaris they were 24 metres by 9 metres. Exiles from England were induced to settle in the new towns by the grant of a plot within the town walls; they were also given farming land outside, and other economic and social privileges. As previously mentioned, Welshmen were specifically excluded from burgess-ship, for the whole point of the *bastide* settlements was to secure Norman dominion over the Welsh nation.

Although each *bastide* town in Wales was planned on gridiron principles, their outlines show considerable variation. Flint, the earliest to be built, has a rigidly regular layout, almost Roman in conception. A central main street divides the town into two and leads to the castle sited independently and somewhat unusually outside the town walls. In the centre of the town and alongside the main street were the church and market.

At Caernarfon and Conwy, the castle and town were more closely integrated. Caernarfon was built on a level promontory between two rivers, with the castle defending the neck of the isthmus. The chequerboard street pattern and town walls have survived to this day along with the new church, which in this case, was built into the corner of the town walls (fig.56). Conwy is on a hilly site, although — like Caernarfon — by the sea's edge. The outline of the town is consequently quite irregular, but within the walls the usual gridiron plan was maintained (fig.57). Altogether, there are twenty-seven powerful towers spaced at 50-metre intervals, and three twin-towered gateways along the length of the town wall. Both the walls and the towers of Conwy are remarkably complete and surprisingly unmodified by later additions or alterations. Taken together, they are the most perfect surviving example in the whole of the British Isles — a kind of Welsh Avila or Carcassonne!

Despite the surviving perfection of these *bastide* towns they are no longer, as Pennant wrote, 'the badge of our subjection,' for ironically, Edward I's policy of conserving their Anglo-Norman character failed. Caernarfon, for instance, is today one of the strongholds of Welsh culture and it is Welsh rather than English that is heard and spoken in the streets. The Anglo-Norman settlers became assimilated within the Welsh community. Indeed, within a few generations, they became completely Welsh.[17] In Caernarfon town the East Gate and West Gate became known as *Porth Mawr* and *Porth-yr-Aur* respectively, while at the royal castle itself, the Eagle Tower had become *Twr-yr-Eryr!*

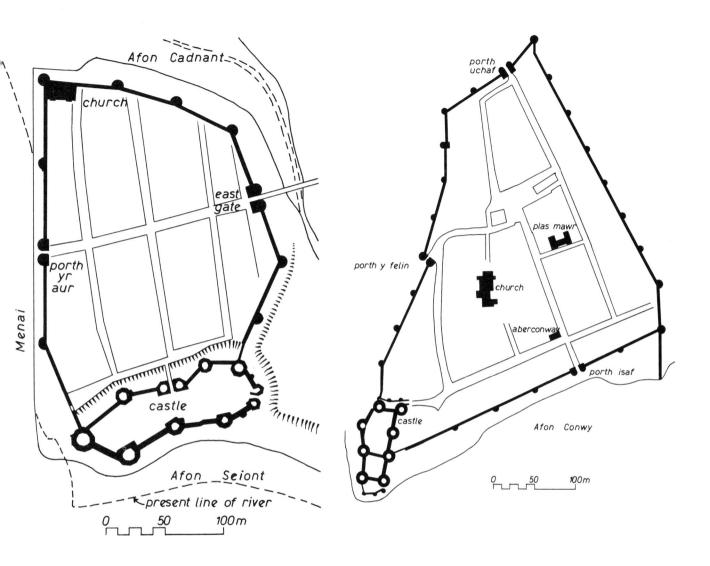

Afon Cadnant

church

Menai

east gate

porth yr aur

castle

Afon Seiont

present line of river

0   50   100 m

porth uchaf

porth y felin

plas mawr

church

aberconway

porth isaf

castle

Afon Conwy

0   50   100 m

56. Caernarfon, Gwynedd: plan of bastide town
and castle

57. Conwy, Gwynedd: plan of bastide town and
castle

81

[1] After the victory at Hastings, and the coronation in the same year of William the Conqueror at Westminster, sporadic English opposition (mainly in the north of England) was under complete French-Norman control within three years and all English landholders of importance were dispossessed.

[2] A. H. A. Hogg and D. J. C. King have listed (in *Archaeologia Cambrensis,* 1963 and 1970) 416 sites in Wales and 196 sites in the Marches of castles erected between 1066 and c.1250.

[3] Pembroke Castle stands on a fine promontory site between two rivers. It was started in 1190 by Arnulf de Montgomery and over a period of a century and a half a very imposing fortress was raised. The splendid exterior, however, belies the interior which is now almost empty except for the Great Keep. An interesting feature is the immense natural cavern under the inner ward which could be supplied from the river in times of need.

[4] Even in the late twelfth-century the hills and valleys of Glamorgan and most of the coastal land west of Swansea was still in the hands of the Welsh princes. In Brecknock the upper Usk valley and the middle Wye valley were attacked from Herefordshire at the end of the eleventh century and held by the Normans for a considerable period, but their hold was not permanent; as late as 1262 all this land had been reconquered by the Welsh princes.

[5] Llywelyn ap Gruffydd (Lywelyn II or Llywelyn the Last), ruled from 1255 until he was killed at Cilmeri, near Builth, in 1282. He was later to be known as 'Ein Llyw Olaf' (Our Last Leader). His grandfather Llywelyn ab Iorwerth (Lywelyn I), also known as Llywelyn Fawr or Llywelyn the Great, died in 1240.

[6] John E. Morris, *The Welsh Wars of Edward I* (1901, reprinted Oxford 1968), p. 310.

[7] Despite the natural strength of Dinas Brân, it was not defended in 1277 but was burnt when the hopelessness of resistance became apparent.

[8] Probably most of the master craftsmen employed by Edward I in building his Welsh castles originated from Savoy and other parts of France. The building accounts refer to names such as William Seysel, Gillot de Chalons, Albert de Menz, Giles of St. Georges (all from Savoy), Bertrand de Saltu (from Gascony), Manasser de Vaucouleurs (from Champagne), and John of Paris and Peter of Tours. The first constables of Caernarfon, Conwy, Harlech and Rhuddlan were also either Savoyard or Burgundian knights.

[9] The four castles built by Edward I following the first War of Independence are Builth (started May 1277), Flint (July 1277), Aberystwyth (July 1277) and Rhuddlan (September 1277). Nothing remains of the castle at Builth, apart from earthworks.

[10] It has been suggested that the model for the *donjon* at Flint was the great Tour de Constance at the Mediterranean *bastide* town of Aigues-Mortes which Edward I had seen on his departure to the Crusade in 1270. Another possible prototype could have been Castel del Monte in Apulia, which though octagonal in plan was also built with segment-shaped rooms around an internal court.

[11] A. J. Taylor, *Caernarvon Castle and Town Wall* (DOE Guidebook, 1953), p. 6.

[12] The tradition is perpetuated in the Roman road still called 'Sarn Helen' which runs from Moridunum (Carmarthen) to Segontium; continuity of culture is reflected in the name Helen which remains very popular to this day in the Arfon district where Caernarfon is situated.

[13] As Professor Dewi-Prys Thomas has pointed out, the geographical siting of Constantinople and Caernarfon is also very similar — while one is at the south-western end of the Bosporus the other is at the south-western end of the Menai Strait with the estuary of the Seiont forming a mini Golden Horn.

[14] Edward I also repaired the Welsh castles of Bere, Cricieth, Dolwyddelan and Caergwrle.

[15] These were: Chirk, Denbigh, Hawarden, Holt and Ruthin in Clwyd, and Carreg Cennen, Haverford, Kidwelly and Llansteffan in Dyfed.

[16] See page 62.

[17] It is symptomatic of the unique situation in Wales that Dafydd ab Edmwnd — one of the greatest poets of the age in the Welsh language and victor at the Carmarthen Eisteddfod of 1451 — was actually the great-great-great-grandson of John Upton, the Anglo-Norman Constable of Caernarfon installed by Edward I in 1306.

20. Castell yr Adwy, Llandegla, Clwyd.
    Earthworks of 'motte-and-bailey' castle.
21. Cardiff Castle. The 13th century 'shell-
    keep' on top of a late 11th century earthen 'motte'!
22. Chepstow Castle, Gwent. Marten's Tower
    and Gatehouse. 13th century.

23. Castell Dolbadarn, near Llanberis, Gwynedd. Early 13th century Great Tower.
24. Castell y Bere, Llanfihangel-y-Pennant, Gwynedd. Aerial view showing its fine site on an isolated rock.

25.   Caernarfon Castle, Gwynedd. The most
      spectacular of Edward I's castles in Wales.
      Started 1283.
26.   Harlech Castle, Gwynedd. Started 1283.

27. Beaumaris Castle, Anglesey, Gwynedd. Castle planning at its most sophisticated. Started 1295.

28. Caerphilly Castle, Glamorgan. Castle planning at its most complex. Protective artificial lakes surround the inner castle and a fortified 'hornwork' (on the left) and an immense barrage wall (on the right) complete the defences. Started 1271.

29. Bishop's Palace, St. David's, Dyfed. Late
    13th century domestic apartments in
    foreground and mid-14th century Great
    Hall and Chapel in background.
30. Raglan Castle, Gwent. The main
    gatehouse. Mid-15th century.

31.   Pembroke. The castle and town from the
      air.

32.   Monnow Bridge, Monmouth, Gwent. A
fortified gateway at the entrance to the
town. Late 13th century.

Chapter 5
Vernacular Architecture

Vernacular architecture is the term applied to buildings that were built without the guidance of a professional architect — buildings erected by local carpenters and builders working in the indigenous manner of the area. Thus one of the features of vernacular architecture is continuity of tradition over a long period. Many of the cottages and farms still existing today were built during the Tudor and Renaissance periods, although their plan-forms may have been derived from earlier medieval models. The buildings that we think of today as ordinary farms and minor country houses were often, when first built, the homes of the gentry and consequently the most important houses in the district. As building methods improved and the gentry became more prosperous they built bigger and better homes, leaving the older houses to degenerate in status.[1] The new houses, whether or not designed by architects, were still largely based on traditional methods of construction and layouts, however, and new styles of architecture were only gradually evolved or hesitatingly borrowed from further afield. Before looking at the larger mansions of the sixteenth, seventeenth and eighteenth centuries, therefore, it is essential to consider the characteristics of vernacular architecture. We must see how the *uchelwyr* (the gentry) originally lived in order to understand how the traditional forms affected the style of later building.

Cruck-Truss and Box-Frame Construction.

Local builders inevitably used the materials at hand. The older houses, farmhouses and outbuildings still seem to reflect the physical nature of the land. They are man-made, but organic, extensions of the earth. Thus the variations in texture and colour of the stones mentioned in Chapter One (Physical Background) may best be observed in rural buildings. Stone, however, is a comparatively difficult material to handle and puts severe limitations on the size and form of buildings to be erected. Wood, on the other hand, is easier to carry and strong in tension; it can be jointed and also provides warm interiors. Wherever possible timber, when available, was therefore used as the basic framework in earlier domestic work (fig. 58).

In Wales the dominant form of timber construction was of the cruck-truss type (fig. 59). This type consists of pairs of boomerang-shaped crucks, their feet resting almost on ground level, set up in the shape of an 'A' and crossed at the apex to form forks supporting the ridge-piece. The structural principle is one of some

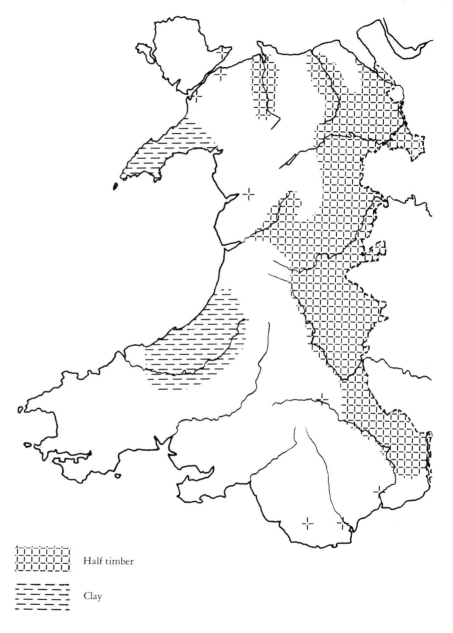

58. Distribution of half-timbered houses and
clay houses (*tai clom*) in Wales

Half timber

Clay

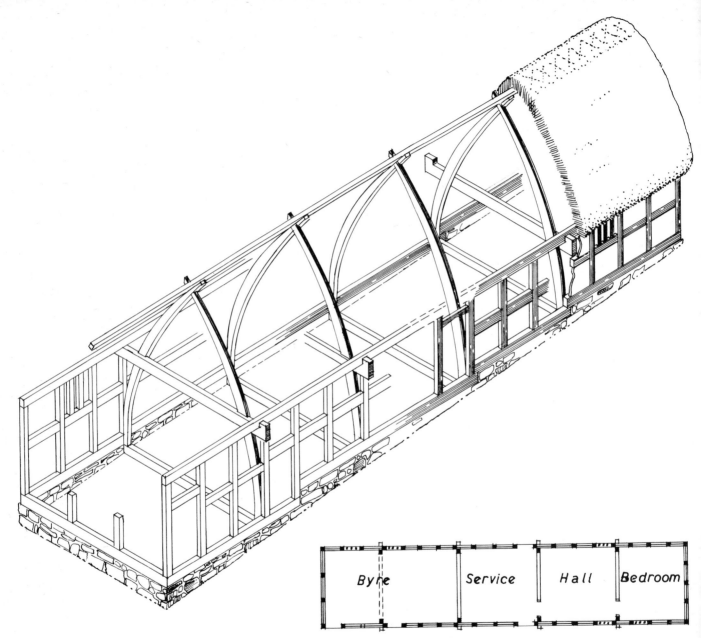

59. Cruck-truss construction: general view and
plan of Hendre'r Ywydd Uchaf farmhouse

Byre · Service · Hall · Bedroom

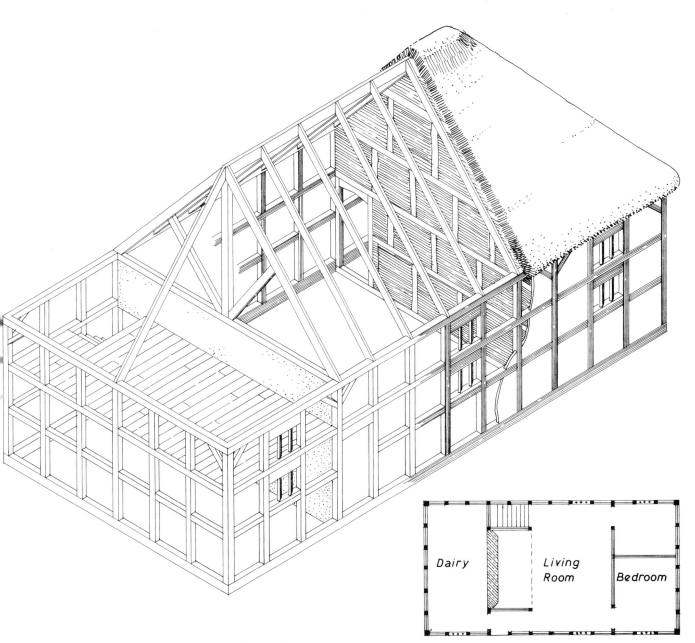

Dairy

Living
Room

Bedroom

60.   Box-frame construction: general view and
plan of Abernodwydd farmhouse

sophistication, in fact, for the entire building is in effect an assemblage of true trusses, the stresses being resolved as in the modern three-pin arch of steel or reinforced concrete. The whole weight of the roof was carried on the crucks by timber purlins and the walls below were merely infill and structurally unimportant — the latter could be of stone or clay, or light-weight panels of wattle-and-daub. An excellent example of a cruck-truss dwelling has been re-erected in the Welsh Folk Museum at St. Fagans. Known as Hendre'r Ywydd Uchaf, a late fifteenth-century house from Dyffryn Clwyd, it was constructed around four cruck-trusses resting on a low stone sill (plate 33). The walls are panelled with wattle-and-daub, the windows are unglazed, the roof thatched; inside, the original open hearth has been re-constructed on the earthen floor. A good example of a cruck-truss dwelling with stone walls is at Leeswood Green near Mold. Other farm buildings were quite usually constructed with cruck-trusses and many fine barns built in this fashion have survived in a number of places. Perhaps the finest extant example of this type is that at Plas Ashpool, near Denbigh, and there is a not dissimilar barn at the Welsh Folk Museum from the same area. The distribution of surviving cruck-trusses shows that this method of building was used generally in Wales with the exception of the south-west where a modified form of jointed cruck was normal. The second main form of timber construction, the box-frame, was, however, restricted to the eastern borderlands. In the Severn Valley it reached as far west as Llanidloes — the westernmost limit of a structural technique distributed over much of southern Britain and the great plains of northern Europe.

In contrast to the cruck-truss, the box-frame was built up from a grid of vertical posts connected by tie-beams (fig.60). The frame itself supported the roof trusses which were made up of separate pieces of timber. The intermediate spaces between the structural posts and horizontal rails were again filled with wattle-and-daub, often painted white, while the timber frame was treated with tar to give the houses their characteristic black-and-white or half-timbered appearance (plate 34).

Box-frame construction in Britain can be grouped into two main schools of carpentry. The greater part of England falls into the eastern school, which is characterised by narrow vertical panels and curved braces. The Welsh borderland area is included in the western school and is distinguished by square infill panels, straight angle braces and curved embellishments at the corners of the panels. A number of houses in the valley of the upper Severn appear to have the tall narrow infill panels belonging to the eastern carpentry school, but in fact their purpose is usually more ornamental than structural, as can be clearly seen at Maesmawr Hall near Caersws where the intermediate members are carved into decorative shapes (plate 35). This preoccupation with an ornamental effect in the western school is significant for it suggests even in vernacular building a vestigal link with the rich artistic roots of the Celtic period. Many excellent half-timbered houses can be seen in Maelor and Dyffryn Clwyd in the north, Presteigne and Knighton in Radnor and especially around Churchstoke, Caersws and Trefeglwys in the Severn Valley. Abernodwydd (now in the Welsh Folk Museum but originally from Llangadfan) illustrates a two-storey box-frame house in its most basic and simple form.

In most parts of Wales — even where stone was used for the outer walls — the interior partitions, screens and floors were usually framed in wood. The earliest extant dwellings built entirely of stone appear to have been in the Normanised areas of the Pembroke peninsulas and the Vale of Glamorgan. In these houses both the external and internal walls were of stone, while around Pembroke and Tenby there are many cases where the first floor is vaulted in stone over an undercroft or cellar, a characteristic which was noted by George Owen as long ago as 1602. To this category also belong the tower-houses, also mainly of the Normanised areas. In the tower-house the main rooms were built above each other at first and second floor levels for defensive purposes but rather surprisingly, when one considers the intermittent wars and feuds that took place in Wales before the sixteenth century, there are very few examples of this type of house, compared with the hundreds in Ireland and Scotland. Only a handful of tower-houses have survived in the north while in the south, a few have survived in Glamorgan and Gwent and near Pembroke.[2] In mid-Wales, there are two tower-houses dating from the late twelfth or early thirteenth century at Talgarth, and near Brecon, as well as the fortified gatehouses in this same area mentioned in Chapter Four (fig. 61).

In former times clay was a common building material and houses with walls made of earth or clay, reinforced with stones or rushes, were probably once widespread throughout the moorland areas and the western peninsulas. The *tŷ-clom*, or clay-house, often had rounded corners to the walls, the latter being generally colour-washed or white-washed and roofed with thatch. Now a rare type, it is mainly confined to localised districts in the Aeron and Teifi valleys of Ceredigion, but even there it is fast disappearing. Usually these cottages are small, single-storey buildings, but occasionally, two storey hybrid examples used stone for the lower walls and clay for the upper walls.

After the departure of the Romans, brick does not seem to have been used again in Wales until the late sixteenth century and even then only exceptionally. It was re-introduced in 1567, when Sir Richard Clough built his own house at Tremeirchion, near Denbigh.[3] While a few other brick houses were built in the same district about 1600, brick did not really become fashionable there until late in the seventeenth century. In Gwent, brick seems to have been first used about 1640 in building the outworks of Raglan Castle, but within the next half-century, only a handful of

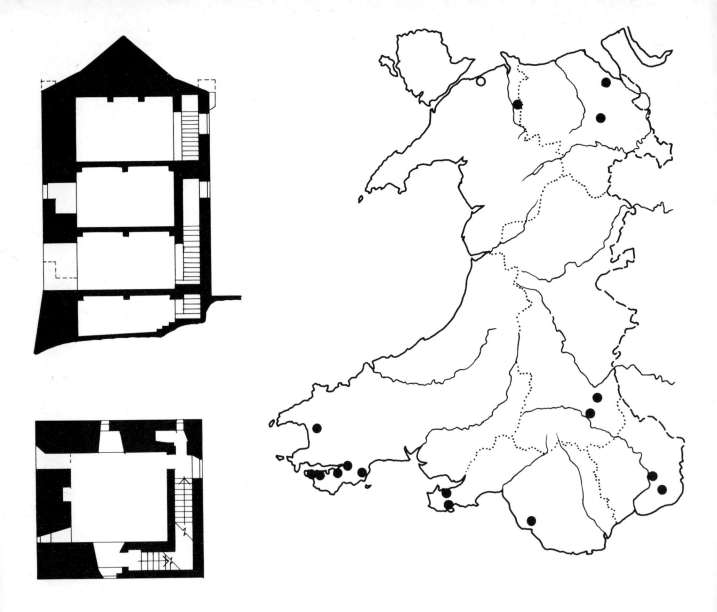

61a. Distribution of Tower-houses in Wales
See Appendix K for list of Tower-houses

61b. Section and first floor plan of the Tower
House, Talgarth, Powys

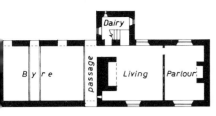

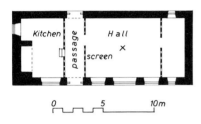

2. Middle House, Llanfilo, Powys: plan of
typical 'long-house' (17th century)

3. Brithdir Mawr, Cilcain, Clwyd: plan of early
'hall-house' (1589)

houses, all not far from the castle, had been constructed in this material. In many parts of Wales brick was not generally employed in house-building until the coming of the railways in the second half of the nineteenth century, or until the advent of the lorry in the twentieth century made it a more economical material to use than the local stone or timber.

Long-House and Hall-house.

The houses of the poorer people during the medieval period were so insubstantial that none has survived in Wales, nor in the rest of Britain for that matter. Moreover, the old custom of building a *tŷ-unnos* in one night (in order to lay claim to the surrounding land) was not conducive to permanence. Consequently, the earliest houses that still exist, other than the castles of the *boneddigion* (nobility), are the houses of the *uchelwyr* (gentry) and these were built in the vernacular tradition. When the uchelwyr were able to build larger and more elaborate mansions, their original houses became the homes of the smaller landowners and eventually were transferred down the scale to the *crefftwyr* (craftsmen) and *tyddynwyr* (small-holders). So the small farm-house we see today may once have been the most important dwelling in its district. Small houses erected later would be built in the same vernacular tradition, perhaps even with the same plan and layout as the prototype. The later houses were often in effect merely copies of the earlier houses belonging to the *uchelwyr*.

In layout, houses developed from single-storey lineal structures — characteristic of the Middle Ages — through a phase of cellular two-storey structures, and finally to compact centrally planned buildings of the seventeenth-century Renaissance. Within these broad categories, there were occupational and regional variations.

In its simplest form, the *bwthyn* is a one-roomed or two-roomed cottage and was the most widespread house type of the Welsh countryside up to the present century. The one-roomed version was usually divided into two areas — one for living and one for sleeping — at first by furniture and later by a screen of lath and plaster or simply by a curtain. Where the cottage formed part of a *tyddyn* (smallholding or croft) it often had a *beudy* (cow-shed) attached to it at one of the pine (gable) ends. In the early medieval period, rooms for special purposes would probably have been built as separate detached structures, arranged along with the house around a central yard as is still the case in many Scandinavian farms. A development of this type was the *tŷ-hir*, or long-house, which consisted of a long rectangular building housing both the family and its cattle under the same roof, but divided at the centre by a common access passage serving both parts of the house (fig.62). This was not

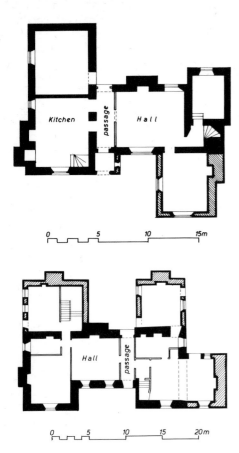

Kitchen   passage   Hall

0 5 10 15m

Hall   passage

0 5 10 15 20m

64.   The Innage, Mathern, Gwent: plan of developed 'hall-house' (late 15th century) — 16th century extensions in hatched shading

65.   Y Dderw, Pipton, Powys: plan of developed 'hall-house' (late 16th century — 17th century extensions in hatched shading)

only an economic way of building; the cattle also helped to keep the house warm in winter. The dividing passage was used as a feeding walk for the cow-house at the lower end, the *pen-isaf*, which as the name suggests, was at a slightly lower level than the living area, the *pen-uchaf*. This arrangement can be seen clearly in Cilewent, a farmhouse from mid-Wales (now at the Welsh Folk Museum), where the *pen-isaf* has an earthen floor and the living area has a floor of local stone slabs (plate 36). Usually, and particularly in southern Wales, the fireplace was placed on the internal wall backing on to the feeding walk.

In the past the custom known as transhumance was practised in the interior parts of the country. The main farmhouse, the *hendre* in the valley was occupied during the winter. In the summer months,.the family together with their animals migrated to the summer pastures on the hills and lived in the *hafod* (plural *hafotai*), a less substantial dwelling.[4] The artificial platforms on which circular or sub-rectangular *hafotai* were built have been found on the slopes of the Brecon Beacons and Mynydd Ddu (Carmarthen Fan), but generally, the remains of these medieval examples are so scanty that it is difficult to date them accurately, or indeed, to distinguish them from Dark Age settlements. Many *hafotai* were probably built in the same manner as a *tŷ-unnos*, the 'one-night' house. According to custom a man could erect a dwelling on common land and therefore claim the surrounding land provided that the house was built (usually of prepared turf with a thatch roof) during one night and had smoke rising from the hearth by the following morning. The ruins of the *tai-unnos,* still to be frequently seen in some upland areas appear to be mainly from the eighteenth century, before the Enclosure Act restricted movement. The remains of a large number of *tai-unnos* along the headwaters of the Afon Tywi (between Tregaron and Llandovery) date, however, only from the mid-nineteenth century, prior to the enclosure of Mynydd Llanddewibrefi in 1888.

Another form of single-storey lineal dwelling is the hall-house. This contained a large room — the hall — in the centre serving as the living area, in which were added service rooms at one end and a sleeping area or parlour at the other end. In its classic form the hall-house was arrranged to form an H-shaped plan, as at Y Dderw in Powys, but more often in Wales it had a T-plan, as at The Innage, Gwent, or a rectangular plan with two or three rooms in line, as at Plas Ucha (c.1400) near Corwen and Brithdir Mawr (1589) near Mold[5] (figs. 63,64 and 65). Between the hall and the service rooms there was usually a lightweight screen enclosed within a timber arch known as a spere-truss (fig.66). The area between the screen and the service rooms, known as the 'screen passage' was in fact an entrance hall with doors at both ends. Originally, the hall was heated by an open hearth in the middle of the floor and the room was visually open to the roof, a fact which explains why the oak roof trusses were so carefully designed for effect and elaborately carved. Cochwillan

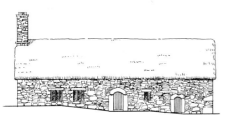

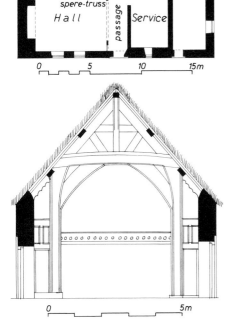

66. Plas Ucha, Clwyd: elevation, plan and cross-section showing spere-truss

(dating from the mid-fifteenth century), near Bangor and Gloddaeth (sixteenth century), near Llandudno, are very fine examples of late medieval hall-houses and both still retain ornate hammer-beam roof trusses over their open halls; Penarth Fawr, near Pwllheli, and Plas Ucha still retain their richly moulded spere-trusses. In later times a wall fireplace and chimney was built at the end of the hall (opposite the screen), or on a side wall, to replace the open hearth.

When more accommodation was required within single-storey houses, the area was augmented by a loft in the roof space, reached by a ladder, built over the sleeping end. This method, very commonly employed in small cottages, resulted in a dwelling known as a *bwthyn croglofft*. Llainfadyn (now in the Welsh Folk Museum) is an excellent eighteenth century example from the Arfon district of Gwynedd (plate 37). Many hundreds of this ubiquitous type have disappeared during this century, though large numbers still remain. Many of our famous men were nurtured on their hearths. Sir Owen Morgan Edwards, for instance, a man of letters, publisher, writer and pioneer educationist, was born in 1858 in a *bwthyn croglofft*, 'Coed-y-pry', at the foot of Aran Benllyn in the heart of Meirionnydd.

Two-storey Houses.

The further development of house layouts resulted in two-storey cellular buildings which are usually referred to as regional house types because their internal arrangement varied from district to district (fig. 67). A type found mainly in the south appears to have been developed from the traditional long-house layout. Here, a cross-passage entrance hall (in place of the feeding walk) separates the main living area from the other rooms, but as in the long-house, the main fireplace backs on to the cross-passage. Often there is also a secondary fireplace in the service room on the end wall. The stair to the upper floor is either in or near the cross-passage or at the side of the central fireplace. In Gwynedd, the predominant type of house plan is related to the hall-house. In this case, the main fireplace is on the end wall opposite to the entrance, which itself is often within the main living area. If there is a secondary fireplace, this is usually on the end wall at the opposite end to the living area. The stair is also on an external wall near the main fireplace. Both of these types of houses were usually built of stone.

Over much of the north-east, there is a third regional type recognisable from the outside by a single central chimney stack. Inside, this type has two centrally positioned back-to-back fireplaces but no cross-passage. More often than not this third regional house is constructed in timber, particularly in the Severn valley area, but stone examples are also found further north.

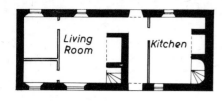

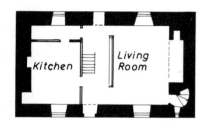

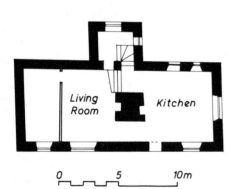

0 5 10m

67. Regional house-type plans:

(a) Southern — Upper Wern Hir, Gwent,

(b) North-western — Plas Du, Gwynedd,

(c) North-eastern — Penisa'r Glascoed, Clwyd

In Dyfed, especially around the St. David's district, a type of stone-built house evolved which appears to have been a fusion of both the 'hall-type' plan and the 'nave-and-aisle' form referred to in the pre-Norman laws of Hywel Dda. Historically, therefore, this ancient type is of peculiar and fascinating interest. The main part of the dwelling is a rectangular structure, up to five metres wide, and sub-divided into various rooms. The internal area of the house was increased by adding side aisles, which in practice became a series of recesses about two metres deep on one or both sides of the central part of the dwelling. A characteristic and most attractive feature of these houses is the boldly sculpted three stage chimneys, the top part of which are cylindrical, built above one of the side extensions.

The final phase of development of house layouts occurred in the seventeenth and eighteenth centuries when classical Renaissance ideas were slowly introduced. The emphasis is on symmetry of plan and elevations. Tu-hwnt-i'r-bont, near Llanrwst, is a charming example of traditional methods and materials being used in the eighteenth century to provide a seventeenth century house with symmetry and extra space by the addition of roof dormers (plate 38). The Renaissance plan was predominantly a layout of the *tai cyfrifol* ('houses of account' or 'gentry houses'). Usually the staircase and entrance hall were located at the centre. Instead of individual rooms being all in line, as with the long-house and the hall-house, the rooms are grouped around the stair and entrance hall, with the living rooms and parlour at the front and the kitchen and dairy at the rear (fig. 68).

In the earliest examples of the Renaissance plan the layout bears a striking similarity to the north-eastern regional type of house for in these the axial planning of the central fireplaces made it relatively easy to give the house a semblance of symmetry with a tall central chimney as a prominent external feature. In new building and the reconstruction of existing houses axial fireplaces were used as a convenient device to achieve the symmetrical 'four-square' type of plan around a central staircase, but in smaller and less complex houses symmetry could be obtained by placing the fireplaces on the two end walls.

The earlier house types of the vernacular tradition continued to be built by smaller landowners throughout the eighteenth century and by *tyddynwyr* until well into the nineteenth century. Occasionally, whole terraces of cottages were built in local stone using the characteristic features of a district. In this way, a remarkable likeness with the older buildings was maintained. A notable example of this continuity of tradition is the row of cottages at Pandy'r Odyn, near Dolgellau built at the beginning of the nineteenth century (plate 39). Its outside appearance is virtually just an elongated version of Tu-hwnt-i'r-bont, at Llanrwst, built a century or more earlier.

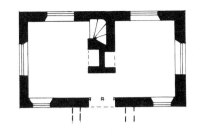

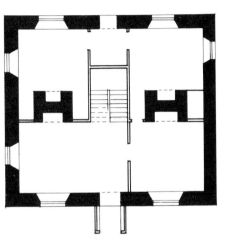

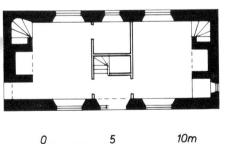

0   5   10m

68. Renaissance house-type plans:
(a) Two-room with axial fireplace (Elmo, Penrhos, c.1640), (b) Four room with axial fireplaces (High House, Gwent, 1675), (c) Two room with end fireplaces (Town Farm, Gwent, 1673).

NOTES TO CHAPTER 5

[1] Plas Ucha, near Corwen, is a good example of this decline in status. L. Monroe described it thus in 1933: 'Plas Ucha is now a humble dwelling retaining but little to indicate that it was ever anything more. That little, however, is sufficient, for a roof truss of such fine proportions and excellent workmanship and the delicate ornamentation of the reset beam could only be found in a house of considerable importance . . .' (*Archaeologia Cambrensis,* June, 1933, p. 87).

[2] A very late example is the interesting four-storey tower (almost circular in plan) added to Pen-y-bryn, near Aber in Gwynedd, in the early seventeenth century.

[3] For the house, known as Bachegraig, see page 7.

[4] While sheep farmers no longer move their flocks, changing their dwelling with the season, it is still the custom for sheep to be farmed out on lower-lying meadows in the winter months — sometimes on other farms 30 or 40 kilometres away.

[5] Plas Ucha was probably first built in the late fourteenth century or early fifteenth century as a timber house; when it was reconstructed in stone during the sixteenth century the original timber roof-truss was retained.

33. Hendre'r Ywydd Uchaf. A 'cruck-truss' farmhouse now re-erected at the Welsh Folk Museum. Late 15th century.

34. Talgarth, Trefeglwys, Powys.

35. Maes Mawr, Caersws, Powys.

36. Cilewent. A 'long-house' now re-erected at the Welsh Folk Museum.
37. Llainfadyn. A *bwthyn croglofft* now re-erected at the Welsh Folk Museum.

38. Tu-hwn-i'r -bont, Llanrwst, Gwynedd.
    Built 17th century and re-constructed 18th
    century.
39. Pandy'r Odyn, Dolgellau, Gwynedd. Early
    19th century cottages built in the
    vernacular tradition.

Chapter 6 **Sixteenth and Seventeenth Centuries**

Tudor and Renaissance

We have seen that during the early medieval period castle building dominated the architectural scene in Wales. In the latter part of the middle ages, the construction of castles gave way to new churches and the extensions of old ones, but by the end of the fifteenth century the spate of church building too was largely over. After the dissolution of the monasteries (1536-40), there was even less new work in this field and it was not until the nineteenth century that religious architecture became again significant. From the sixteenth to the eighteenth century the dominant form of building was domestic in character.

The change of emphasis with the Renaissance from military fortifications and churches to domestic architecture coincided with the development of more settled conditions generally. Castles had by then outlived their purposes and a slowly growing affluence enabled more attention to be paid to house building.

The accession of the partly-Welsh family of Tudor to the English throne in 1485 led to a decrease in the oppressive feudal power of Marcher lords. The 'Act of Union' of Wales and England in 1536 and 1542 took a further step forward in this respect by abolishing the harsher penal laws inflicted upon the Welsh. They were now accorded 'equal rights' with other citizens in spheres other than the all-important ones of culture and language. The incorporation of Wales within a much larger state prevented the possibility of her developing further a national culture (including the arts and architecture) based on her own administrative, ecclesiastical and educational institutions, such as no doubt would have evolved if Glyndŵr's bid for independence had been successful. The result, nevertheless, was an improvement in trade and greater opportunities than had hitherto been the case for individual Welshmen to make their fortunes.

By the sixteenth century, the total population of Wales was no greater than that of Cardiff today. Agriculture was still the main source of livelihood. Concerned largely with sheep and cattle rearing, the country was comparatively prosperous. Wool was highly priced and exported to England in great quantities. The cattle drovers, important members of the community, helped in the spreading of new ideas and fashions. Evidence of the long journeys travelled by Welsh drovers may be seen even in distant Hampshire where a painted inscription on an inn still welcomes their custom with *'Gwair tymerus, porfa flasus, Cwrw da a Gwal cysurus'*.[1]

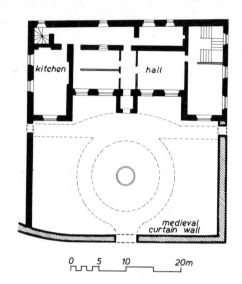

kitchen

hall

medieval
curtain wall

0   5   10   20m

As a result of the breakdown of the manorial system in the Marches, along with the decay of the old native system of land ownership, some individuals were able to acquire large estates. Others enriched themselves through trading activities in the towns. In this way, a new class of squires and merchants emerged which was to dominate Welsh life until the nineteenth century. The changes were reflected in architecture by the phenomenon known as the Great Rebuilding, an intense period of house building which appears to have started in the border districts during the latter part of the sixteenth century, or even later.[2] During this time older sub-standard houses were either deliberately demolished and rebuilt or were altered and enlarged by adding another floor, or extended with an extra wing. Fireplaces with chimneys replaced open hearths, and as in other parts of Britain glass was used extensively for the first time in windows. By the end of the seventeenth century, improvements in communications enabled the gentry to travel further and more quickly than before. Their greater mobility allowed them to become acquainted with new ideas and new fashions in architecture. At the same time, professional architects working with drawing-board and pattern books began to replace the old master-craftsman working with his hammer and chisel.

Sixteenth Century: The Tudor Era

Tudor architecture was an interim style transitional between the indigenous manner of the late medieval period and the Renaissance manner of foreign influence. It was part of the metamorphic transition from military and ecclesiastical buildings to the more sedate compositions of classically inspired country mansions. As a result, it was an unresolved amalgam of both native Gothic and alien Renaissance ideas. Looked at in one way, the Tudor style was a continuation of late Gothic methods of building in which large windows, gabled roofs and an overall emphasis on the vertical were prominent features. Looked at another way, the Tudor style was the beginning of Renaissance formal planning, when comfort was of more concern than defence and dignified appearance was considered even more important than comfort.

St. Fagan's Castle, near Cardiff, built between 1560 and 1580, exemplifies the dual nature of Tudor building, particularly in Wales, where high-pitched roofs and tall gables tended sensibly (if only for climatic reasons) to linger longer than in England (plate 40). The mansion of St. Fagans, erected within the stout curtain-walls of a medieval castle, has a hall-house layout.[3] The plan, however, has been arranged to give a symmetrical disposition of rooms with a projecting porch and cross-passage in the centre (fig. 69). On one side of the passage is the hall with a withdrawing-room beyond; on the other side is the buttery and a kitchen. Both the withdrawing-

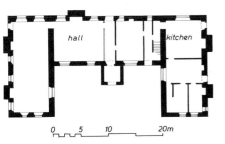

0 5 10 20m

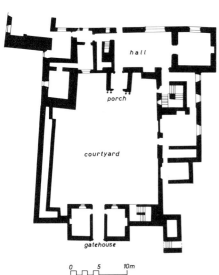

hall

porch

courtyard

gatehouse

0 5 10m

70. Old Gwernyfed, Powys: plan

71. Beaupre Castle, Glamorgan: plan

room and the kitchen project in front of the rest of the house so that the whole building has a plan like a letter 'E'. The symmetrical main front displays many large rectangular windows. A steep multi-gabled roof gives it a picturesque rather than solemn air. Old Gwernyfed, near Hay-on-Wye, was built slightly later (probably between 1600 and 1613), but has an almost identical layout (fig. 70). In place of a castellated curtain wall in front, it has a rectangular forecourt with round towers (one of which is a dovecot) at the angles.

Other castles were converted into mansions of a more rugged character. Oxwich Castle in the Gower peninsula was rebuilt in the first half of the sixteenth century with a large hall at first-floor level, and a long-gallery above, but still retained part of the original fabric of the earlier castle. Similarly, Powys Castle, Welshpool, is largely an adaptation of a massive thirteenth-century fortress, the core of which was a *castell* of the Welsh princes. An attractive long-gallery with a superbly decorated plaster ceiling was added between 1587 and 1592 and about the same time, fashionable new windows were inserted (plate 41).

Beaupre in the Vale of Glamorgan was rebuilt in the last years of Elizabeth's reign as a 'fortified' house by Rycharde Bassett.[4] The courtyard in front of the house is guarded by a large gatehouse, built in 1586 with an unresolved mixture of late Gothic windows and early Renaissance surrounds to the archway (fig. 71). The house itself is plain, but was fronted in 1660 by a striking and very ornate three storey porch in the 'Italian' manner with pairs of superimposed columns, as at Kirby Hall (1575) in England (plate 42). Less highly decorated porches and gatehouses were still being added to mansions in northern Wales until well into the seventeenth century, eg Plas Mawr (1595) at Conwy, Cefnamlwch (1607) in the Llŷn peninsula, Cors y Gedol (1630), near Barmouth and Plas Rhiwaedog (1664) near Bala.[5]

Fortifications of any kind were the exception in the sixteenth century, however, and in most cases attention was concentrated on the appearance of the house. Llanfihangel Court, a southern example near Abergavenny, is a stone-built fifteenth-century manor house, the front of which was rebuilt and extended in 1559 to give a symmetrical facade. It has an 'H' plan with the hall in the centre and projecting gabled wings at the side.

It was in the north-east — the 'Tuscany of Wales' and the cultural heart of the country at this period according to Mr. Peter Smith[6] — that new architectural ideas based on Dutch Renaissance designs first made their appearance in Wales. The new architecture was introduced by Sir Richard Clough during the second half of the sixteenth century when he built two houses near Denbigh. The first of these was

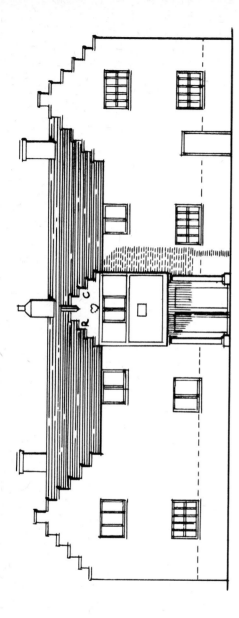

Bachegraig, erected in 1567/8 at Tremeirchion. As previously mentioned, it was also the first Welsh house to be constructed in brick — reputedly with materials and craftsmen specially imported from Holland.[7] The design, aptly described as a 'Flemish château', was most unusual with its tall main floor, an almost pyramidical roof containing two tiers of dormer windows, its very tall chimneys and (at the apex) a single square room under a cupola. Except for the much altered brick-built gatehouse and stables, built two years later, nothing has survived. [8]

The second of Sir Richard Clough's houses — Plas Clough at Henllan — appears to have been built at the same time as Bachegraig and was also constructed in brick. The layout of Plas Clough is unexceptional. What makes this house unusual was the incorporation of crow-stepped gables at each end of the main front and on the first floor room (now altered) over the entrance porch (fig. 72). In the sixteenth century crow-stepped gables were commonly used in Dutch buildings in and around Antwerp, but Plas Clough is the earliest known house of the Renaissance period in Wales to be built in this manner. Following the success of Plas Clough crow-stepped gables soon became a popular feature of other large houses in Clwyd and Gwynedd, such as Plas Mawr (1576) in Conwy, Golden Grove (1578) near Prestatyn and Faenol Fawr (1597) near Rhuddlan. The fashion for decorative stepped gables eventually spread as far west as the Llŷn peninsula and the south-western corner of Meirionnydd, but apparently never any further south.

In the Severn Valley, half-timbered houses of outstanding quality were being built throughout the period and continued to be erected well into the seventeenth century. Lymore, near Montgomery, for instance, was a very large framed house with a three-storey symmetrical facade, built as late as 1675. This house was demolished as recently as 1935 — a major architectural loss.

Inside the Tudor mansions the emphasis was on greater comfort and privacy. Flat ceilings, replacing open roofs, were panelled in timber or plaster covered with decorative patterns. The hall became a dining-room and other rooms were added to cater for new amenities. Most of the rooms were panelled in wood and handsome fireplaces were installed. In many of the larger houses, a long-gallery, reached by an impressive oak staircase, was built over the hall to serve as a passage to upper rooms and as an area to display paintings and decorations. Sanitation was still in its infancy in Wales as in Europe generally, but at Carew Castle, near Pembroke, where a large northern wing with great semi-circular oriel windows was added between 1588 and 1592, there was an interesting piped system of water supply to the kitchen and brewhouse from an outside fountain.

72. Plas Clough, Clwyd: elevation based on drawing by Moses Griffiths, 1770

The towns in Tudor times, though still small, were relatively prosperous. Most of

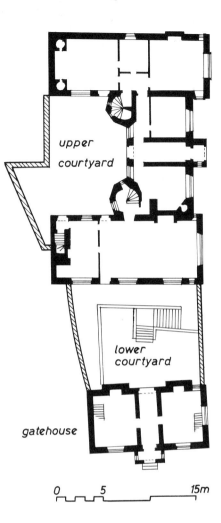

upper
courtyard

lower
courtyard

gatehouse

0   5   15m

them still retained their protective walls intact. The largest town was probably Denbigh with a population of about 3000; few other towns had much more than a thousand people. Within the town walls most houses were detached and many stood in their own grounds.

One of the best preserved town-houses of the Elizabethan period in Britain as a whole, is Plas Mawr in Conwy (plate 43). It was built by Robert Wynn of Gwydir [9] in two parts, in 1576 and 1580, to an 'H' plan with an upper courtyard at the rear and a terraced lower courtyard between the side of the house and the gatehouse (fig.73). Inside, the most notable features are the elaborate 'Italian' fireplaces and the boldly decorated plaster ceilings in many of the rooms. The main hall is in the centre block at first floor level above an open, cobbled passageway, leading to the upper courtyard. On the ground floor, a large gallery in the eastern wing overlooks the lower courtyard. At the rear of the central part of the house, there are two spiral staircases, medieval in feeling, which lead to a watch-tower. Externally, the mullioned windows with their 'classical' pediments and elaborate crow-stepped gables and dormers give the house its very rich appearance, uncertain in style, though trying to be *avant-garde* renaissance.[10]

Also in Conwy is Aberconwy, a half-timbered house dating from about 1500. The two lower floors are built in stone, while the over-sailing second floor is of timber (plastered over), and is supported on numerous wooden brackets carried on stone corbels. Ruthun still has quite a number of half-timbered town-houses, most of which date from the seventeenth century. Exemewe Hall (now a bank), is earlier, dating from about 1500, while the Court House and Nantclwyd House are earlier still.

In southern Wales, most of the Tudor town-houses have disappeared in successive rebuildings over the centuries. Newport, Gwent, still has its Murenger House, a four storey half-timbered building with the two upper storeys oversailing each other. Reputedly built in 1541 (by Sir Charles Herbert of Troy, near Monmouth), but possibly earlier, it has been restored and is now a restaurant. Tenby has retained its town walls and has a medieval street layout, but there are few early buildings. Plantagenet House, early fifteenth century in date, has the characteristic Pembroke-type round chimney while the three-storey Tudor Merchant's House alongside, of the late fifteenth or early sixteenth century, has a corbelled chimney on the gable end. Both of these very attractive houses have the irregular and unaffected appearance of typically vernacular buildings, although here and there features such as a Tudor hood mould over a window display a touch of fashionable extravagance.

73.   Plas Mawr, Conwy, Gwynedd: plan

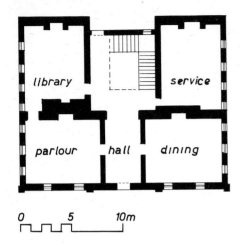

library   service

parlour   hall   dining

0   5   10m

74. Plan of Pen-pont House, Powys (1670),
before 19th century additions

110

Seventeenth Century: The Renaissance

Wales has pitifully few good seventeenth-century Renaissance houses. Most of those that were built have been either destroyed or altered to a degree which makes it impossible to get a clear impression of what they looked like when first built. Pen-pont, near Brecon, is a case in point. Built about 1670, with a typical four-square Renaissance plan around a lofty central staircase, its main elevation was completely altered in the nineteenth century by the addition of a third storey and a colonnade running across the front of the house (fig. 74).

The main reason for the poor representative of seventeenth-century houses in Wales, however, stems from the inevitable sinking of national fortunes following the temporary euphoria of the Tudors and the death of Elizabeth, last of her dynasty. Losing the pace-setters of patronage, Wales started to decline architecturally for, as Dr. Peate points out in *The Welsh House*, 'a nation bereft of its sovereignty cannot promote the growth of fine arts except by indirect and generally innocuous means.'[11]

A further reason for the poor showing of seventeenth-century architecture, is that the Renaissance style came late on the whole to Wales. Even in the middle Wye Valley, which was an area open to outside influence, there are no full-blooded examples. Trefecca Fawr and Tredwstan Court, both near Talgarth, are the nearest approach in this region to the image of a Renaissance house. But despite their hipped roofs and symmetrical elevations in the new manner, they were in fact built in the latter part of the seventeenth century with roughly 'L' shaped plans and did not attain their existing regular appearance until additional wings were added in the early eighteenth century. Abercynrig, near Brecon, received its present formal expression somewhat earlier when the house was completely refurbished at the end of the seventeenth century, but even then, the reconstructors found it impossible to achieve perfect symmetry for they built one of the projecting wings narrower than the other.

The earliest mansion in the new style in Wales is again found in the north-east. Built at the beginning of the seventeenth-century, Plas Têg near Mold, stands out as an impressive example. Solid and square on plan with square towers at the corners, it presents a castle-like appearance, but the grimness of the high stone walls is relieved by rows of tall windows and by elegant curved lead roofs supporting a cupola on each of the four towers (plate 44). Inside, there is an elaborate staircase built around three sides of an open well; a typical and important feature of a number of Renaissance houses.[12]

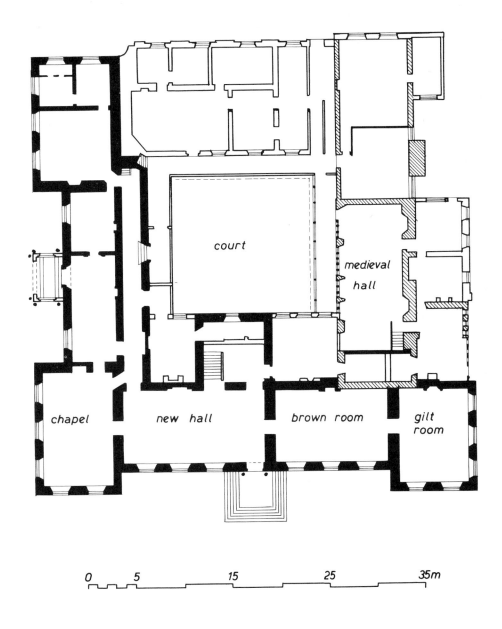

court

medieval
hall

chapel   new hall   brown room   gilt
room

0   5   15   25   35m

75. Tredegar Park, Newport, Gwent: plan
showing medieval work shaded and seventeenth
century work in black

111

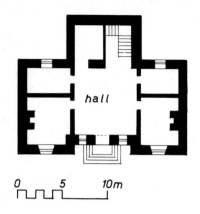

0 5 10m

Erddig, near Wrexham, was built on a much larger scale than Plas Têg and more obviously belongs to the Renaissance period. It dates from 1684 when Josua Edisbury of Pentre-clawdd started building it to designs by Thomas Webb.[13] Although situated on the crest of a hill overlooking the vale between Wat's Dyke and Offa's Dyke the mansion (with its 365 windows) and outbuildings were laid out to a very formal plan. This in turn was complimented by rigidly formal gardens with long parallel lines of trees and an axially planned lake at the rear (plate 45).

The largest Renaissance house in Wales is Tredegar House, near Newport, largely rebuilt by Sir William Morgan about 1670 around an open court and added to a medieval range (fig. 75). The two main fronts (north-east and north-west) comprise long two-storey buildings, constructed in warm red brick and Bathstone dressings, with slightly projecting wings at either end (plate 46). Attic floors with curved dormer windows are contained within a fairly low hipped-roof. Superimposed in a Baroque manner, on these basically simple elevations, are floridly designed central porches with twisted columns and window embellishments in the form of lavishly decorated pediments and apron swags. Inside, the entrance hall is comparatively plain, but leads to a splendidly carved staircase and a series of stately rooms which still retain most of their original decoration. The Gilt Room was lavishly decorated at the end of the seventeenth century with carvings, paintings and sculptures copied from Continental examples, while the Brown Room with its elaborate carved wall panelling was probably decorated in the early years of the eighteenth century.[14]

While Tredegar House is doubtless amongst the best of the larger houses that were built during the seventeenth century in Wales, pride of place for fine proportions and urbanity must go to the Great Castle House at Monmouth, built in 1673 within the grounds of Monmouth Castle. The dignified main facade is three storeys over a basement and is divided into three bays and covered by a steep hipped-roof with curving eaves (plate 47). The central bay, which is recessed, contains a two-storey feature incorporating superimposed classical pilasters around the doorway and window. Internally, the planning reflects true Renaissance formality, with a very large entrance hall occupying a central position (fig. 76). The rooms themselves are of particular interest, with excellent woodwork and richly decorated plaster ceilings.

In view of the number of Welsh Houses traditionally associated with Inigo Jones, it is perhaps surprising that the Great Castle House is the only one which bears any semblance to his ideas. In fact the only domestic building that can be reliably attributed to Jones is the finely proportioned and symmetrically planned gatehouse (1630) at Cors y Gedol, near Barmouth, where the owner was a personal friend of the architect[15] (fig. 77).

76. Great Castle House, Monmouth, Gwent: plan

Another building which has long been reputed to be the work of Inigo Jones is Ruperra Castle, north-east of Cardiff. Although there is no documentary evidence for the attribution it is difficult to ignore the idea altogether for despite the mansion's castellated roof-line it was a most unusual building for its period.[16] The projecting porch follows the tradition of Beaupre in its mixture of late Gothic and Early Renaissance, but the rest of the building is completely alien to anything else in the area, and would be difficult to date on stylistic grounds alone. In fact it belongs to the early seventeenth century and has more than a hint about it of Jones's theories on massing even though it lacks his architectural style as we know it.[17] Its perfectly square plan with four almost identical elevations was, for instance, a new-fangled innovation at a time when wholly symmetrical plans were rare anywhere in Britain (fig. 78). Added to this novelty is the solidity of its appearance emphasised by the smooth, round towers at the four corners and by the simply detailed windows of round-headed triplets. Nothing could be in greater contrast to the animated elevations of the mansions that had been built up to this time. Whether or not Ruperra Castle was designed by Jones it at least fulfilled one of his foremost principles that 'ye outward ornaments oft to be solid, proposionable according to the rules, masculine and unaffected.'

77. Cors-y-gedol Gatehouse, Gwynedd

113

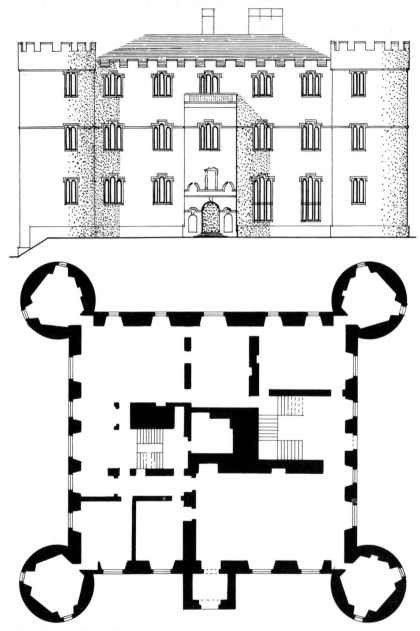

78. Ruperra Castle, Glamorgan: plan and
elevation

Inigo Jones (1573-1652), the first great professional architect in Britain, is reputed to be from Llanrwst, where a number of buildings are attributed to him, although it seems more likely he was born in London. He visited Italy twice to study the work of Palladio and as a result, brought back to Britain a genuine Italian Renaissance style quite different from anything built in these islands before. His first major work, the Queen's house in Greenwich (1616), was an absolute break with medieval tradition and it does not seem unreasonable therefore to credit Jones with the design of Pont Fawr, Llanrwst, the first bridge to break away from the medieval vernacular (plate 48). Pont Fawr was actually built in 1636 but had been ordered two years earlier by the Privy Council when Jones was still Surveyor-General to the king, and at a time when he was not particularly busy with other work. The bridge itself is beautifully proportioned and rises to a point, at the centre, marked by armorial tablets on the parapet walls. The three spacious arches (13m,18m and 13m wide) spanning the Afon Conwy with their narrow hexagonal piers and low parapets give the bridge an unusually slender appearance. Throughout Wales, many other bridges were built or rebuilt in the sixteenth and seventeenth-century, but none approaches the supreme confidence of the Pont Fawr at Llanrwst, nor its elegance.

One other building in the valley of the Conwy also deserves mention, namely the Gwydir Uchaf Chapel, built in 1673 as a private chapel for Sir Richard Wynn. It is notable for its four bay timber ceiling boldly painted with primitive cherubs and scrolls which, in the words of the Ministry Guide, forms 'one of the most remarkable examples of this class of seventeenth century art in Britain.' The chapel is small but has some well executed carvings and fittings in addition to the ceiling paintings and at the west end there is a gallery.

Public buildings were still few and far between and fewer have survived. During the early part of the seventeenth century, the traditional Tudor style, still under way, resulted in good examples of half-timber work in the more prosperous agricultural areas. The Old Market Hall (1609) at Llanidloes, for instance, has tall vertical timber and plaster panels to the upper floor, which is carried over an open ground floor, on heavy oak arches (plate 49). Brecon Town Hall, built in 1624 by the famous carpenter, John Abel, has long since disappeared; had it survived, it would have been a fascinating and bizarre example of the way Tudor and Renaissance elements were sometimes combined. Here classical-looking columns on both floors, together with elaborately carved bracketing, contrasted with the rest of the building which was of traditional timber-frame with a multi-gabled roof.

[1] 'Seasoned hay, tasty pasture, good beer and a comfortable bed.'

[2] R. W. Brunskill concludes that the period of the Great Rebuilding in most parts of rural England was between 1570 and 1620 (*Illustrated Handbook of Vernacular Architecture*, p. 27). In Wales it was generally considerably later; Moelwyn I. Williams suggests that in Glamorgan, for instance, the Great Rebuilding did not take place until about 1680 to 1730 ('A General View of Glamorgan Houses' in *Glamorgan Historian,* vol. 10, p. 162).

[3] St. Fagans Castle, the property of Nicholas Herbert and Sir Edward Lewis in the seventeenth century, is now the home of the Welsh Folk Museum.

[4] The original seat of the Bassets, a little distance away, had itself been a rebuilding, following the insurrection of Llywelyn Bren, in the early fourteenth century. One branch of the Anglo-Norman Basset family became, paradoxically, thoroughly Welsh in culture and language, marrying into the family of the great Lord Rhys of Dinefwr. The Beaupre branch, however, became more and more anglicised, as did many of the gentry following the death of Elizabeth I, and Rycharde Basset's plaque on the main house is inscribed in English.

[5] Plas Rhiwaedog occupies an ancient site, associated with Llywarch Hen in the Dark Ages.

[6] Peter Smith: *A few reflections on Gellilyfdy and the Renaissance in North-Eastern Wales,* p. 21.

[7] Sir Richard Clough (d.1570), the son of a Denbigh glover, was a merchant who had settled in Antwerp in 1552. There he became acquainted with Flemish building techniques and was responsible on a number of occasions for the delivery of Flemish building materials to Britain. In 1567 he returned to Wales, married the famous Katheryn of Berain (Catrin o Ferain) and began building Bachegraig and Plas Clough. Sir Richard Clough also hoped to make the Clwyd navigable for small ships as far as Rhuddlan, but before this could be accomplished he had returned to the Continent where he died at an early age.

[8] The Middleton Arms at Ruthin, also said to have been built by Sir Richard Clough, is reminiscent of Bachegraig and still retains its high Flemish roof with four tiers of dormer windows, although the rest of the building has been much altered.

[9] Robert Wynn was the third son of John Wyn ap Maredudd, the builder of Gwydir Castle. Robert was probably familiar with the architecture of Bachegraig through his sister-in-law Katheryn of Berain who, after the death of Sir Richard Clough, married Robert's elder brother Maurice Wynn.

[10] Plas Mawr reflects architecture in trauma — the 'classically' transitional house. At the same time, it exudes the pride of the Wynns in their noble ancestry, being directly descended from Owain, King of Gwynedd, and their pride also in the Tudor inheritance of the British throne.

[11] Iorwerth C. Peate: *The Welsh House,* p. 3. Typical of the *boneddigion* who became estranged from their Welsh background were the Cecils and the Herberts. William Cecil, famous descendent of the Sitsyllts (Seisyll) and Vaughans, Lord Treasurer (1572-98) and pillar of Elizabeth's court harped with pride on his Welsh ancestry and corresponded with Morys Clynnog in Welsh; but the great houses of the family, Burghley and Hatfield, were built in England. (The materials for Burghley House were imported from Antwerp by Sir Richard Clough.) Similarly, the Herberts of Raglan Castle as Earls of Pembroke became completely anglicised and moved to Wiltshire where they commissioned Inigo Jones to design one of his best houses, Wilton.

[12] One of the best staircases of this period, at Taliaris, near Llandeilo, dates from 1638 when the house was first built.

[13] In 1713 Erddig was bought by John Mellor who added (in 1723) wings to the house. In 1774 the west front was refaced in stone and internal alterations were carried out by Joseph Turner and James Wyatt.

[14] Another mansion with fine interior decoration dating from the late sixteenth century was Emral in Clwyd. The vaulted plaster ceiling (superbly sculpted to illustrate the life and labours of Hercules) and panelling of the hall at Emral was rescued by Clough Williams-Ellis and has been re-erected in the Town Hall at Portmeirion.

[15] An account of 1770, describes Inigo Jones as being 'very intimate with' the builder and records that he 'gave (William Vaughan, the owner) the design for the gatehouse at Cors-y-Gedol' and also that for the tomb in Llanddwywe Church, set up in 1616 in memory of his father. The aesthetically pleasing design of the gatehouse was somewhat obscured by the use of coarse rubble stonework in its construction.

[16] Ruperra Castle is now a shell, but all the exterior walls remain intact. The castellated parapet that completely surrounds the building was probably added in the late eighteenth century after the interior of the house had been largely destroyed by fire. An early drawing of Ruperra (dated 1684) shows castellated parapets on the angle towers only. The rest of the walls were two storeys high with a third floor lit by dormer windows.

[17] The same can be said of Plas Têg which is also sometimes attributed to Inigo Jones.

40.　St. Fagans Castle, near Cardiff. Built
between 1560 and 1580. Now the home of
the Welsh Folk Museum.

117

41. Powys Castle, near Welshpool, Powys.
The Long Gallery, 1587-92.

42.   Beaupre Castle, near Cowbridge,
       Glamorgan. 16th century with porch
       dating from 1660.

43. Plas Mawr, Conwy, Gwynedd. Built
between 1576 and 1580.

44. Plas Teg, near Mold, Clwyd. Sometimes
    attributed to Inigo Jones, it dates from the
    early 17th century.
45. Erddig House, Wrexham, Clwyd.
    Engraving by Thomas Badeslade showing
    the house and gardens c.1740. Built 1684
    (Thomas Webb).

46. Tredegar House, Newport, Gwent.
Rebuilt c.1760.
47. Great Castle House, Monmouth, Gwent.
Built in 1673 within the grounds of
Monmouth Castle.

122

48. Pont Fawr, Llanrwst, Gwynedd. Built
    1636 (attributed to Inigo Jones)
49. Market Hall, Llanidloes, Powys. Built in
    the vernacular style in 1609.

Chapter 7
Eighteenth Century

The Romantic Era

The period known as 'Georgian' in England (an unsatisfactory term architecturally as it expresses little except the names of Hanoverian kings reigning between 1714 and 1820), was in Wales a period of educational and religious revival, of literary renaissance and of economic revolution. Much of the architecture of the period was characterised here, as in the rest of Britain, more by romantic excursions into historicism than by continuity of tradition — many architects being more concerned with emotional appeal than with intellectual abstraction. For much of the eighteenth century the more important buildings were again domestic in character, but from the middle of the century onwards the first stirrings of the industrial revolution, with its consequent need for improved transport, could be felt. This was paralleled in religion by the growth of Nonconformity, one of the most potent factors in the life of Wales to the present day. Both these forces — the industrial and the religious — span the period from the late eighteenth century to the twentieth century and are discussed in the following chapters.

In the domestic field the eighteenth century was a period of great activity, partly as a result of increased prosperity following the introduction of scientific methods of agriculture on the more important estates. Though there is little to compare with the palatial mansions of favoured English shires, Wales has a number of country mansions that were designed on a smaller scale in the fashionable style of the period. The architects employed were more often than not from England, for the gentry were becoming more and more estranged from their Welsh background and now organised their way of life on English patterns.

This was also an important period for urban building. Again, there is nothing to compare with the fine terraces and crescents of the planned parts of London, Bath and Edinburgh, but many of our market towns owe much of their urbane character to the elegant 'Georgian' and 'Regency' houses that were built then. The essence of these houses' appearance was in their simplicity and fine sense of proportion matched by tall sash windows and pedimented doorways set in stuccoed facades. Abergavenny, Monmouth and Cowbridge in the south-east; Carmarthen, Laugharne, Haverfordwest, Tenby and the earlier parts of Swansea in the south-west; Montgomery and Welshpool in mid-Wales — all these contain good examples of domestic street architecture of the time.

Montgomery is perhaps the best unspoilt example of an eighteenth century town, for it has seen comparatively little change. It still retains its modest and well-proportioned late 'Georgian' town-hall and houses, all built around a central square with cobbled pavements. Carmarthen also has a particularly good town-hall with large Venetian windows, built in 1767. At Aberystwyth and Beaumaris the best domestic architecture belongs to the nineteenth rather than the eighteenth century, but it is still in style derived from and similar to that of the earlier period.

Baroque and Palladian

In England, the Renaissance spirit had given way in the late seventeenth century to the floridness and pomposity of Baroque Classicism. Even this, however, was tame in comparison with the exuberant architecture found on the Continent, particularly in Austria and southern Germany. The Baroque phase in England lasted until about 1730, after which there was a reaction and a return to the more sober Palladian style introduced by Inigo Jones in the early seventeenth century. In Wales, apart from the exception of Tredegar House already mentioned, there were few such excursions into the plasticism of Baroque architecture.[1] One of these, only 15 kilometres from Tredegar House, was at Penhow Castle where a highly decorated parlour was added about 1720. Baroque art in Wales in fact was virtually confined to the marvellous wrought-iron gates and screens that ornament the entrances to a number of parks and churches in Clwyd. These are the work of the talented brothers Robert and John Davies of Bersham, near Wrexham. Robert Davies (1675-1748) is reputed to have been a pupil of Tijou, the famous French wrought-iron smith. The art of the Davies brothers is seen at its most magnificent at Leeswood Park, near Mold, where they provided both the White Gates and the Black Gates. The White Gates and Screen, thirty metres in length, are superbly executed with elaborate crestings and delicate tracery and are amongst the finest in Europe. Other gates and screens by the Davies brothers are at St. Giles's Church (Wrexham), St. Peter's Church (Ruthin), Erddig Park (near Wrexham), Chirk Castle and at Eaton Hall just across the border in Cheshire.

Despite the fine gates at Leeswood, the Hall itself is typically Palladian in its angular composition, even though it has lost its outer wings and the upper floor of the three storey main block. Built between 1720 and 1730 — reputedly to designs by Francis Smith of Warwickshire — the main block now consists of a balustraded two-storey central portion with projecting side bays embellished by curved pediments over the lower windows and giant Corinthian pilasters at the corners. Another mansion in the Palladian spirit is Nanteos, near Aberystwyth, built in 1739 (plate 50). Externally, it is an austere stone building, square on plan and three

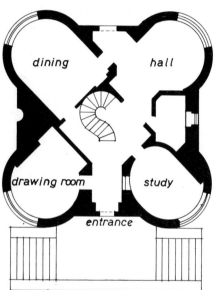

storeys high with balustraded parapet. The main entrance is marked by a colonnaded porch of Doric columns while tall round-headed windows above accent the position of the elegantly decorated Salon within. Two other notable mansions belonging to this period are Wynnstay, near Ruabon, rebuilt in 1736-9 by Francis Smith, and Broadlane Hall, Hawarden, designed by the local architect Joseph Turner in 1752. Both houses were later rebuilt; Wynnstay (for the second or third time) in 1789 by James Wyatt and Broadlane Hall in 1809 when it was replaced by Thomas Cundy's Hawarden Castle.

Towards the middle of the eighteenth century, John Wood (the Elder) of Bath was working at Llandaf. His main work there was a rebuilding of part of the cathedral in Classical style (1734-52), as a rather mean Italianate temple within the walls of the ruined nave. Funds ran out and the domed tower and pedimented porch of the 'temple' were never built. Nearby, a large new house, Llandaf Court, was built between 1744 and 1751, also probably to designs by Wood (fig. 79). Even plainer than Nanteos, it comprises a three-storey rectangular block with rows of tall windows and a Doric porch on the south side. Of the smaller houses the most remarkable is Moor Park, near Crickhowell, built in 1760 by John Powell (fig. 80). It is noted for its peculiar plan. Square, with round towers at the corners, it is divided into four partly-circular rooms on each floor grouped around a fine spiral staircase.[2]

The most impressive public building of the early eighteenth century is the Shire Hall at Monmouth, built in 1724 (fig 81). Two storeys over an open arcade, the facade is divided by Ionic pilasters into six bays, the centre pair being united under a single pediment. In urbanity, scale and unity of design the Shire Hall stands alone among Welsh public buildings of its period yet, surprisingly, the architect's name is unknown.

Late Classicism

At Taliaris, a seventeenth-century mansion near Llandeilo, Palladian influence survived until late into the eighteenth century when the building was gracefully re-fronted (about 1780) in ashlared limestone (plate 51). At the same time a two-storey block with Venetian windows was added.

But Taliaris was the last of a line. Already in 1753 William Thomas had introduced a more romantic version of Classical architecture at Stackpole Court near Pembroke. Thomas illustrated the mansion in his book *Original Designs in Architecture*, which he wrote and published in 1783.[3] The entrance bay is unexceptional despite its fine pediment and Ionic pilasters, but the wings on either side are most unusual.

79. Llandaff Court, Cardiff

80. Moor Park House, Powys: plan

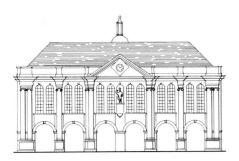

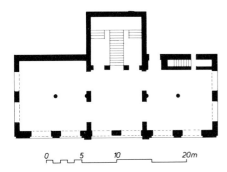

81. Monmouth Shirehall, Gwent: ground floor plan and elevation

They appear as large flat surfaces relieved, not by windows, but by round-headed niches and sculptured plaques (plate 52).

Generally, architects in the latter part of the century appear to have been mostly concerned with the interiors of buildings. Interior decoration at its most stately may be seen in Chirk Castle, a forbidding border fortress of the Edwardian wars, where state rooms with fine stucco ceilings and an Ionic entrance hall with a graceful staircase were built into the existing medieval structure between 1763 and 1773. The result is an interior totally at variance with the exterior character of the drum-towered castle. The alterations were probably designed by Joseph Turner of Hawarden and are similar in style to the work of Robert Adam, the Scottish architect who was then one of the most accomplished exponents and practitioners of interior design. The magnificent ceilings at Chirk are either coffered or coved and are elaborately, but delicately, decorated with shallow carved floral mouldings and painted panels while the walls have carved timber panels and richly moulded door casings (plate 53).

In mid-Wales, the library at Trawscoed, Cardiganshire, also has a richly panelled ceiling with floral bas-relief medallions on the side panels and frescoed cherubims on the coved centre panel, all supported on fluted Corinthian columns. Nannau (1796), near Dolgellau, is another mansion with Adam-style interior decoration and a fine wrought-iron staircase balustrade.

The finest example in southern Wales of architecture as 'interior decoration' is at twelfth-century Fonmon Castle in the Vale of Glamorgan. Here in the mid-eighteenth century a new library, sub-divided by panelled arches, was constructed with a superb Rococo plaster ceiling, possibly designed by Thomas Stocking of Bristol (plate 54). At the same time, a more restrained but delightfully decorated Stair Hall was inserted with an elegant staircase and gallery.

An exceptional building of this period, and one of the finest of its type in Britain, is the Orangery at Margam, which was erected in 1787 to give protection to the delicate orange trees during winter. Its elegant and well-disciplined design is attributed to Anthony Keck (plate 55). The great length of the Orangery (reputed to be one of the largest in the world) punctuated by a raised parapet with floral carvings over the centre bays, is terminated by pedimented pavilions at the two ends. Numerous tall round-headed windows, which might otherwise have seemed too interminable, are neatly linked together with rusticated piers contrasting with a simple frieze and cornice running along the whole length of the building.

The best late eighteenth-century public buildings are the work of Joseph Turner, an

Hawarden architect practicing from Chester. A number of domestic and public buildings in Clwyd can be attributed to him, notably the Old County Gaol (1755) and the refined single-storey Roman Doric County Hall (1785) in Ruthin and the elegant bridge (1770) at St. Asaph.

Romantic Gothic, Landscape Gardening and the Picturesque

Soon after 'normal' Georgian trends reached their apogee — which in Wales may be dated to the 1760's (when the interiors of Chirk Castle and Fonmon Castle were being so richly reconstructed) — domestic architecture experienced an extra-ordinary *volte-face*. During this phase, which started off as a flickering flame but was to become a forest fire in the nineteenth century, architects retreated, at first somewhat lightheartedly, to medieval buildings for their inspiration. Perhaps the earliest Welsh work in the 'Gothick' manner was a small summer-house with a castellated upper storey erected in Llandaf sometime before 1776. The first major work, at nearby Cardiff Castle (1777), had some quasi-scholarly justification because the commission entailed restoring the original fifteenth-century domestic apartments as well as adding two wings in similar style. The architect was Henry Holland, normally regarded as a classicist. Holland's other work near Cardiff, at Wenvoe Castle, had less real justification for adopting a pseudo-medieval stance, for this was in all respects a completely new building, albeit on the site of a genuine castle. A large mansion, it had a three-storey centre block and long two-storey wings on either side with towers at each end. Quite lacking in conviction no great loss has been suffered through its demolition. Its Gothic character was skin-deep, consisting mainly of embattled parapets used purely for ostentatious display. The rear courtyard and stables — which have fortunately survived — were, however, designed in a dignified Classical manner with pedimented arches and a formal staircase. An important adjunct to the country mansions were the parks which, during the latter half of the eighteenth century, were landscaped in as naturalistic a manners as possible. This new style of landscaping was in direct contrast to the formal layout of gardens which hitherto, under French influence, had characterised the surroundings of large houses. The most famous of the late eighteenth-century landscape-gardeners was Lancelot Brown, otherwise known as 'Capability' Brown, father-in-law of Henry Holland. Brown was responsible for laying out the vast grounds of Cardiff Castle and also in 1777 the park at Wynnstay, near Ruabon, where he introduced a lake, plantations and an artificial waterfall. In their desire to persuade nature to imitate romantic art (for this is really what it amounted to) landscape gardeners contrived sinuous lakes and artificial grottoes, adding 'follies' — often in the form of 'Gothick' ruins — to aid the 'naturalistic' appearance of the parks. One of the best known romantic follies in Wales, for instance, is a sham castle near Abergavenny, known as Clytha Castle. Erected as a memorial to the owner's wife, it was built in 1790 with three boldly castellated towers to designs by Edward Haycock (fig. 82).

In the informal new style of landscape-gardening, the park was meant to be seen *from the house* as a 'natural' extension of the 'natural' countryside; any buildings erected within the park were intended to merge pictorially into this scene. In Wales many of the country parks were planned on a small scale, for in most parts there were already expansive views and splendid natural scenery; it was pointless therefore to plan on a grand scale parks which would inevitably be dwarfed by their natural surroundings. Thus Humphrey Repton wrote in 1793 concerning Rug, a neo-Grec house in the upper Dee valley, 'the views from the house should aim at comfort and appropriation of landscape, rather than extensive prospect' and instead of creating a large park there he concentrated the landscaping in a 'lawn' of only 50 acres.[4]

Eventually, the latent anachronism in the relationship of a neo-classical 'formal' house with an 'informal' park setting was appreciated. It now seeemed necessary that the house too should form an integral and informal element within the whole scene. Henceforth, symmetry was to be avoided in designing houses, just as it was shunned in landscape-gardening. The artistic attitudes which brought about this merger of architectural and gardening ideals had been developing for some time but were not clearly defined until theories relating to the *Picturesque* were formulated at the end of the eighteenth-century. Although the Picturesque movement was not strictly an architectural one it had a profound effect on architectural thinking and is of especial interest here because three of the principal figures concerned with it were of Welsh stock and were intimately connected with work in Wales. The three were Sir Uvedale Price of Aberystwyth (1747-1829), Thomas Johnes of Hafod (1748-1816) and John Nash of Carmarthen (1752-1835). Between them they crystallised the aesthetic theory of the Picturesque and put it into practice. It was Price who gave deeper meaning to the word 'picturesque' and, together with his Herefordshire neighbour Payne Knight, he is generally regarded as the originator of the cult. In 1794 Price published his *Essay on the Picturesque.* Extolling the virtues of an emotionally romantic approach to landscape, he considered Gothic architecture to be better fitted than Grecian on the grounds that a rough and rugged ruin is more naturally 'picturesque' than an artificially neat and smooth new building. Even before the *Essay* however, Knight had built (in 1774) a neo-Gothic castle in Herefordshire while the ideals of the Picturesque had already been partly manifested by Thomas Johnes in the secluded and beautiful valley of the Ystwyth at Hafod Uchtryd less than twenty kilometres from Aberystwyth. Johnes, whose family originated from Llanfair Clydogau (near Tregaron), was a cousin of Payne

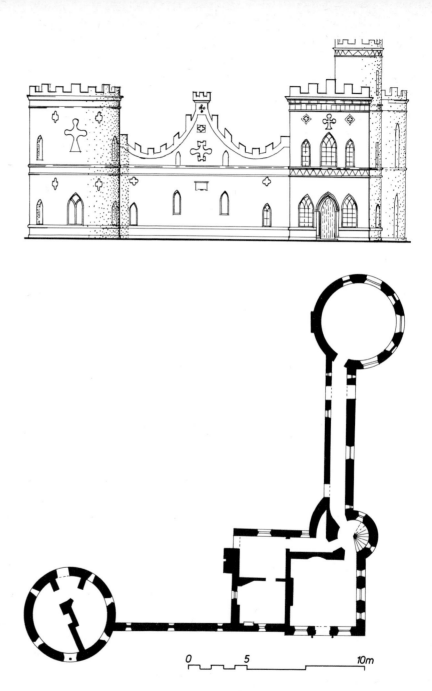

82. Clytha Castle, Gwent: plan and north elevation

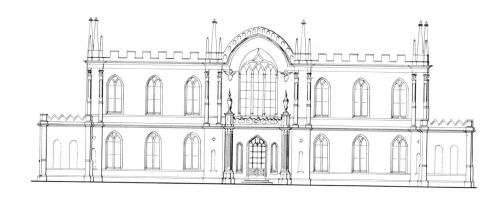

Knight and a friend of Uvedale Price. At Hafod, Johnes was able to develop the
ideas of Price and Knight — relating to the combination of romantic architecture in
a landscape setting — in a remarkable way (plate 56). The house itself was romantic
almost to the point of being bizarre; for though the details were 'Gothic' the
building as a whole had a distinctly Oriental flavour. This was partly because
different architects worked on the house at various times. The first was Thomas
Baldwin of Bath who erected a Gothick pavilion in 1786 complete with pointed
windows, embattled parapets and weird pinnacles (fig. 83). Behind this an
octagonal library — with a coffered dome and Doric columns — was erected,
apparently to Johnes's own design.[5] In 1793 John Nash, then a comparatively
unknown architect, added two low Gothick wings. In 1807, a fire destroyed most of
the interior, including the library with its priceless and irreplaceable collection of
Welsh and French manuscripts. Stunned but unbeaten, Johnes commissioned
Baldwin to rebuild the house as before.

On the landscaping side, Johnes drained bogs in order to improve the land and
planted some four million trees between 1796 and 1813 to provide shelter for his
estate. In 1853 an Italianate campanile and terrace were added to the house by
Nash's pupil Anthony Salvin.[6] A year later George Borrow described it in *Wild
Wales* as 'a truly fairy place . . . beautiful but fantastic . . . the walls were of
resplendent whiteness, and the windows which were numerous shone with
beautiful gilding'. Tragically, the house has now been demolished and almost all
that remains of Johnes's resplendent creation are some trees.[7]

83.   Hafod Uchtryd, Dyfed: elevation of main
front by Thomas Baldwin

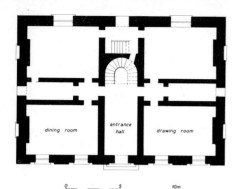

84. Whitson Court, Gwent: plan

85. Ffynone, Dyfed: plan

John Nash In Wales

John Nash was Welsh on his mother's side and he himself is thought to have been born at Cardigan, though there is no proof of the fact. He was brought up and educated in London, but after a brief and financially calamitous period working there he returned to Wales and set up his office in Carmarthen in 1784. Nash's architectural talents were many sided and it is significant that his life span covers a period of extraordinary fertility in British architecture. Born three years before Walpole's first Gothick exercises at Strawberry Hill, Nash could show by the beginning of the nineteenth century that he, like so many scores of architects afterwards, could turn his hand to any style required of him, 'Gothic' or 'Picturesque Vernacular', 'Italianate' — even 'Hindoo' — all styles were grist to Nash's mill and he treated them with equal gusto. We are concerned here with Nash's neo-Gothic, Romantic Classical and Picturesque Vernacular experiments, for these were the three modes which he first essayed while working in Wales. Wales was, as it were, the crucible of his developing expertise.[8]

While Nash was designing additions for Johnes at Hafod, he was also carrying out work at St. David's Cathedral and at Aberystwyth for Uvedale Price.[9] His contribution at St. David's involved rebuilding the west front (since replaced by a new front designed by Sir George Gilbert Scott), and it is interesting to note that the draughtsman responsible for the working drawings was Charles de Pugin (father of the indefatigable Augustus Welby Pugin), who was then working for Nash at his Carmarthen office. The building for Price at Aberystwyth was Castle House, a peculiar Gothic-styled villa based on a triangular plan (in order to exploit the views on all sides) with octagonal towers at the corners. The building has long since disappeared, its site now being occupied by the University College of Wales building (1864-85), which, appropriately, was designed in a tough version of Victorian Gothic.

More significant in Welsh terms than the small Aberystwyth villa is Kentchurch Court at Pontrilas (near Abergavenny), the ancestral home of the Scudamores. Like the Scudamore's' other mansion at nearby Monnington Court, it is closely associated in history with Owain Glyndŵr and though now on the English side of the Monnow, it is here that the descendants of Glyndŵr's daughter and her husband, John Scudamore, still live. The house was extensively remodelled by Nash about 1795 with castellated towers and 'Tudor' windows to give the effect of a Gothic castle, while carefully retaining the ancient tower in which Glyndŵr is reputed to have spent his last years. With these alterations at Kentchurch, Nash's reputation as a creator of castellated-gothic houses became established.

Most of Nash's works in Wales contrast strongly with Kentchurch. They come under the heading of 'Romantic Classical' and include the houses known as Ffynone, near Cardigan (1793), Llysnewydd in the Teifi Valley (1794) and Whitson Court, near Newport, Gwent (1795). Each was built to a square plan with simple elevations which were nevertheless well mannered and quite handsome. Internally, the rooms are planned around semi-circular staircases with fine balustrading. At Whitson Court the stairwell is lit from above by a large dome in the ceiling (fig. 84). The inside of Ffynone is Nash at his 'Classical' best and is splendidly set off by an octagonal vestibule with an attractive vaulted ceiling and archways with delicately detailed circular fanlights (fig. 85). The exteriors of both Ffynone and Llysnewydd have been drastically altered by later changes; Whitson Court on the other hand has suffered only slight alterations to its appearance (plate 57). The layout is very formal, comprising the three-storey red-brick house itself as a central block flanked by enclosed courts which are terminated by two-storey pavilion-like wings. The rather severe design of the group is relieved by arched recesses on the ground floor of the house and wings.

Nash's third architectural experiment was with the 'Picturesque Vernacular' or 'Rustic Cottage'. There is one Welsh example in the Lodge at Whitson Court and that is early enough (c.1795) to pre-date Nash's later partnership with Humphry Repton, the landscape gardener from whom Nash is generally supposed to have learned the principles of Picturesque disposition.[10] The Lodge — a stuccoed cottage with an open portico — was probably Nash's first attempt to exploit the picturesque cottage style. After Whitson, Nash developed the Rustic Cottage idea further in a number of other places, eventually reaching a culmination in 1811 in the Hamlet at Blaise Castle (near Bristol) where he laid out a group of nine cottages, all different, in an irregular cluster.

As well as designing other houses in Wales, Nash was also responsible for the gaols at Carmarthen (1789-92) and Cardigan (1793) and the bridge at Aberystwyth (1798), but all have now been replaced. The first town planning exercise by Nash was for a small town improvement scheme at Abergavenny which resulted in a new market (1795) to his design. Later he is reputed to have had a hand in the layout of the new town at Aberaeron (1808) where he also designed one or two country houses.

In 1796 Nash returned to London to set up a large and fashionable practice. He kept his Carmarthen office open for a few years and re-visited Wales periodically to see to his contracts. In London, as chief exponent of 'Picturesque' attitudes, he became one of the greatest virtuoso architects of early nineteenth-century England. He is particularly renowned for his grandiose town planning schemes in London and the Oriental-style remodelling of the Royal Pavilion at Brighton. It should not be forgotten, though, that his earlier schemes were nearly all built in his mother's country and that it was in Wales that his inimitable genius showed its first flowering.

[1] At Tredegar House a new and elegant stable block — with tall rectangular windows to the ground floor, circular windows to the first floor and curved dormers at roof level — was built alongside the mansion c.1725.

[2] A number of other houses in the middle Usk and Wye valleys were rebuilt or fashionably re-fronted on a modest scale in the early eighteenth century. The best of these is Pen-yr-wrlodd, near Hay, which was enlarged by the addition of a dignified new wing with a slightly projecting entrance bay.

[3] William Thomas (d.1800), a native of the Pembroke district, was one of a number of Welsh architects to publish a work on architectural design. He appears, however, to have had little real influence on Welsh architecture although it is interesting to note that one of the original subscribers to his book was a certain Mr. Nash, possibly John Nash. Other Welsh architect-authors in the eighteenth century were James Lewis (c.1751 — 1820) of Brecon who also wrote a book entitled *Original Designs in Architecture* (2 vols., 1780 and 1797) and Edward Oakley of Carmarthen who published *The Magazine of Architecture, Perspective and Sculpture* (1730 to 1732), *Every Man a Compleat Builder* (1738) and *Ornamental Architecture in the Gothic, Chinese and Modern Taste* (1758).

[4] In the south-east, where the scenery is more subdued, parks were often laid out on a much larger scale, thus Bute Park, Cardiff, is 350 acres and Tredegar Park, Newport, is 1,000 acres in extent.

[5] A number of writers have attributed the library to either Baldwin or Nash, but Malkin (writing a few years after the library was built) states categorically that Johnes 'was in this instance his own architect; and this library is the triumph of the place'. B. H. Malkin: *The Scenery, Antiquities and Biography of South Wales,* (1804), p. 359.

[6] Salvin also designed Pennoyre (1846), a large house in a more reticent style near Brecon, which still stands.

[7] Perched on a rocky spur amongst the trees there also remains the pathetically overgrown terraces of a once delightful private flower-garden that Johnes constructed for his invalid daughter Mariamne.

[8] During the period 1785 to 1798 Nash designed or altered at least 23 buildings in Wales. Apart from the renovation of 17 Bloomsbury Square in London, these were Nash's earliest works.

[9] Nash also remodelled (1792-95) Dolaucothi for John Johnes, the brother of Thomas Johnes's wife.

[10] As we have seen, Nash was working at Hafod two years previously and it is much more likely that he learned about Picturesque principles there.

50. Nanteos, near Aberystwyth, Dyfed. Built 1739.
51. Taliaris, near Llandeilo, Dyfed. Re-fronted c.1780

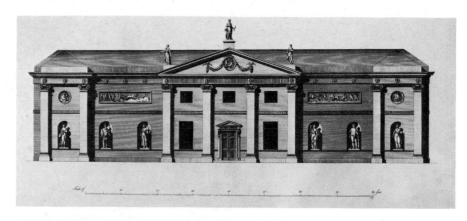

52. Stackpole Court, near Pembroke, Dyfed.
   Built 1753. Drawing by William Thomas
   from *Original Designs in Architecture*.
53. Chirk Castle, Clwyd. First Floor Saloon
   (between 1763 and 1773), probably by
   Joseph Turner.

54. Fonmon Castle, Penmark, Glamorgan.
The Library (mid-18th century), possibly
by Thomas Stocking.

55. The Orangery, Margam, Glamorgan. Built
1787 (attributed to Anthony Keck).

57. Whitsun Court, near Newport, Gwent.
John Nash, 1795.

56. Hafod Uchtryd, Ysbyty Ystwyth, Dyfed.
Watercolour by Nash, c.1807. View from
the south showing the main house
(Thomas Baldwin, 1786) and the
Octagonal Library (Thomas Johnes).

Chapter 8 Industry and Planning in the Eighteenth and Nineteenth Centuries

From about the middle of the eighteenth century Wales was involved in a period of change which was to transform much of its landscape and townscape. This was primarily due to the development of industry which, although small in scale at first soon expanded rapidly as a result of new methods of iron-making, the use of steam-power and the change-over from domestic manufacture to the factory system. The full impact of the Industrial Revolution became felt in the nineteenth century when the old pattern of building development was often overlain and largely obliterated. In southern Wales, in particular, beautiful secluded valleys were transformed into monotonously drab sprawls of ironworks, coal mines and terraced houses. To a lesser extent, parts of the north-east, and north-west were also radically changed by the iron industry, coal mining and quarrying. With the coming of new industry went the need for improved communications and these also left their mark on the countryside in the form of canals, turnpike roads, railways, bridges and tunnels.

Change was not limited, however, to the industrialised areas. In the remaining rural parts of Wales the landscape was permanently affected by innovations brought in by the Agricultural Revolution and then later by the enclosure of common land.

Building activity was vastly affected by these changes. Not only was there more urgent building activity than ever before; new types of buildings were required and new forms of construction were evolved. Apart from some revolutionary engineering projects, architectural progress was generally limited and architects, when employed, often favoured romantic versions of past styles. Social demands also affected building development. The growth of religious nonconformity coloured the picture as did an awakening interest in education. A number of town planning experiments were aimed at creating ideal environments either for the needs of employees or in order to attract trade.

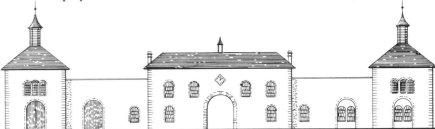

86. Dinorwig Quarry Workshops, Gwynedd:
north elevation

Within the wide range of buildings that were erected during this period the most exciting are those which are directly concerned with industry and transport — the engineering structures. As Elisabeth Beazley has written, 'Wales, by chance of time and geography, saw structures that were to amaze the world. A history of industrial revolution building might be written using Welsh examples only.'[1]

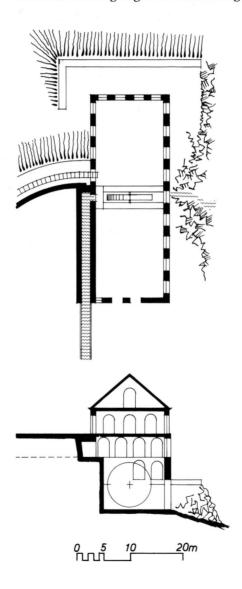

87.   Cwm Ystradllyn Slate Mill, Gwynedd: plan and section

Industrial Buildings

Industry in the form of iron-making had existed of course in Wales from as early as the Iron Age; in the latter part of the sixteenth century it was reintroduced, but this was on a very small scale in scattered furnaces using charcoal. The Industrial Revolution proper may be said to have started when the iron-making process was radically improved by using coke instead of charcoal as a fuel for smelting the ore. The earliest recorded use of coke in Wales was in 1753, at Bersham near Wrexham, and a few years later, in 1759, at the new Dowlais Ironworks near Merthyr Tydfil. In the following years additional ironworks were established at Merthyr (the Plymouth Ironworks in 1763, the Cyfarthfa Ironworks in 1766 and the Penydarren Ironworks in 1784) and it developed rapidly to become the largest and most important town in the Principality, a position which it maintained from about 1800 to the 1860's. The iron industry spread out from Merthyr along the northern rim of the coalfield from Hirwaun in the west to Blaenafon in the east so that by 1839 over a hundred furnaces had been built within this narrow strip of land. Southern Wales had become the leading iron-producing area in Britain.

With the exception of Ebbw Vale all the ironworks were closed long ago and now little remains to be seen except for the derelict ruins of furnaces and engine houses. The two largest ironworks at Cyfarthfa and Dowlais covered vast areas of ground and must have been awe-inspiring sights in their heyday with rows of monumental blast furnaces billowing clouds of glowing smoke from the fires below.

The ironworks' buildings were solidly built and functional and though rarely pretentious they were often of a high standard of design when compared with the workers' housing built close by. Paintings of the Cyfarthfa Ironworks in the early nineteenth century by Penry Williams show that small circular openings in groups of three were here used as a unifying motif on both the stone and iron-framed buildings. Few of these buildings now remain in any form, but at the four-storey stone engine-house of the Ynysfach Ironworks (a subsidiary of the Cyfarthfa company) in Merthyr Tydfil one can still recognise something of the dignity of these early industrial buildings. In this engine-house a simply repeated pattern of arched openings is outlined in ashlared limestone against a background of Pennant Sandstone rubble. By contrast the nearby blast-engine house at the Dowlais Ironworks (erected in the latter part of the nineteenth century), is built in red and yellow brick with a large porch carried on cast-iron columns. More unusual were the blast furnaces at Rhymni, which were designed in the style of Egyptian temples.

Allied to iron making was the tinplate industry. This came to be concentrated in western Glamorgan and around Llanelli. There a number of early tinplate buildings still stand, although they have now been adapted for use by other industries. Many of the buildings of the famous tinplate works established by the Crawshays in 1835 at Trefforest, in the Taff Valley, also survive and are of interest for their spidery wrought-iron roof trusses and the disciplined architectural treatment of their external walls. Five long, narrow, whitewashed stone buildings remain and each is punctuated by a pattern of very tall round-headed openings and smaller circular windows in the Cyfarthfa manner.

In many other parts of Wales industrial development proceeded with similarly disastrous effect on the landscape, though generally on a localised scale. Thus there was iron-making in the districts around Wrexham, lead mining in mid-Wales, extensive copper mining in the northern part of Anglesey, with copper smelting at Holywell and Swansea, and slate quarrying in Gwynedd. Slate quarrying, 'the most Welsh of Welsh industries', was developed on a large scale from about 1780 onwards and had a major influence on the building industry by allowing for the first time a really cheap and weatherproof form of roofing. The result is to be seen in industrial towns everywhere, in the rows of terrace houses roofed with the thin grey-blue slates of Wales. Slates were also exported in immense quantities from specially built docks, and at Port Penrhyn there is a charming late Georgian Port Office with a Doric porch designed by Benjamin Wyatt. Occasionally the buildings at the slate quarries themselves were designed with some concern for appearance. Thus at Llanberis the old quarry workshops (now a museum) were planned around an open rectangle with a symmetrical two-storey main front and corner towers topped by steeples, all built with local granite walls and slate roofs (fig. 86).

Industrial buildings were normally, however, starkly functional and utilitarian. One of the most impressive monuments of the slate industry is the Cwm Ystradllyn slate mill, built in 1855. It now stands roofless, gaunt and isolated amongst the mountains above Porthmadog (plate 58). It is a massive three-storey building honeycombed on all sides with rhythmic rows of great round-headed windows that give it a strong masculine character. A curving railway on a high embankment brought the raw slate in at the top floor level; here it was sawn. On the middle floor the sawn slate was dressed and then carried out on another railway running parallel with the upper one. On the ground floor there was a giant water-driven wheel for working the machinery (fig. 87).

Industrial architecture of quite a different and self-consciously romantic kind can be seen at Llandybie, near Ammanford, where R. K. Penson (a Welshpool architect better known for his churches and schools) designed some unusual kilns alongside the limestone quarries in the 1850's. The high sloping walls of the kilns are pierced by pointed arches and elaborated with deep buttresses and corbelled parapets, so

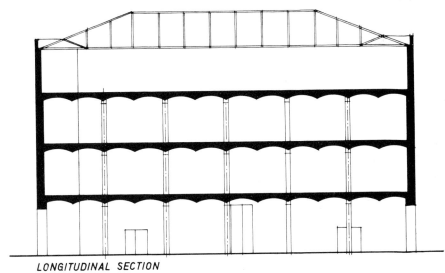

LONGITUDINAL SECTION

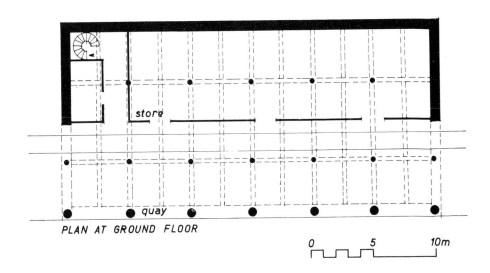

PLAN AT GROUND FLOOR

0   5   10m

88.   Bute Warehouse, Cardiff: plan and section

that at first glance they look like the extensive and very impressive remains of a medieval castle (plate 59).

The earliest multi-storey mills belong to the textile industry of northern Wales. At Holywell the cotton industry was first established in 1777 and within a few years (by 1790) four large cotton mills had been erected on the banks of the river there. Up to five storeys in height with rows of identical rectangular windows, these buildings must have appeared immense and completely out of scale with their rural surroundings when first built. At about the same time Newtown in mid-Wales became the centre of the Welsh flannel trade. Although the industry has now ceased the multi-storey brick warehouses where the handloom weavers worked still stand, while an early example of a cottage factory also survives at Newtown as a textile museum. In this building the lower floor was used for living accommodation and the upper floor, reached by a staircase at the rear, was equipped with machinery to form a weaving loft for the family.

It is appropriate to mention here that Robert Owen (1771-1858), the great social planner, was born at Newtown. Brought up in the traditions of the local weaving industry he later settled in Scotland where he became famous for his pioneering development of New Lanark (near Glasgow) as a model industrial village. In 1825 Owen established a co-operative settlement at New Harmony in the United States of America, and in 1841 he began the development of a similar colony (designed by Joseph Hansom) at Queenswood in Hampshire. Both attempts at social planning were, however, short-lived. In Wales 'Owenite' communities, as they came to be called, were set up at Pant Glas near Dolgellau in 1840 and at Garnllwyd near Carmarthen in 1847.

The buildings of the large industrial ports of Wales are rather disappointing on the whole, although both Cardiff and Swansea have examples illustrating the technological progress that was made in the nineteenth century. Seen from the outside the Bute Warehouse at Cardiff, designed by W. S. Clark in 1861, is a neat four-storey rectangular brick building with an open ground floor (fig. 88). Inside, round cast-iron columns at regular centres support a grid of iron beams which are spanned by brick vaulting carrying the floors. The Maritime Museum at Swansea is housed in another interesting but less adventurous warehouse. A vast two-storey 'shed' it has an exceptionally wide span roof. The most interesting industrial building in Swansea is Weaver's Flour Mill, built in 1897 to the designs of the French engineers, Hennebique and Le Brun. This was the first multi-storey reinforced concrete building to be erected in Britain and the materials for constructing it had to be imported from France. Even at this early date in the story of modern concrete the structural possibilities of the new material were exploited by deeply cantilevering the end bays.

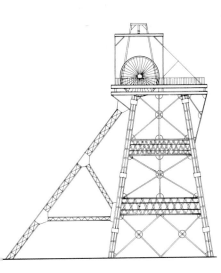

Until comparatively recently, a familiar feature of all the Glamorgan and Gwent Valleys was the colliery with its winding-house and high winding-towers. Most of the collieries that still exist were developed towards the end of the nineteenth century, or during the early part of the twentieth century, for before the 1840's the coal industry was a secondary adjunct to the ironworks and was concerned almost entirely with providing fuel for their furnaces. The winding-houses are usually simple, straight-forward stone buildings with round-headed windows picked out in red or yellow brickwork. In some of the later winding-houses a large semi-circular arch adorns the main front, as at National Colliery (1890), Rhondda, giving them an appearance strongly evocative of Nonconformist chapels of the same period.

The most distinctive feature of any colliery is the winding-tower used for winding the cages up from the coal-face to the surface. Originally winding-towers were constructed in timber but as pits became deeper, stronger towers were needed and complex steel lattice structures were used. One of the earliest, at Deep Duffryn Colliery, Mountain Ash, was built in 1842 and still exists. A later and very elaborate example may be seen at Merthyr Vale (1875) (fig. 89). In the early twentieth century simpler and less interesting winding-towers were introduced made entirely of standard rolled-steel joists. Eventually, after the 1939-45 War, these too were superseded by reinforced concrete towers.

The early twentieth century produced one industrial building that was remarkably advanced in design, indeed 'the most advanced British building of its date', according to Nikolaus Pevsner[2]. This was the boiler factory designed by H. B. Creswell for Williams and Robinson at Queensferry in 1901 (plate 60). Its 'Egyptian' appearance was largely fortuitous, unlike the self-conscious historicism found in earlier buildings. The straightforward simplicity of the design was in fact very much in keeping with the functional needs of the factory, for the battered buttresses that frame the building were structurally necessary. This, however, was a singular example of functional logic in a twentieth century industrial building and was not to be repeated in Wales for a half century until the famous rubber factory at Brynmawr was completed in 1951[3].

Bridges, Viaducts and Dams

The major industries of the late eighteenth and the nineteenth centuries were often sited in remote and almost inaccessible places because this was where the raw materials were extracted and processed. In order to transport the finished goods to other parts of Britain, it was necessary to improve the existing communications and this resulted in some magnificent works of engineering.

89. Merthyr Vale Colliery Winding Tower, Glamorgan

Even before the industrial development of districts away from the coast the roads and bridges of Wales were being gradually improved. The finest by far of these early bridges was the one that William Edwards of Groes-wen, a chapel minister and self-taught mason, built across the Afon Taf at what is now Pontypridd — the town itself being named after the bridge. His first two attempts at spanning the Taf, in 1746 and 1751, ended in dismal failure but at his third attempt, in 1756, he built a slender curved bridge of a single arch spanning 43 metres which at the time of its construction was probably the longest span in Europe. The bridge is in stone and to reduce its self-weight — and also to allow the passage of flood-water — Edwards pierced the spandrils with large cylindrical holes, three on each side, thus contributing to the structure's extraordinary grace (plate 61). Later, Edwards built other bridges of similar design, including those at Dolauhirion (1773) near Llandovery, and at Morriston (1780) near Swansea, but none was as large or as daring as the one at Pontypridd.

The first major improvement in Welsh transport was achieved in the latter part of the eighteenth century through the construction of canals from the manufacturing centres to the ports. More often than not their construction involved expensive cutting and embanking along narrow twisting valleys, as in the case of the Glamorganshire Canal built between Merthyr Tydfil and Cardiff in the 1790's. In its comparatively short distance of 40 kilometres it traversed a landfall of 150 metres and incorporated 40 locks.

In the north Thomas Telford built a canal from Llangollen to Ellesmere (to join the Shropshire Union Canal there) which included two superb aqueducts. The first, at Chirk (1796-1801), is the smaller and consists of ten stone arches carrying the canal above the Afon Ceiriog. The bottom of the narrow waterway is made of iron plates bolted together, instead of the more usual method of forming a channel with heavy puddled clay. Telford's other aqueduct, the justly famous Pont Cysyllte (1794-1805) below Llangollen, is more dramatic and crosses the valley of the Dee in nineteen splendid arches high above the river (plate 62). The canal, together with its cantilevered towpath, is carried on cast-iron webbed arches supported on tall hollow stone piers, a very economical and weight-saving form of construction which has well withstood the test of time. Telford's chief claim to fame in Wales lies with the Holyhead Turnpike Road which was built (1815-29) to improve the stage-coach route from London to Dublin. The first important crossing along this route is the beautiful Waterloo Bridge (1815) at Betws-y-Coed. The cast-iron spandrils of this bridge are elaborately decorated with giant leeks, roses, thistle and clover and bear the inscription that *This arch was constructed in the same year the battle of Waterloo was fought.* Telford then completed (1822) an elegant suspension bridge with castellated towers lower down the river, at Conwy. This, however, was only a foretaste of his greatest bridge Pont-y-Borth (1819-26) — joining the mainland of Wales to the Isle of Anglesey — across the Menai Strait, which was the first really large iron suspension bridge in the world (plate 63). The centre span, 170 metres long and 30 metres above the tide (due to shipping requirements), is suspended by massive chains from limestone towers at each end and is approached by arched stone viaducts from both sides of the Strait.[4]

Other fine iron road bridges can be seen at Chepstow in Gwent, and in the Severn Valley. The former was designed by John Rennie in 1816 and has five shapely cast-iron arches resting on stone piers. The bridges over the Severn at Llandinam (1846) and Aber-miwl (1852) were designed by Thomas Penson of Welshpool and are both single arch braced cast-iron structures, similar to the Waterloo Bridge in appearance but less self-consciously decorative.

Although the world's first load carrying steam locomotive made its pioneering run in Wales as early as 1804 — at Penydarren near Merthyr Tydfil — the railway mania proper did not arrive until much later. Because of the mountainous nature of the country, railway building when it commenced involved the construction of many viaducts and tunnels. These were mainly in the south, but two of the most notable railway bridges were built in the north, both by an engineer in association with an architect, Robert Stephenson and Francis Thompson. Both were alongside Telford's road bridges across the Afon Conwy and the difficult Menai Strait. In each case, Stephenson's answer to the engineering problem was in the form of continuous rectangular tubes through which the trains pass; they represent a new landmark in the world development of bridge building. Like Telford, Francis Thompson designed castellated towers at each end of the Conwy Tubular Bridge (1846) in deference to the great medieval castle alongside. The Britannia Tubular Bridge over the Menai Strait, was built (1845-50) with two separate metal tubes, one for each track, and is in four spans with five great stone pylons where, as H. R. Hitchcock rightly says 'Thompson handled his material with a superbly rational elegance'.[5] The bridge has a total length of 460 metres. Again there was a stipulation that the bridge had to be 30 metres above water and this necessitated building the long centre spans on land, floating them out on pontoons to the required positions and then slowly hauling them up by hydraulic pumps. In 1970 the great wrought-iron tubes were badly damaged by fire and are now propped up by deplorably cumbersome steel arches between the masonry towers, which had survived the holocaust intact.

At Chirk and Cefn Mawr, Telford's aqueducts were similarly paralleled by great stone railway viaducts built in 1848 by Henry Robertson. In mid-Wales good stone viaducts may also be seen on the old London and North Western Railway at Cynghordy, near Llandovery, and at Knucklas, near Knighton.

About the middle of the nineteenth century Isambard Brunel, perhaps the greatest of the railway engineers, built the South Wales Railway from Gloucester to Swansea, the Vale of Neath Railway and the Taff Vale Railway, but little of architectural interest remains. His tubular bridge at Chepstow (1852) has been replaced, and his wooden 'fan' viaducts at Neath (1851) and Aberdare (1854) have been demolished as well as his long (27 spans) wooden viaduct (1850) over the Tawe at Swansea.[6]

Not surprisingly, the viaducts which have lasted longest are the stone arched structures, for these are the most difficult to dismantle. A number of fine examples, Roman in scale, still exist in the mining valleys of the south. The longest, at Ystrad Mynach, was designed in 1857 by Liddel and Gordon and strides majestically across the Rhymni valley for 260 metres. More graceful, perhaps, is the Cefn Coed Viaduct, near Merthyr Tydfil, a slim fifteen arch structure laid out on a curve to the designs of Conybeare and Sutherland in 1866.

The finest of all British viaducts, that across the deep valley of the Ebbw at Crumlin, for the Taff Vale Railway, was destroyed in 1965. Built in 1857 and designed by T. W. Kennard, it was in two sections the longest of which was 325 metres in seven equal spans, a hair-raising 64 metres in height. The piers consisted of cast-iron tapering pylons; they carried wrought-iron trussed girders all of which from a distance looked deceptively slim and fragile. The other two great girder viaducts at Llanbradach (730 metres) and Taffs Well (472 metres) were not built until 1901 and 1905 and have likewise been demolished. Both were designed by Szlumper with steel lattice girders resting on enormous solid piers.

A most unusual bridge is the Transporter Bridge at Newport. This is really a suspension bridge with the main span, in the form of a continuous truss, supported at a very high level on deceptively slender latticed pylons (plate 64). The legs of the pylons are tapered to points at the base and are delicately balanced on top of stone piers. Hovering over the water and suspended from the main span 54 metres above is a travelling carriage that transports loads across the Usk river. The bridge was built between 1902 and 1906 to the designs of the French engineer, F. Arnodin, who was also responsible for the slightly earlier and more famous (but now destroyed) transporter bridge over the harbour at Marseille. Of the very few bridges of this type now left in the world, the Newport Transporter is probably the finest example.

Other major engineering works of the nineteenth century are the reservoirs constructed in remote valleys to supply water to the industrial parts of southern Wales and England. The largest of these is Vyrnwy (or Llyn Llanwddyn as it is

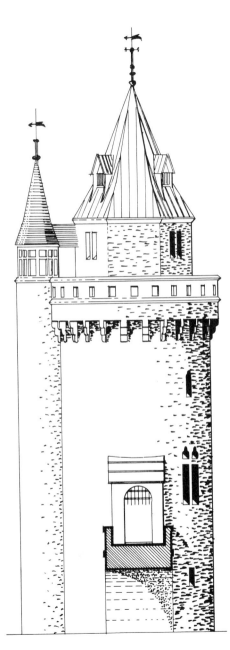

90. Valve Tower, Vyrnwy Reservoir, Powys

known locally), on the eastern slopes of the Berwyn range. It was constructed between 1881 and 1892 and is about eight kilometres long and nearly a kilometre in width. Architecturally, one of its more interesting features is the circular valve tower built out into the lake and designed to evoke the appearance of the medieval castle of Chilon on Lake Geneva (fig. 90). The massive dam with its 31 arch road viaduct is in comparison very restrained. In the Elan valley, near Rhaeadr, a chain of three large reservoirs was constructed amidst superb scenery between 1893 and 1904; since then a fourth reservoir on the adjacent Afon Claerwen has been built. Both the lower reservoirs, Caban Coch and Penygarreg, have simple stone dams without any undue elaboration (except for the domed valve towers) while Craig Coch reservoir is held back by a curved dam carrying an arched road viaduct. Reservoirs on a somewhat smaller scale were constructed in other parts of Wales, mainly in the Brecon Beacons and Mynydd Hiraethog. Though undistinguished in architectural terms, the use of natural stone and the incorporation of the occasional romantic feature has enabled the dams of these reservoirs to merge more sympathetically into their surroundings than most modern concrete dams seem able to do. Perhaps, when considering the sublime scenery in which most reservoirs are set, the use of 'picturesque' principles in determining the appearance of dams was better justified here than in any other sphere of nineteenth-century architecture or engineering.

Renaissance and Industrial Town Planning

The new ideas of urban design that were introduced into England in the seventeenth-century, and reached fulfilment in the planning of Bath and Edinburgh in the following century, did not have the opportunity of gaining acceptance in Wales until the late eighteenth and early nineteenth-centuries. Indeed, until the end of the eighteenth-century there had been no urban development of any consequence in Wales and pre-planned layouts were hardly necessary. Even when adopted, formal planning was but a faint echo of the ideals of Renaissance town planning which had been originally formulated in Italy and France for despite the new layouts the buildings themselves are generally small in scale and lacking in grandeur.[7]

Milford, Aberaeron and Tremadoc are three small towns which were built according to some of the basic principles of Renaissance formal planning; they grew out of the eighteenth-century spirit of improvement. They are all ports on the west coast and were mainly the work of enthusiastic individuals who wished to develop their estates and make them into outlets serving the surrounding districts.

Milford came into being in 1790 when an Act of Parliament was obtained *to make and provide Quays, Docks and Piers and other erections and to establish a Market with proper Roads and Avenues thereto.* Little seems to have been done however until 1797 when a French architect, Jean-Louis Barallier, was employed to design the new town. The layout which Barallier devised was simply a grid-iron pattern of three parallel streets crossed by shorter streets at right angles. This has survived, giving the centre of Milford its distinctive character, although the buildings themselves were only developed slowly and haphazardly. The larger houses were in the lower street, shops in the middle street and smaller houses in the upper street. At the end of the lower street a plain Gothick church (1802-8), probably designed by Barallier, was built to terminate the vista. A quay, custom-house, market-hall and chapels were also built. In addition it was hoped to found a naval and engineering college, but of this only an octagonal observatory appears to have been completed.

Aberaeron is considerably smaller in population than Milford. Yet although it has a more urban character, even this peters out away from the earliest development. Aberaeron is reputed to have been planned by John Nash though there is no written evidence to support this fact. Nevertheless, it is obvious that the layout of the town is the work of one man and Nash was certainly engaged to design one or two of the country houses in the neighbourhood at about the same time.[8] The character of some of the terraces, built by David Samuel of Caer Bislan, is such that they might well have been designed in Nash's office. The plan of Aberaeron is based on two large open-ended squares, on either side of the main coast road, partially enclosed by mainly two-storey terraces of houses (fig. 91). The new enclosed harbour was the first part of the scheme to be constructed between 1807 and 1811. This was then followed by the open square around the harbour and the adjacent rectangular grid of terraces. During this phase the Town Hall (1835) was erected in a prominent position facing the harbour. Finally, after 1840, Alban Square was laid out around a large public green which, though pleasant in itself, fails completely as a controlled urban space. Only three sides of the intended *piazza* were completed, but apart from that the terrace houses are far too small for such a grandly conceived project. Although the terraces are symmetrically accented by larger houses in the middle, and at the ends, this is hardly sufficient to overcome the lack of an appropriate urban scale.

Tremadoc is the smallest of the three west coast 'new towns'. It remained as a town centre alone, without any concomitant development, because its purpose was immediately negated by nearby Porthmadog which grew rapidly as a result of slate exports. Small though it is, Tremadoc has a more definitely urban character than either Milford or Aberaeron (plate 66). It is certainly prouder, more rugged and masculine and this is partly due to its siting below a dramatic backcloth of near precipitous cliffs. The new town was the creation of W. A. Madocks of Dolmelynllyn. It was built, apparently from rough sketches contained in letters to

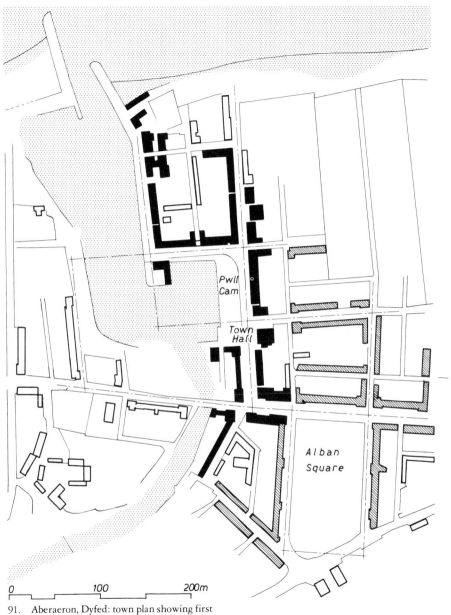

Pwll
Cam

Town
Hall

Alban
Square

0   100   200m

91.   Aberaeron, Dyfed: town plan showing first
main phase of development (pre-1840) in black
and second main phase of development (post-
1840) hatched

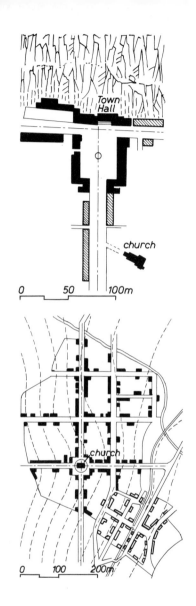

92. Tremadoc, Gwynedd: plan showing earliest buildings (c.1810) in black

93. Morriston, Swansea: town plan c.1850 (Contours at 5m. intervals)

his agent between 1800 and 1811, as part of a successful venture in reclaiming the Traeth Mawr estuary. In layout, Tremadoc is simply a 'T' plan with a rectangular market place in the form of a Renaissance *piazza* at the junction itself (fig. 92). Enclosing three sides of the market place, there is a continuous terrace of two-storey houses and shops. The north side of the market place is completed by an attractive town hall-cum-market-cum-theatre with an open arcade on the lower floor. On the outskirts of the town, Madocks built a Gothick church on one side of the road, and on the opposite side a neo-classical chapel. Here, apart from a four-storey woollen mill built further away on another road, the original development ended and very little was added until recently.

With the exception of one notable example, town planning in the industrial areas was mostly limited to small housing estates. The exception is Morriston, near Swansea, founded by Sir John Morris about 1768 to attract and house labour for his copper works. William Edwards of Groes-wen was employed by Morris to design the layout and this he did according to a grid-iron plan (fig. 93). Although Edwards had built a new bridge (1780) and a chapel (later rebuilt) for the new town, the main development does not appear to have really got under way until about 1790. Streets were laid out on spacious lines and plots of land were leased on condition that the lessees built according to prescribed plans. As the main focus of the town, a church was erected on an island at an intersection of the main street. Later, the visual importance of the church was reduced by the tower and spire of Capel-y-Tabernacl (1873) which now dominates the main street. Once started, Morriston flourished and grew. By 1796 there were already 141 houses with a population of over 600. By 1815 the size of the community had almost doubled.

Generally, the industrialists in the coalfields showed little inventiveness in laying out their estates of terrace housing. Long lines of terraces were first built around the pit-heads and then continued along the sides of the valleys following the contours as far as possible. Gradually, the lines of terraces coalesced to form continuous linear settlements, with little to break the monotony apart from the colliery winding-towers or the frequent chapels. The Rhondda Fawr, with a built-up area 16 kilometres long and never more than a kilometre wide, is the classic example of such a linear mining town in its narrow valley. The two-storey terrace houses of these districts, though unimaginative and stereotyped, are usually neat and soundly built and according to the standards of the day, well designed with entrances at back and front. In the south most terraces are built in rust-brown sandstones giving them a strongly idiosyncratic air which, when looked at without bias, has considerably more character than that of most council-house terraces or private semi-detached houses built during the twentieth century. In north-eastern Wales most of the industrial terrace houses were built in hard red brick. Two terraces (built in 1816) have survived at Holywell with an unusual architectural treatment of alternate large and small arches to the doorways (fig. 94). The noisome back-to-back terraces and miserable tenement courts found in so many of the English industrial towns were rarely built in Wales.

Occasionally, an attempt was made to produce something which was visually more stimulating. Thus the new core of Tredegar in Gwent was planned in the manner of a Renaissance *piazza* as an open market square at the intersection of four roads with the town-hall at one corner of the square (fig. 95). Later the square became a circle and a cast-iron clock tower, 22 metres high was placed in the centre as a decorative focal point (1858). Y Drenewydd, at the upper end of the Rhymni valley, is an interesting example of estate planning in a 'Classical' manner. It was built as a model community to house the workers of the nearby ironworks. The design of the estate is reputed to have been drawn up by R. Johnson, the manager of the ironworks, between 1802 and 1804 and was intended to be the start of a new town (hence its original Welsh name of Trefnewydd).[9] Four parallel terraces were planned to start with, but only three were built. The simplicity of the layout is compensated for by an impressive scale and symmetry in the terraces each of which has projecting end units, a middle section raised a storey higher than the rest and wide over-hanging eaves (fig. 96). In complete contrast to the classical symmetry of Y Drenewydd is the stark simplicity of the early housing estates built for iron-workers at Blaenafon and at Pentre-bach, near Merthyr Tydfil. Both, however, have the appearance of being planned. The earlier of the two, Stack Square at Blaenafon, was started in the 1790's and comprises three sides of an open square overlooking the ironworks. The Triangle, at Pentre-bach, was started about 1810 and consists of three similar two-storey terraces arranged around a triangular court and a longer curved terrace at the rear.

In the more rural areas early nineteenth-century model estate villages were sometimes given a 'vernacular' picturesqueness as at Llandegai and Llanfachreth with their rustic *cottages ornées*, both in Gwynedd. Marford, near the English border in Clwyd, is a fanciful hamlet of Gothick cottages (originally thatched) with ogee arches, cross 'arrow slits' and curious eye-shaped windows (plate 67). It was built in 1805 by George Boscawen with money inherited by his wife ten years earlier. Like those in the north, a number of model estate villages built in the south were also treated in a 'picturesque' manner. The best known are in Glamorgan at Margam Groes, near Port Talbot, and Merthyr Mawr, near Bridgend. Margam Groes was developed in the 1830's with semi-detached cottages with tall chimneys and also had an unusual octagonal chapel. Merthyr Mawr was built about ten years later with low thatched cottages grouped around a delightful little church designed by Benjamin Ferrey.

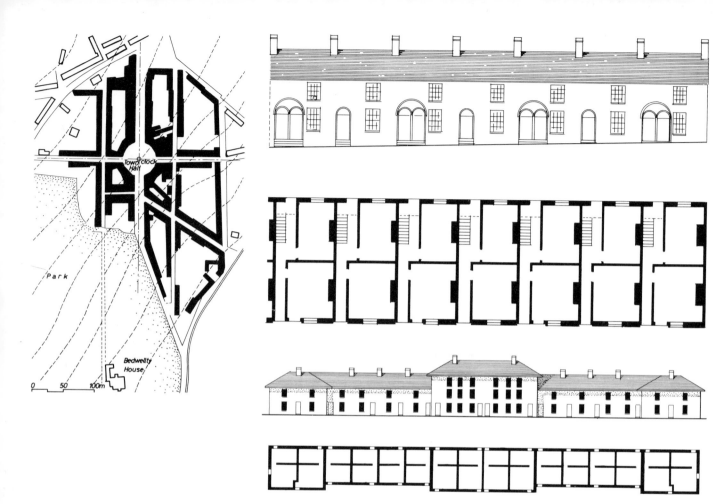

94.   Panton Place, Holywell, Clwyd: plan and elevation.

95.   Tredegar, Gwent: town plan, c.1850. (Contours at 5m. intervals)

96.   Y Drenewydd (Butetown), Rhymni, Glamorgan: plan and elevation of terrace

154

Not all of the model villages, however, had been designed in such a whimsical and wistful manner. The outstanding exception is Tregynon where, about 1870, Henry Hanbury-Tracy of Gregynog built a series of cottages and a village school entirely of concrete, then a daring and novel method of construction. Not only were the walls and floors of concrete (unreinforced) but so also were the roof slabs (covered by slates), staircases, chimneys and mouldings. Some of the detailing is based on traditional construction, such as the Victorian Gothic porches and occasional pseudo-black-and-white-timberwork, but generally the mouldings are simple and in keeping with the new material (plate 68). Thomas Nicholas claimed that Mr. Tracy had set 'the landowners of Wales an example in *cottage-building,* which it is to be hoped will be extensively followed'.[10] Unfortunately, the Hanbury-Tracys were eventually forced to sell the estate for over-extending themselves in various industrial and commercial experiments including the concrete houses.

The latter part of the nineteenth century produced a new type of town — the planned seaside resort — which, if not grander in conception than some of the earlier ports and industrial estates, was at least better able to fulfil its expectations.[11] The outstanding example in Wales of a planned seaside resort is Llandudno, sited on a narrow neck of land between the sea and the estuary of the Conwy and between the limestone headlands of the Great Orme and the Little Orme.

Llandudno, like nearby Colwyn Bay, was made popular and brought within easy reach of the industrial parts of north-western England by the opening of the Chester/Holyhead railway in 1849. Both towns were developed by local landowners from their country estates and taken together they represent a unique attempt at creating garden-cities-by-the-sea, half a century before the Garden City Movement of Ebenezer Howard. The layout of Llandudno is a grid of streets artfully adjusted to follow the long, crescent-shaped curve of the beach. Two main thoroughfares (The Promenade and Mostyn Street), lie parallel with the sea and are intersected at one end by a broad boulevard (Gloddaeth Avenue) which links the north shore, facing the sea, with the west shore facing the estuary. Development was controlled by an Act of Parliament (1854), the basic framework of the streets having already been established by Lord Mostyn in his sale plan of the Gloddaeth estate (1849) which showed the layout of the 179 plots he was selling. Strict building regulations were laid down stipulating generous widths of streets and pavements and also the maximum size of houses. A basic intention of the regulations was to secure *in the laying out of the various plots of ground, order and uniformity.* This was largely achieved in the development, at least up to about 1918. On the Promenade a great crescent of mainly three-storey hotels and houses sweeps boldly along the front of the bay ending in a fine pier (1876) at the foot of the Great Orme. Behind this is the main shopping street (Mostyn Street) with its four- and five-storey terrace blocks and iron-and-glass arcades. Later development has not robbed the town of its sense of spaciousness, its pleasant scale and consistent order. Though there are few buildings of individual merit Llandudno is still the most rewarding Welsh example of a planned town built since the Middle Ages.

NOTES TO CHAPTER 8

[1] Elisabeth D. Beazley: 'A Tour in Wales', in *The Architect's Journal,* (vol. 129, p. 860-883), 1959.

[2] The Brynmawr Rubber Factory (designed by the Architect's Co-Partnership) was, according to Reyner Banham, 'one of the first major pieces of post-war British architecture'. *(Guide to Modern Architecture* (1962), p.62).

[3] Nikolaus Pevsner: 'Nine Swallows — No Summer', in *Architectural Review* (vol. 91, p. 109), 1942.

[4] The suspension chains were originally wrought-iron, but steel was substituted in 1938.

[5] Henry-Russell Hitchcock: *Architecture: Nineteenth and Twentieth Centuries* (p. 69), 1958. The entrances to the bridge are flanked by enormous stone lions sculptured by John Thomas.

[6] The Bute street Station in Cardiff, built in 1841, was possibly designed by Brunel; it is probably the earliest surviving station in Wales. Fortunately, one of Brunel's stone viaducts is still in use at Quakers Yard, near Merthyr Tydfil. Built in 1841 for the Taff Vale Railway, it spans the Afon Taf and the track of the old Penydarren Tramroad in a fine sweeping curve of six arches across one of the most attractive stretches of the valley.

[7] Victoria Terrace, (by Hansom and E. Welch, 1835), Beaumaris, is a worthy exception. Three storeys high and grand in scale it has a projecting centre block embellished with niched pilasters and a wide pediment.

[8] One of these houses was Monachty (c.1808), built for the Rev. Alban Jones Gwynne, the founder of Aberaeron. Gwynne inherited money in 1805 and then proceeded to obtain an Act of Parliament in 1807 to build piers and provide shipping facilities.

[9] For many years this village was known as Butetown. The original name was revived in 1973.

[10] Thomas Nicholas: *Annals and Antiquities of the Counties and Families of Wales,* (vol. II, p. 805), 1872.

[11] Swansea and Tenby had been fashionable watering places at the beginning of the nineteenth century, but they were not planned as resorts. Both towns have interesting buildings dating from this period. The Public Baths (now Laston House) at Tenby was erected for Sir William Paxton in 1811 (to designs by S. P. Cockerell) to take advantage of the current vogue for sea bathing. The Assembly Rooms at Swansea (designed by William Jernegan, c.1810), were built on the sea front near the mouth of the Tawe; the building is now completely surrounded by later development.

58. Cwm Ystradllyn Slate Mill, Dolbenmaen,
    Gwynedd. Built 1855.
59. Lime Kilns, Llandybie, Dyfed. R. K.
    Penson, c.1850.

60. Boiler Factory, Queensferry, Clwyd. H. B. Creswell, 1901.
61. Pontypridd Bridge, Glamorgan. William Edwards, 1756.

62. Pont Cysyllte, Ruabon, Clwyd. Thomas Telford, 1794-1805.

63. Pont y Borth, Menai Bridge, Gwynedd. Thomas Telford, 1819-26.

64.   Transporter Bridge, Newport, Gwent,
      F. Arnodin, 1902-6

65.   Transporter Bridge, Newport, Gwent.
      Detail.

66. Market Hall and Square, Tremadoc,
     Gwynedd. Built between 1800 and 1811.
67. Cottage Ornee, Marford, Clwyd. Typical
     cottage, built c.1805.
68. Concrete Farmhouse, Tregynnon, Powys.
     Built c.1870.

Chapter 9 Chapel and Church in the Eighteenth and Nineteenth Centuries

Capeli Cymru

Within two centuries of the Act of Union, the Church in Wales — now Anglican, ruled by absentee English bishops and organised from Canterbury — was ailing and dispirited. Certain native clerics flashed like meteors through this spiritual gloom; Griffith Jones of Llanddowror (the great pioneer of Welsh education), Daniel Rowland (the most eloquent and popular of Welsh preachers), William Williams Pantycelyn (celebrated hymn-writer and poet) and Thomas Charles of Bala (organiser of Sunday Schools). Throughout the second half of the eighteenth century these 'methodists' in the Church attempted to reform official indolence from within, but in 1811 the inevitable schism took place and they began ordaining their own ministers. Thus the 'methodists' became Methodist — Welsh Nonconformist — and seceded from the Church.

The earliest nonconformist chapels, however, date from as far back as the seventeenth century for the first appearance of nonconformism in Wales is generally associated with the historic meeting held at Llanfaches, Gwent, in 1639 when William Wroth organised his followers into a Puritan church. Yet even before this there seems to have been a *tŷ-cwrdd* (meeting-place) converted from a barn at Blaencannaid near Merthyr Tydfil. With the support of the Commonwealth Parliament the nonconformist movement continued to grow slowly, mainly in the early industrial centres of the south. In 1649 the first Baptist chapel was established at Ilston in the Gower peninsula. After the Restoration of the monarchy in 1660 the movement suffered something of a decline until the passing of the Toleration Act in 1689. Nevertheless, at the time of the Religious Census held in 1669 the Merthyr Tydfil district was estimated to have between 300 and 600 people attending secret conventicles. By the end of the seventeenth century a few other chapels had been established in different parts of Wales. Two of these still survive. The Baptist chapel at Llanwenarth, near Govilon in Gwent, was built in 1695 and enlarged during the mid-eighteenth century. In Powys the Independents erected a *capel* (chapel) at Maes-yr-onen, near Hay-on-Wye, in 1696/7. This was a new building — utterly simple in appearance — attached to the end of an older farmhouse. Despite its simplicity, the striving after symmetry and formality (and perhaps approval) which can be detected in the main elevation — three tall windows centrally placed between two 'pedimented' doorways — heralds the shape of things to come in later chapel designs (fig. 97). Astonishingly, Capel Maes-yr-onen has survived intact complete with its original furniture and remains the oldest unaltered nonconformist meeting-place still in use in Wales.

Throughout the eighteenth century the nonconformist movement continued to gather strength and momentum. In the early part of the century a number of small chapels were erected in the industrial parts of the south-east culminating in 1742 in the erection of Capel Groes Wen, near Caerphilly, the first Calvinistic Methodist chapel in Wales. During the second half of the eighteenth century new chapels, albeit small in size, were being erected in all parts of the country. Some, such as Capel Pen-rhiw[1] at Felindre in Dyffryn Teifi, were simply conversions of farmyard barns (fig. 98). Most appear to have been new buildings, but rarely (except in special cases such as William Edwards's Capel Libanus erected in Morriston in 1782) were they professionally designed. Generally the early chapels seem to have been built to a similar plan as that used at Maes-yr-onen; that is with the pulpit placed in the middle of one of the long walls, either between or facing the twin entrance doorways.

By the end of the eighteenth century probably well over a hundred new chapels had been built in Wales. Many of these were in the industrial south. In the Merthyr Tydfil district alone five *capeli* had been established before 1797 when the first English language chapel was opened there. Almost all of the early chapels were later rebuilt, enlarged or remodelled and only an odd one here and there in the more isolated districts has survived unaltered. Typical of these dissenting forerunners were Capel Pen-rhiw (1777), already mentioned, and Capel Newydd (1769) at Nanhoron in the Llŷn peninsula. The latter edifice is again a barn-like structure with twin entrances, an earthen floor and box pews; it is a simple but singularly moving monument to a past religious fervour. Two of the earliest Quaker meeting-houses have also survived. These are at Dolobran (1700), near Meifod, and at Llandegley (1717), near Llandrindod, both in Powys.

During the nineteenth century the rising tide of Nonconformity displaced Anglicanism as the main religious force in Wales and the *capel* took the place of the church in the lives of the people. This is as true of the agricultural uplands in the north and west as of the mining valleys in the south. In rural villages and mining towns throughout Wales the *capel* became the most important public building, both spiritually and culturally as well as physically.

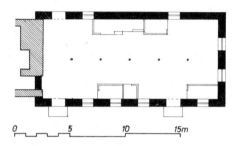

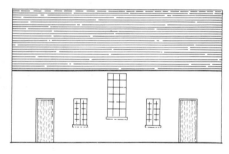

In the south, the rapid urbanisation of the mining valleys was paralleled by an equally rapid growth of Nonconformist *capeli*. There are far more chapels in southern Wales than in any other part of Britain. In the two Rhondda valleys alone, more than a hundred and fifty chapels were built during the nineteenth century, mostly between 1870 and 1900. By 1905 there were over 1,600 chapels in the industrial areas of the south.

The intense activity of the chapel-builders gave rise to a distinctive style of religious architecture. The development of this style may be seen most clearly in the industrial towns where, because of the phenomenal increase in population within a few decades, there was an extreme concentration of chapels. For most of the nineteenth century there were comparatively few English-language chapels in Wales and at first they were designed in the same fashion as the Welsh-language chapels. Later, the development of the English chapels was naturally influenced by the great architectural 'battle of the styles' of England, so that from about the middle of the nineteenth century onwards both neo-Classical and neo-Gothic designs were used. The Welsh-language chapels, more conservative and suspicious of an architecture traditionally associated with the state church, remained true to the 'Classical' tradition until well into the twentieth century. There were a few Welsh 'Gothic' exceptions of course, mainly in the northern coastal resorts, and also an occasional example in places as far afield as Caernarfon (Ebeneser, by John Lloyd in 1826), Croes Goch (1858) near St. David's and Cardiff (Pembroke Terrace, by Henry C. Harris in 1877). But these were atypical departures from the norm and cannot be considered as part of the vigorous mainstream of chapel development in Wales.

Although by the mid-century there were many Nonconformist sects in Wales there is a unity of expression, in the design of the chapels, which forms a kind of Celtic vernacular. The majority were not architect-designed, but were generally the products of local builders, often chapel members, who gleaned their ideas from the illustrated catalogues of their period. Thus there is a common character to the *capeli*, although they vary locally in particular details such as window tracery.

From about the middle of the century onwards more and more chapels were designed by professional architects, especially in the larger towns. The best known of these architects are William Gabe, who worked in the Merthyr Tydfil area, Evan Griffiths in Aberdare, John Humphreys in Swansea, George Morgan in Carmarthen and David Jenkins in Llandeilo.

Quite often the designer of the *capel* was the minister himself. In a number of cases the minister had been originally apprenticed as a carpenter or builder and was

97. Capel Maes-yr-onen, Powys: plan and elevation

98. Primitive chapel facade: Pen-rhiw, Dyfed. (1777)

99.   Primitive chapel facade: Croes-y-parc, Glamorgan (early nineteenth century)

100.   Transitional chapel facade: Llanddewi Velfry, Dyfed (1832)

responsible for the design of many chapels other than his own. The most prolific of all the chapel designers was the Rev. William Jones of Capel Jerusalem, Ton Pentre, in the Rhondda. He is reputed to have designed over two hundred chapels during the latter part of the nineteenth century and to have inaugurated a new trend in their architecture by designing large, open chapels. The Rev. Thomas Thomas of Landore, better known as Thomas Glandŵr, was designing a number of chapels at about the same time in the Swansea area as well as further afield in Newcastle Emlyn, Tal-y-Sarn, Buckley and London. Earlier in the century the Rev. Thomas Morris of Llandeilo Fawr was building or enlarging chapels in Cowbridge, Pontypool, Newport and London, while the Rev. Evan Harries was responsible for a large number of Calvinistic Methodist chapels in the Merthyr Tydfil area. Other preacher-designers in southern Wales were the Rev. William Davies and his son the Rev. Aaron Davies in the Rhymni valley and the Rev. William Humphreys in the Swansea valley.

The basic form of the Nonconformist *capel* — a rectangular box with pitched roof and gable ends — is much the same in all parts of Wales. In their essential simplicity the chapels are buildings in a class of their own, eschewing any attempt to imitate the medieval Gothic of a church which was now seen as estranged. There is, though, a strong similarity between the less pretentious chapels and some of the colliery buildings which were built during the same period, probably by the same craftsmen.

The chapel avoided the kind of ceremonial ritual associated with traditional church worship. It did not therefore require an elaborate layout. Instead, it was designed simply as a kind of People's Theatre to cater for the most important element of the service — the *pregeth,* the sermon. Consequently, the *oriel* — the galleries or balconies on three sides — is an important feature in all but the smaller chapels. The basic layout is a reflection of the theological basis of Nonconformity which was intended to reassert the fundamental message of Christianity — *y Gair,* the word. It also provided a neutral background to the hell-fire *hwyl* of the preaching. As a community centre it was the venue of the *seiat* once a week, frequent *cyfarfodydd gweddi* (prayer meetings), the occasional *cymanfa ganu* (singing festival) and, of course, the unique cultural festival of Wales, the *eisteddfod,* scores of which (lasting a day or more) are still held every year in chapels throughout the length and breadth of the land.

Apart from their generally unobtrusive box-like form the facades of chapels display a wide variety of designs ranging from sophisticated simplicity to exotic mannerism. Facadism is, in fact, the basic element in the external appearance of nearly all Welsh chapels apart from the earliest buildings.

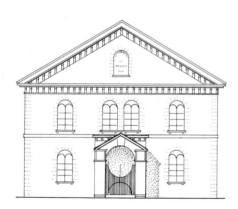

101. Sub-classic chapel facade: Sardis,
Pontypridd (1852)

102. Sub-classic chapel facade: Tabernacl,
Pontypridd (1861)

The established rules of proportion were disregarded and in their place new principles were applied to each building. The gable-ended roof, traditional in Wales and easier to construct, became the dominant feature and culminated in massive pediments over a single-storey or two-storey front. In the centre of the facade most chapels found room for a stone or slate plaque announcing the name of the 'connection' and the date when it was built, or rebuilt (often two or three times to cater for increasing membership), but never the name of the designer or builder. The plaques, with their bold lettering, are of every conceivable shape and size.

The design of the main facade characterises the development of chapel architecture more than any other single feature. There was a continuous development through four main phases, ascending from the primitive barns of the early meeting-houses through to a golden age in chapel design and then descending to the usual debasement associated with the latter years of all architectural styles.

In the earliest, the Primitive, phase the domestic-looking long-wall facade, which had been adopted by the eighteenth-century meeting-houses was continued and the traditional position of the pulpit, in the centre of the long-wall, was retained (fig.99). Windows and doors were arranged symmetrically on either side of the pulpit, with often a pair of tall windows placed above the pulpit. Most of the earliest chapels, such as the Unitarian (1795) Bridgend, and Gellionen (1801) Pontardawe, appear to have been built in this manner although they have now nearly all been replaced by later rebuilding. Bwlchnewydd chapel (1833) near Carmarthen and Capel Cymer (1834) in the Rhondda are typical of many smaller examples built in a similar style in the early part of the nineteenth century. Some *capeli* in the remoter uplands, such as Soar-y-Mynydd (1822) near Tregaron, were built with a house and stable under the same roof. In other chapels, such as Trinity (1829) Defynnog, in the upper Usk valley, the 'primitive' facade was retained externally when the interior was re-orientated to provide a balcony.

In all the later phases the main architectural emphasis is reserved for the gable-end of the chapel which by then had become the main entrance front. In the transition to the Sub-Classic phase the pulpit is still sometimes placed between the doors, on the entrance front, but more often it is at the opposite end (fig.100). Windows are nearly always tall and round-headed and are positioned in a symmetrical relationship to the central door or doors (fig.101). From about 1830 onwards this form became the dominant chapel type. It is unnecessary to mention particular buildings, we have a superfluity of examples. Generally the roof ridge extends to the gable wall and the triangular wall-space is decorated by the name plaque or by a circular window. In two-storey versions the window arrangement varies considerably from a single window above the door to a whole row of windows (fig.102).

The third, or Classic, phase is distinguished by the frequent use of neo-Classical features such as pediments, columns or pilasters, cornices and balustraded parapets (fig. 103). Capel Peniel (1810) Tremadoc, is an exceptionally early and dignified example which appears to have been based on Inigo Jones's design for St. Paul's Church, Covent Garden, although it was no doubt independently inspired by the neo-Grec movement (plate 69). Crane Street Baptist Chapel (J. H. Langdon, 1846) Pontypool, is probably the most unequivocal expression of neo-Grec influence in a Welsh chapel. On the outside there is a bold and very correct Doric portico while inside the only natural lighting is from above in the manner of a Greek temple. Generally the earlier Classic chapels, such as the Congregational (1820) Ruthin, Naval (1834) Pembroke Dock[2], Zion (1841) Merthyr Tydfil, Tabernacle (1850) Bridgend, Zion (1857) Llanelli and Seion (Rev. T. Thomas, 1862) Tal-y-Sarn, have flattish facades with pilasters and a simple pediment or balustraded parapet. Another interesting chapel that stylistically belongs to this period is Cefnywaun (1869) at Deiniolen, Arfon, the main front of which is an exercise in the orchestration of circles: a fine wheel window in the centre flanked by two smaller circular windows and another small circular window in the pediment.

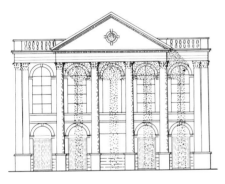

In later chapels of the Classic period the main features are fuller and more emphatic and the whole facade becomes boldly articulated[3] (fig. 104). These chapels were nearly always designed by professional architects like George Morgan whose chapels at Carmarthen (English Baptist, 1872) and Swansea (Mount Pleasant, 1875) have majestic Corinthian porticos (plate 70). Capel Bethesda (by W. W. Gwyther, 1863) at Mold and the Baptist Chapel (1881) at Newtown were also designed in grand style with similar porticos. Capel y Tabernacl (J. Hartland, 1865) Cardiff, has neither column nor pediment, but has a refreshingly unusual appearance due to its original arrangement of staircase towers flanking the entrance hall and the careful Classical detailing of minor elements. A mannerism found in chapels designed by John Humphreys — and peculiar to him — was the use of semi-circular arches, instead of a horizontal architrave, to link columns together over the entrance portico. Humphreys was responsible for a number of rather rich chapels in the Swansea area the best known of which is Morriston's famous Tabernacle (1873), 'the great Cathedral of Welsh Nonconformity'. Another excellent example of Humphreys's work is Zion (1878) at Llanidloes (plate 71).

Even before some of the above chapels were completed the signs of stylistic decadence were showing themselves. During the latter part of the nineteenth century there was a general deterioration in chapel design. The sense of proportion and of style was lost. Elevations, tending to over-decoration and over-statement, became gaudy and heavy. Often the lower line of a pediment was broken by a semi-circular arch and the mannerist result was usually coarse and clumsy.

103. Classic chapel facade: Zion, Llanelli (1857)

104. Classic chapel facade: Mount Pleasant, Swansea (1875)

105. Decadent chapel facade: Tabor, Maesycwmer (1876)

106. Eccentric chapel facade: Heol y Crwys, Cardiff (1899)

Where, however, the device was used with care and understanding it could form the basis of a dramatic facade as with the later chapels of the Rev. Thomas Thomas at Maesteg (Siloh, 1876) and at Maes-y-cwmer (Tabor, 1876) (fig. 105). Where elements of different styles were used in conjunction, as happened in many chapels at the end of the century, the outcome was nearly always disastrous. Even amongst these there were some notable exceptions as, for instance, Capel Salem (1899) Senghennydd (near Caerphilly), where the result of mixing styles is boldly effective (plate 72).

Of all the later chapels, the Calvinistic Methodist Capel Heol y Crwys (J. H. Phillips, 1899) Cardiff, is perhaps the most unusual. A grotesque but nevertheless lovable building with *Art Nouveau* undertones (influenced by Coates Carter of Penarth and Baillie Scott) it stands like a toy castle in front of a railway terminal (fig. 106). It was, indeed, the end of the line for the neo-Classical tradition in Welsh Nonconformist architecture. Although a few chapels vestigially in this tradition continued to be built in the twentieth century, along with the rare neo-Gothic chapels, none compares in quality with the *capeli* built in the great age of enthusiasm.

Anglican Churches

The State Church, the Church 'of England' in Wales, had for centuries occupied all the ancient sacred places — many of them the sites of Christian cells since the Age of Saints. Despite dwindling congregations and English bishops, and the fact that it was not until 1870 that the special needs and claims of the Welsh Church were officially recognised,[4] there was much rebuilding. Many of the older churches were in an advanced state of dereliction through neglect. Most of the completely new churches, in new parishes, were required to serve the immigrant populations drawn to expanding towns in the industrial areas.

Whereas chapels were mostly designed on neo-Classical lines in the nineteenth century new churches were, by contrast, either neo-Romanesque or neo-Gothic. During the seventeenth and eighteenth centuries there had been very little new church building in Wales and the Renaissance style found in town churches in England had therefore small chance of establishing itself here. In Britain as a whole Gothic architecture had ceased, by the middle of the seventeenth century, to be the prevalent style for churches. Yet a trickle in the Gothic tradition continued in Wales in a few places on the comparatively rare occasions when any new churches were erected.[5] As late as 1706, for instance, a completely new Gothic church with battlemented tower was built at Llanfyllin in Powys. The Gothic details are sparse and weak; there is a mixture of round-headed and pointed windows and the building has an overall plain appearance, but even more significant is the fact that it is built entirely of red brick instead of stone. Llanfyllin church represents the watershed between the old and the new; the last survival in the long line of Gothic tradition and at the same time the first of the new 'Georgian' churches in Wales. Welsh 'Georgian' churches were nevertheless few and far between and the Renaissance-derived style which was used without question in domestic work and other public buildings never really caught on for ecclesiastical work. True, a part of the cathedral at Llandaf had been rebuilt in the early eighteenth century in a Classical manner, but the building was never completed and was, moreover, disliked by contemporary critics. St. Mary's Monmouth, was also partly rebuilt about the same time (1737), in a similar style; it lasted somewhat longer, until 1883. In the north a few more Late Renaissance churches were built, notably at Bangor Is-coed (Richard Trubshaw, 1726), at Dolgellau (1716), at Worthenbury (Richard Trubshaw, 1736-9) and at Amlwch (1800). Of these only Eglwys Fair at Dolgellau, with its unusual timber columns and ceiling and St. Deiniol at Worthenbury, with its red brick walls and stone dressings, have survived without major alteration. These were exceptions, mainly confined it should be noted, to the eastern borderlands.

When church building resumed in earnest during the first half of the nineteenth century, it continued in a revived tradition of medieval church architecture.

Nearly all the nineteenth-century churches were designed by professional architects. In Glamorgan and Gwent the most important Anglican church architects were John Prichard, John Norton and G. E. Halliday.[6] In Dyfed the favourite architects were R. K. Penson, R. J. Withers and E. H. Lingen-Barker. In the north they were George Alexander, John Douglas, John Lloyd and John Welch. In mid-Wales the territories of the church architects seem to have been more restricted, with comparatively little overlapping; the most popular were E. B. Ferrey, J. B. Fowler, the Pensons, Sir George Gilbert Scott, Edmund Street and S. W. Williams. Many of these architects worked in more than one part of Wales while English architects of note, other than those already mentioned were sometimes called in to design individual churches. There were also occasional clerical architects such as the Rev. W. E. Jelf and the Rev. J. L. Petit, who together in the 1860's built St. Philip in the grand setting of the Mawddach valley, at Caerdeon not far from Barmouth, on the model of an Alpine village church.

The early Revival buildings of the Established Church, such as Morriston (1795) and Milford Haven (1808), tend to be plain and raw. Few books had, by then, been published on medieval architecture and architects were consequently very unsure of the correct handling of stylistic details. Tremadoc (1806) is one of the earliest in the 'Gothic' style and is surprisingly well handled, although the stumpy tower and spire are far less convincing. Capel Colman at Boncath, near Cardigan, designed by Daniel Davis (1835), is more typical of the unsure touch. Though quite large for such a tiny parish, its cut-price appearance results from a strange mixture of rendered walls, round-headed openings, naive slate pinnacles and clumsy parapets.

In the fast-growing industrial towns of the south, churches in the cheapest 'Romanesque' style were built by the Iron Companies for their workers at Dowlais (1827), Tredegar (J. Jenkins, 1836), and Glyntaf (T. H. Wyatt, 1838). The visually more satisfying church of St. David at Rhymni (Philip Hardwick, 1839-43) should also be mentioned here as being probably the last neo-Classical church to be built in Wales.[7] Romanesque was also the style sometimes favoured for the 'economical' churches built, in the 1830's and 1840's, under the Church Building Act of 1818 with the aid of Parliamentary grants to serve the expanding population. In Wales, the best of these 'Commissioners' Churches' (as they were known), is St. Mary's, Butetown, Cardiff, (John Foster of Liverpool, 1843). At the east end it has two large and powerful towers with pyramidical stone roofs, while between the towers there is an arcade of sham windows fronting onto a small apse. The bold and cavernous interior has massive round columns with Byzantine capitals supporting stark semi-circular arches; these in turn support a flat ceiling. This Cardiff church at least avoided the shallow flimsiness of churches usually associated with the name of the 'Commissioners'.

In the north, John Welch could turn his hand with equal facility to both Romanesque and Gothic styles. His most interesting church, built at Betws-yn-Rhos in 1838, has a charming twin bell-turret capped by steeplets. Betws Garmon church (1841) by George Alexander is again 'Romanesque' and though small has quite a strong Celtic flavour that is completely in keeping with its wild surroundings.

Three churches by Thomas Penson in the Severn valley give a hint of the way in which church architecture was later to develop in the use of contrasting materials and verbose decoration. Llanymynech (1843) and Christ Church Welshpool (1847), heavily 'Romanesque', show rubble stonework outside but elaborate terra-cotta decoration inside. St. David's at Newtown (1847) on the other hand, is Gothic Revival in yellow brick with a strong vertical emphasis. Inside, it has elaborate, but delicate, decorative mouldings to the nave arcade arches.

With the exception of Llandaf, all the Welsh cathedrals were restored by Sir George Gilbert Scott — the most prolific of all Victorian architects — between 1860 and 1875. The most important of these was St. David's where, in 1862, Scott rebuilt

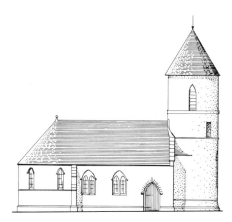

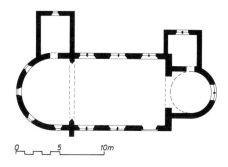

Nash's Romanesque west front with a watered down but stylistically purer, if rather dull, version of the medieval original. The most delightful of Scott's many church restorations in Wales was the rebuilding of Pen-pont (1865) near Brecon. The original round tower was rebuilt and capped by a circular spire; an apsidal chancel to the full width of the church was added at the east end and the building itself covered by a steep roof with a high waggon ceiling (fig. 107).

The cathedral at Llandaf was rebuilt in 'Early Gothic' by the local architect John Prichard between 1843 and 1867.[8] Mostly the work was a conservative and well-executed restoration but at the west end Prichard was inspired to add a splendid tower with a lofty octagonal spire (59.5m high). A similar tower and spire had been designed previously by Prichard at St. John's Newport (1859). Although he was not one of the most original of architects; nearly all his churches are the fruit of true scholarship and are excellently detailed. One of his finest works is St. Catherine's (1882) at Baglan, Glamorgan, a cruciform church with a tall spire and a rich and elaborate interior.

Most of the better churches in the industrial valleys are by John Norton. His Christchurch (1859) at Ebbw Vale, is a really bold structure, built in red sandstone. The tower and spire (added 1884) is unusual in having circular turrets and spirelets at the corners. St. David's (1865) Neath and St. Catherine's (1886) Pontypridd, are both large churches by Norton with black and red polychromatic brick decoration inside. Their spires form prominent landmarks, challenging the engulfing tides of Welsh Nonconformity around them. Another good church (although rather harshly detailed) with a fine spire is St. Elvan's at Aberdare (A. Moseley, 1852).

Polychromatic architecture, or 'constructive colouration', as it was sometimes called, was a popular feature of up-to-date Victorian churches in the latter part of the century. One of the finest examples in Britain of this form of decoration is to be seen at St. Augustine's Church, Penarth, designed by William Butterfield (1866). Inside Butterfield used yellow bathstone and pink sandstone for the columns and arches and raw red brickwork filled with black and white diaper-work for the walls to produce a warm and colourful space, in marked contrast to the sober but well-mannered grey-white limestone exterior (plate 73).

The most striking mid-nineteenth century church in northern Wales is without doubt the so-called Marble Church at Bodelwyddan, near Abergele (plate 74). It was designed by John Gibson (1856), Barry's assistant on London's new Houses of Parliament. From the outside it is extraordinarily neat and tidy, 'Middle-pointed Gothic', perfectly symmetrical from the west end, and dominated by a tall slim tower and beautiful spire (62m high) all built in white limestone and all completely

foreign to the *genius loci*. A nearby building which also deserves mention is G. E. Street's rather harsh, but visually effective, church at Towyn. This was designed in 1873 as part of a group which also contains a school and vicarage. The church is neatly linked to the vicarage by its vestry. Both the strongly patterned roof and gable tower of the church are unusual in this part of Wales.

Although there was a considerable amount of church building at the close of the nineteenth century — when the population of Wales was still rising steeply — there are few churches that have either the conviction or inventiveness of the churches built during the middle years of the century. Two, however, stand out among the many mediocre and uninspired examples. The first is G. F. Bodley and T. Garner's St. German's Church (1884) in Cardiff. In Decorated Gothic style, its graceful interior has a welcome simplicity and soaring spaciousness that gives it a moving and cathedral-like atmosphere emphasised by clusters of tall slender columns supporting a panelled waggon ceiling. The side chapels are roofed with graceful ribbed stone vaulting. This church even has flying buttresses.

The second example, St. Mark's (1896) at Brithdir near Dolgellau, designed by Henry Wilson, makes no attempt to ape past styles (plate 75). The architects intended that it should look 'as though it had sprung out of the soil, instead of being planted on it' and as far as possible, they used indigenous materials — the native granite and local slate — and avoided columns and medieval mouldings. The high roof slopes steeply down almost to head level, echoing the hills, and on the west gable it projects out to shield a massive stone cross. The windows are tall angular slots in the granite wall. Inside, the dimly lit chancel walls are rendered with rough-cast and painted red ochre. The interior is furnished with fittings in an elongated but modulated *Art Nouveau* manner.

As with Nonconformist chapels, the merest hint of *Art Nouveau* seems to have brought original thought in church design almost to a full stop. Except for a singular design by Herbert North for a new church at Caerhun near Conwy — unfortunately never carried out — the style was not developed further in Welsh religious architecture. North had a strong feeling for the vernacular architecture of north-western Wales and in the Caerhun church (1902) he tried to achieve something of the intimate spirit of the older churches in the district.[9] The tall, narrow windows, the porch doorway and the double-nave roof are all local features; in the design they have been combined in an entirely new way to produce a new vernacular inspired both by tradition and *Art Nouveau* attitudes (fig. 108). Had the church been built, it would surely have been a jewel amongst the hills. The nearby Parish Hall, which North also designed (to an unusual and original plan), was, however, built.

The Established Church — fearful and uncertain about the future — was by this time, however, in no mood for a new architecture. The voices of Disestablishment were very loud in the land. In 1914, under the pressure of public opinion, the Church question — which had been one of the main sources of discontent since the Reform Act of 1867 — was finally settled by the Act which disestablished and disendowed the Church of England in Wales.

NOTES TO CHAPTER 9

[1] Capel Pen-rhiw has been re-erected at the Welsh Folk Museum, St. Fagans.

[2] The Naval Chapel at Pembroke Dock is now a motor museum.

[3] This period also produced some of the best chapel interiors, many of which have richly decorated ceilings.

[4] From 1714 to 1870, when Dr. Joshua Hughes was appointed to the See of St. Asaph, none of the bishops elected to any of the Welsh sees had been able to preach in Welsh.

[5] The two Gwydir Chapels at Llanrwst were built in 1633 and 1673 and the Bod Owen Chapel at Llangadwaladr (Anglesey) was built in 1661, all in the Gothic tradition.

[6] Most of the Roman Catholic churches in southern Wales were designed by J. J. Scoles.

[7] Another interesting church, of which only a few crumbling walls now stand, was the octagonal chapel-of-ease built in 1803 by the Crawshays at Georgetown, Merthyr Tydfil.

[8] John Prichard (1817-86) was appointed Diocesan Architect in 1847 and was responsible for the restoration and building of many churches throughout the diocese. He was buried in the churchyard at Llandaf and a brass plate inside the cathedral is inscribed "In Memory of a Great Architect, John Prichard, Restorer of this Cathedral . . .' Most of Prichard's churches were built in Glamorgan. Occasionally he was employed further afield such as for the church at Penegoes (1877) near Machynlleth.

[9] In 1924 North (together with Harold Hughes) wrote *The Old Churches of Snowdonia*, a classic study of the local churches.

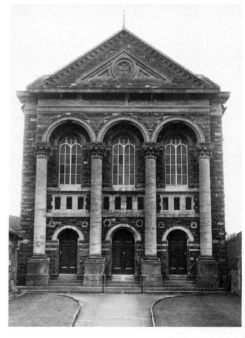

69. Capel Peniel, Tremadoc, Gwynedd. Built 1810.
70. English Baptist Chapel, Carmarthen, Dyfed. George Morgan, 1872.
71. Capel Zion, Llanidloes, Powys. John Humphreys, 1878.

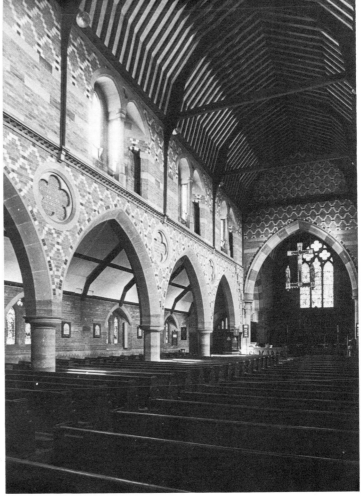

72. Capel Salem, Senghennydd, Glamorgan.
    Built 1899.

73. St. Augustine's Church, Penarth,
    Glamorgan. Interior. William Butterfield,
    1866.

74. 'Marble Church', Bodelwyddan, Clwyd.
John Gibson, 1856.
75. St. Mark's Church, Brithdir, Gwynedd.
Henry Wilson, 1896.

Chapter10 **NineteenthCentury Historicism**

Castellated Mansions

In the early part of the nineteenth century revived medieval styles took on a new lease of life in the castellated mansions of the great estate owners and the newly rich industrialists. These vast houses were built to impress. They implied a pedigree, even if none existed. They also represented the attainment of the romantic ideal, and in this their picturesque outlines were admirably suited to the often wild and beautiful surroundings in which they were set.

The pattern which had been started by Nash at Aberystwyth and at Kentchurch Court at the end of the eighteenth century was followed in 1809 by Thomas Cundy's 'Gothic' transmutation of Broadlane Hall into Hawarden Castle and was then firmly established by G.A. Busby's Gwrych Castle at Abergele in 1814. Gwrych Castle was a completely new 'fortress' — an imposing structure consisting largely of long battlemented walls and frowning towers (eighteen in all) strung out along a wooded hillside with an eccentric disregard either for cost or for military logic. The tallest tower in the chain, known as the Hesketh Tower, was named after the original owner Lloyd Bamford Hesketh, himself a noted amateur architect who probably collaborated closely with Busby in the design. A long list of genuine and lengendary historical events connected with the locality is inscribed on the entrance gateway in an attempt to give the baronial lair an air of respectable authenticity.

For George Pennant, the inheritor of an extensive and slate-rich estate, Thomas Hopper designed a much more convincing 'Norman fortress' at Penrhyn Castle near Bangor.[1] It was built around the great hall of an earlier 'castle' (designed by Samuel Wyatt, c.1782) which in turn incorporated the remains of a medieval mansion built by the Tudors of Penmynydd in the early fourteenth century (and enlarged by Gwilym ap Gruffydd in the fifteenth century) on the site of the palace of Rhodri Molwynog, the eighth century Prince of Gwynedd.[2] An immense structure by any standard, Hopper's Penrhyn Castle took thirteen years (1827-40) to complete. It was built to a very irregular layout displaying a panoply of rectangular, round and octagonal towers with a monumental 'keep' (based on that of Hedingham in Essex) tagged on at one end (plate 76). The 'Romanesque' detailing is generally very sound, but it is in the general massing and handling of forms that Hopper was at his best and thus where a more picturesque skyline was required, he unashamedly used late medieval crenellations. The interior rooms are vast and elaborately decorated with deeply-cut Norman chevron, billet and double-cone ornament; they are, however, nightmarishly oppressive and most uninviting as places in which to live.

Hopper's other works in Wales at Llanover (in Gwent) and Margam (in Glamorgan) were inspired by the Tudor style. Llanover Court (1828) took almost as long to build as Penrhyn Castle but was unfortunately demolished in 1935. Margam Abbey (built alongside the ruined Cistercian Abbey in 1830) is dominated by a great octagonal tower in the centre. The main part of the house is infinitely varied in appearance, with pinnacles and chimneys of all shapes, bay windows, oriel windows, hooded windows and arched windows, gables, crenellations, buttresses and set-backs, all designed to give the venerable impression of a building which is the fortuitous result of the accumulation of centuries. The irony of Hopper's work is that it should have replaced the enormous residence of the Mansels which, started about 1537, was the genuine result of additions and stylistic alterations over many generations.[3]

In the north-east Chirk Castle was given a neo-Gothic touch between 1835 and 1837 by A.W. Pugin when he replaced part of the east range with a fine suite of rooms. He also re-vamped the entrance hall of the castle with oak-panelled walls, a panelled ceiling and an ornate stone chimneypiece.

The best of the early nineteenth-century castles in the south is Robert Lugar's Cyfarthfa Castle near Merthyr Tydfil, built in 1825 for Wiliam Crawshay, the notorious 'Iron King'. A mixture of 'Norman' and 'Late Gothic', it is not only less overpowering than Penrhyn Castle but is also much inferior in its detailing. Nevertheless, the general massing of the main front is quite spendidly composed on the hillside and gives the building a striking appearance from a distance. Maesllwch Castle (1829), in Powys, also by Lugar, is in similar style, now much reduced in size. Hensol Castle (by Thomas Henry Wyatt, 1835) near Llantrisant, is entirely 'Late Gothic'. Outwardly rather evocative of Cyfarthfa Castle, the impression of medieval authenticity is again spoiled by over-provision of too many large and out of character windows. However, we should remember that pedantic exactitude could not be easily satisfied in the architect's brief. The client wanted a medieval fortress; at the same time he demanded much more light than his ancestors, or his tenant farmers and his iron-workers.

Very few of the great houses were built in the neo-Classical manner during the nineteenth century. Occasionally, as at Plas Newydd in Anglesey (1795-1806), it was a fusion of Classical order and symmetry with Gothic details as though the architects (James Wyatt and Joseph Potter) were unconvinced of what the final outcome ought to be. The best neo-Classical houses date from the early years of the century. At Rug, near Corwen, Lord Newborough rebuilt his mansion in a neo-Grec manner about 1800, probably to designs by Joseph Bromfield.[4] A later extension gave it an odd symmetrical appearance, but originally it was a simple rectangular two-storey block built in light-buff coloured Cefn sandstone. A high portico with four giant Ionic columns masks the main entrance and behind this, on the garden front, there is a projecting semi-circular bay with Ionic half-round columns. The northern extension, added about 1890, continued the proportions of the main building with the addition of another projecting bay on the entrance front and a five-bay Corinthian arcade on the garden front. Far less pleasing to the eye was Lord Newborough's other and larger mansion at Glynllifon, near Caernarfon. Erected in a rather dull and minor-key Palladian style in 1836, with rows and rows of monotonous equal-sized windows, it is now an educational institution of the Gwynedd authority.[5]

A more scholarly building, albeit on a much smaller scale, is Glan Severn (by Joseph Bromfield) at Berriew, near Montgomery. The main facade of the excellent and quite delectable house is reminiscent (in a simplified and more Grecian form) of the Petit Trianon at Versailles, built forty years earlier. It was finished about 1807 but the neat and purely Greek entrance lodge appears not to have been started until the middle of the following year.[6] Perhaps our best example of the neo-Grec movement is Clytha House, Gwent, designed by Edward Haycock and built in 1830 (plate 77). The splendid main front has a notable Ionic portico (semi-circular in plan) framing an entrance which leads into a lofty top-lighted hall containing a cantilevered grand staircase. This was probably the last 'Greek' house in Wales and a worthy swansong of the movement inspired, largely, by the arrival of the Elgin Marbles in Britain at the beginning of the century.

Pure 'Classical' architecture was altogether too restrained, too intellectual and ascetic, for the grand and fustian tastes of most Victorian empire builders. They wanted something more showy, more extravagant. The seductive châteaux of the French Renaissance — with their high curving, almost Gothic, roofs — were ideal exemplars of pomp. Wynnstay, near Ruabon, was rebuilt for Sir Watkin Williams Wynn in 1861 by Benjamin Ferrey in such a way, although in this building the vertical emphasis of the centre and end bays is too pronounced to look convincing.[7] Kinmel, near Abergele, by W. Eden Nesfield (designed before 1870 but not built until 1871-4) is handled much more confidently and elegantly in pink brick with a light stone trim. Architecturally, it was one of the more important buildings of its time in Britain and greatly influenced Richard Norman Shaw — one of the most successful of Victorian architects in England — and consequently much of late

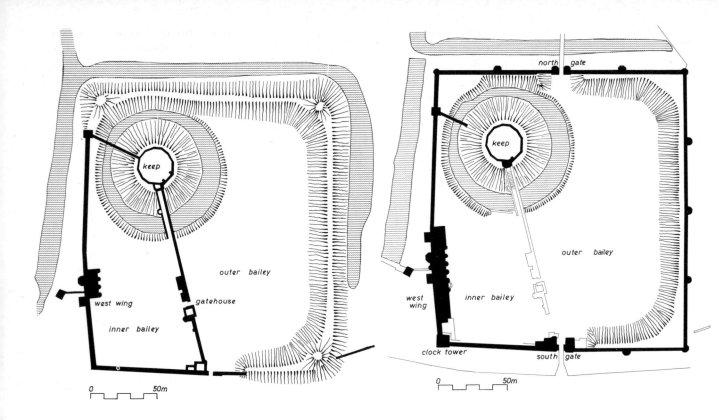

109.   Cardiff Castle, Cardiff: plan during the late
medieval period

110.   Cardiff Castle, Cardiff: plan after
nineteenth-century extension and restoration

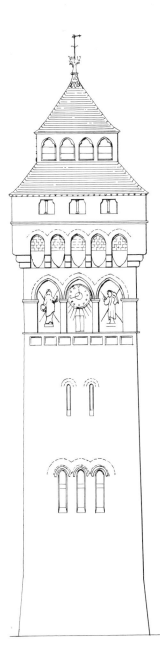

111. Cardiff Castle: elevation of Clock Tower

nineteenth-century domestic work.[8] The symmetrical entrance facade, proud, high-roofed and dominated by a central pavilion, echoes Francois Mansart's Château de Balleroi but the more loosely composed garden facade is reminiscent of the Dutch influenced 'William and Mary' style of late seventeenth-century England. More Dutch than French also is the delightful and richly carved gate-lodge at the entrance to Kinmel Park, also by Nesfield (plate 78).

Another important house, Bodrhyddan Hall (an ancient Welsh seat near Rhuddlan), was remodelled and enlarged by Nesfield in red brick at about the same time (1872-73). More *petite* and prettier than Kinmel, its small-paned sash windows and high pitched roof and coy dormers suggest not only the beginnings of the 'Queen Anne' style but prophesy also the coming of the neo-Georgian style which eventually was to find favour, in our century, as the official British style for municipal housing between the two World Wars.[9]

Most of the residences so far discussed were comparatively small-fry in romantic escapist terms compared with what was yet to come. For sheer ostentatious extravagance and sumptuous theatricality, Cardiff Castle and Castell Coch were easily the most remarkable mansions to be resurrected during the nineteenth century. In their way they were symptomatic of their age and illustrate perfectly one side of the dichotomy that existed between the arts and industry. The division was a result of the traumatic reaction of the wealthier classes to the brutal reality of the Industrial Revolution, the new source of their expanding wealth. Industrialisation represented a rational development of new technological forces; the Arts came to be represented as the opposite — irrational, emotional and romantic. Large sections of the wealthier classes failed utterly to appreciate artistic design and retreated into cosy rooms stuffed with bric-a-brac — those who could afford it withdrew to country mansions, there to escape from the industrial proletariat (whom they also failed to appreciate, except as a means of furthering their fortunes); a dedicated and literate minority retreated as far as possible into the past from the commercialism and misery of their own age. The transformation of Cardiff Castle (started 1867) and Castell Coch (1872) was the ultimate in nostalgic escapism from the industrial squalor that everywhere accompanied the sources of wealth.

Both castles were now partly altered and partly rebuilt in exotic restorations by William Burges in conjunction with his excessively wealthy but highly cultured patron, the Marquess of Bute.

Bute and his architect were both 'hopelessly in love with the Middle Ages' and in these two castles they gave full vent to their passion. The internal restorations of

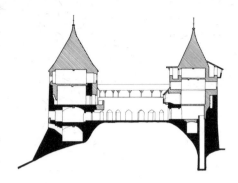

the castles were on such a scale as to completely alter the character of the rooms. They became (in the words of Henry-Russell Hitchcock) 'more like settings for Wagnerian opera than anything the Middle Ages actually created.' At Cardiff — which had been tentatively Gothicized and enlarged by Henry Holland 90 years previously — Burges re-vamped two existing towers and added two new towers at the south-west angle, the result of which may be seen in today's magnificently romantic skyline (plate 79 and figs. 109 to 111). Inside he added new rooms and divided existing rooms, embellishing them with coffered and vaulted ceilings, massive and ornate fireplaces and walls decorated with rich carvings, stained glass, marble and inlaid precious stones.

At Castell Coch (8 kilometres to the north at Tongwynlais) Burges indulged in a similarly sumptuous extravaganza of interior decoration, although externally his restoration there was a serious attempt to reconstruct the castle as it was originally built, complete with working portcullis and drawbridge (fig.112). Perhaps the only questionable interpretation of what the castle originally looked like on the outside is in the flamboyant design of the chimneys and conical roofs over the three round towers (plate 80). In the latter respect Burges had been directly prompted by Viollet-le-Duc's reconstruction of the Château de Pierrefonds. Indirectly, indeed, Burges's whole romantic approach to the restoration of the two Welsh castles was largely inspired by Viollet-le-Duc and his restorations of French castles. Ironically Viollet-le-Duc had himself been inspired by the popularisation in French romance of Arthur the half-legendary Welsh hero figure in the Dark Age campaigns against the Anglo-Saxon invaders of Britain. 'Romantic Military' architecture stemming from Arthurian (as well as Troubadour) attitudes reached its culmination on the Continent in Pierrefonds (started 1857 for Napoleon III) in France, and the even more fantastic Schloss Neuschwanstein (started 1869 for Ludwig II) in the Bavarian Alps. Just a few years later it was transmitted back to Wales in the guise of Cardiff Castle and Castell Coch.

Civic and Commercial Pomp

Some of the most successful works of architecture of the nineteenth century were the public and commercial buildings erected in the more prosperous county towns and in the growing centres of importance. As with chapels, churches and mansions, the outward appearance of these buildings reflected the historic styles of the past. In the earlier part of the century most buildings could be clearly identified with one or other of the historic styles; educational buildings were 'Gothic' or 'Tudor', inspired by the manner of medieval colleges in Oxford and Cambridge, and public buildings were proudly 'Classical' to symbolise the civic virtues. In the latter part of the

112. Castell Coch, Glamorgan: section showing the remains of the medieval castle (in black) and William Burges' restoration (shaded)

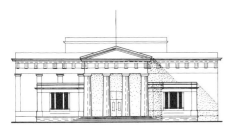

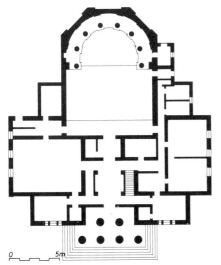

113. County Hall, Brecon, Powys: plan and elevation

century, the range of buildings was far wider and the question of which was the most 'appropriate' style became more difficult to decide. Many — such as libraries, museums, offices, banks, hotels, railway stations and hospitals — were virtually new types of buildings. They required new and more flexible solutions. By then archaeological knowledge had deepened and become more precise, so there was a bewildering range of styles and periods from which to choose. Each had its own adherents who often tended to use it irrespective of the building's function. Thus a hotel might be based on the design of a French Renaissance château or a Venetian Gothic palace, and an office building might be a revival version of Greek, Elizabethan or Flemish.

The Greek Revival was rather a late starter in Britain for already in the late eighteenth century the 'Greek' movement had been popularised in Germany by Winckelmann and Gilly and in France by Nicholas Ledoux. Academically purer than Renaissance architecture and less eclectic than Baroque the 'noble simplicity and quiet grandeur' of the neo-Grec manner made it an ideal vehicle of design for civic and cultural buildings. The rather stately Royal Institution of South Wales (Frederick Long, 1841) at Swansea, with its Ionic portico, is a good example (plate 81) as is also the more impressively sited Shirehall (Wyatt and Brandon, 1842) at Brecon (fig. 113). The earlier Shirehall at Dolgellau, built in 1825 (by John and Edward Haycock), with Doric pilasters of tough local granite and wide and attractive overhanging eaves, is more homespun.

Without question one of the most powerful neo-Grec public buildings not only in Wales but in Britain was the superb Town Hall at Bridgend, Glamorgan, designed by David Vaughan in 1842. Probably the most Ledoux-like building in these islands, its colossal unfluted Doric columns appeared to be influenced by the image of the great temples in the western Greek colonies (e.g. Paestum and Segesta) rather than by the precepts of Athens. The Bridgend Town Hall was ungraciously demolished in 1971, after having been officially scheduled as a building of exceptional architectural interest.

After the mid-century, 'Greek' influence gave way to a more ponderous and Roman-inspired neo-Renaissance style, examples of which can be seen in the Doric portico of John Thomas's County Hall and Assize Court (1862) at Caernarfon, and the Tuscan colonnade of the Guest Memorial Library (now the GKN Recreation Centre) designed by Charles Barry at Dowlais in 1863. Later in the century civic architecture was to employ a greater variety of styles, but almost without exception the result was mundane building. The exception is William Griffiths's fine neo-Jacobean Town Hall at Llanelli (1885), a carefully composed design which out-did anything that any of the other iron and coal towns could offer (plate 82).

Many of these architects were remarkably versatile and were able to produce 'Classical' or 'Medieval' designs to the clients' order. Thus next to his Library at Dowlais, Barry had already built a large school in 'Perpendicular Gothic' (1855). At Swansea, Thomas Taylor designed the old Guildhall (1841) in 'Roman Corinthian' style and the Bishop Gore Grammar School (1852) in 'Tudor' style. St. David's College (1827) Lampeter, is another example of a Classicist, C.R. Cockerell, deigning to design a building in 'Late Gothic' and 'Tudor' this time in the form of a stuccoed quadrangle with small cupola towers at the corners and an arched entrance gateway (fig. 114). Howell's School at Llandaf is a romantically rambling structure in stone and, as a result, has a more convincing medieval collegiate atmosphere. It was built in 1860 to a design by Herbert Williams, which somewhat surprisingly had been based on plans drawn up by Decimus Burton, another Classicist architect.[10] Of all our educational buildings the most unusual and interesting is the rather bizarre University College on the sea front at Aberystwyth (plate 83). It was begun in 1864 by J.P. Seddon as a fantastic neo-Gothic hotel incorporating Nash's house for Uvedale Price. Funds ran out before completion and the building was taken over, in 1872, to realise one of the great unfulfilled dreams of Owain Glyndŵr and became the first college of the University of Wales.[11] Seddon was recalled to make the necessary alterations to the hotel. These were intended to make it an even more extravagant mixture of Gothic styles with pinnacled roofs and castellated towers. In 1885, a large part was burnt down, but the triangular southern wing, terminated by turret and spires, and the richly decorated facade of the northern wing remain — along with the boldly arched entrance and the great round staircase tower at the rear.

In many towns new market halls, often with airy cast-iron interiors and glazed roofs, were built. Some of the best are at Caernarfon (John Lloyd, 1836), Wrexham (T. Penson, 1848) which is neo-Jacobean in style and Cardigan (R. J. Withers, 1859) — stone arched under a 'Gothic' Guildhall. At Monmouth the Market Hall (G.V. Maddox, 1838), was fronted by an elegant arcade of pilasters and inset Doric columns and had a pedimented upper floor.[12] Shops and offices varied enormously in attractiveness and in style. Occasionally plate-glass and iron were used to advantage to produce large areas of window space to display goods, but more often historic styles were ineptly adapted without any relevance or meaning. Of the office buildings the banks were generally the best, for they employed competent architects well versed in the detailing of historic styles, usually 'Classical' but not inevitably so.

Two of the most impressive office blocks are the Pierhead Building, Cardiff and the Port Building, at Barry. The Pierhead Building, designed by Wiliam Frame in 1896 for the Bute Dock Company, is a spiky 'French Gothic' landmark with pinnacled turrets and a castellated tower, all in a florid red brick. The Port Building, designed by A.E. Bell (1898) for the Barry Railway Company, on the other hand is formal, grand, elaborately neo-Classical and faced largely in white Portland stone. Built at the end of the century within two years of each other, a few miles apart, and serving precisely the same function, these two buildings in Wales epitomise the double-faced nature of nineteenth-century architecture throughout the whole of Europe. Here, in the Pierhead Building, Gothicism and Romanticism remind us of churches and castellated mansions, while the Classicism and sober formality of the Port Building remind us of chapels and civic pride. Curiously, they also reflect, in their own ways, the different personalities of the men who promoted the Companies for which they were built.[13] Significantly, the architecture of neither building, however, has anything to do with the industry and engineering that were their reason for being.

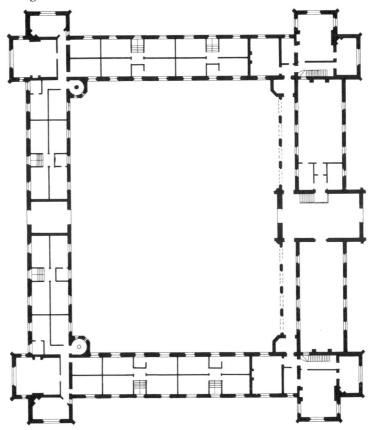

114.   St. David's College, Lampeter, Dyfed: plan at ground floor level

[1] The Pennant family had in the previous century made vast fortunes from the slave-run sugar plantations in Jamaica. In the nineteenth century they made even vaster fortunes from the slate quarries while the quarrymen themselves laboured in appalling conditions. There could be few starker contrasts than that between a quarryman's *bwthyn* on the raw hills and the baronial fortress of the quarry owner at Penrhyn. The small houses and housing conditions of the quarryworkers is discussed in a thesis prepared by D.G. Jones at the Welsh School of Architecture in 1972.

[2] A barrel-vaulted cellar under the present Penrhyn Castle appears to be a fragment of the fourteenth-century dwelling; according to Mr. Douglas Hague this building can 'be regarded as probably the most important home of the Royal Tudors of Penmynydd' in medieval times. (D.B.Hague: 'Penrhyn Castle' in *Transactions of the Caernarvonshire Historical Society*, 1959, p.35).

[3] The older house was demolished in 1793.

[4] A letter (in the National Library of Wales) from the Shrewsbury architect Joseph Bromfield to A.D. Owen refers to stair balusters used at Rug and to the completion of work there in 1801.

[5] Glynllifon was extended in 1890. The most interesting buildings are in the surrounding park. Fort Williamsburg, built between 1761 and 1776, is a roughly rectangular enclosure with angle bastions, a castellated tower and barrack building. The uncompleted Newborough Mausoleum was begun in 1826 as a truncated cone standing on a podium, but the chapel intended to crown the structure was never built.

[6] The house had been commissioned six years earlier. In 1801 Bromfield wrote that he had not finished his work at Rug and was not yet in a position to start designs for a new house for Mr. A.D. Owen.

[7] Ferrey's building was built on the foundations of a house designed in 1789 by James Wyatt, which in turn replaced the house designed by Francis Smith in 1736.

[8] It can be argued that, despite its French overtones, Kinmel was the seed of the stylistic movement, later known as 'Queen Anne', which under Shaw's leadership was to prove so popular with younger architects in England at the end of the century. See Mark Girouard: *The Victorian Country House* (1971). Kinmel was destroyed by fire in 1975.

[9] A slightly earlier precursor of the Georgian revival was Cefn Bryntalch (by G.F. Bodley, 1869), a fine house overlooking the Severn valley near Abermule. See Elisabeth Beazley & Peter Howell: *The Companion Guide to North Wales* (1975), p. 290-1.

[10] Burton was originally commissioned to design the school, but he withdrew after quarreling bitterly with the building committee.

[11] Glyndŵr had, as far back as 1404, proposed two universities, one in the north and the other in the south.

[12] The Market Hall was largely destroyed by a fire in 1963, but the arcade has been successfully retained in a new development.

[13] The 3rd. Marquess of Bute (1847-1900), heir to the Bute Docks and founder of the Bute Dock Company, was a multi-millionaire aristocrat, scholar, High Tory and Roman Catholic convert. David Davies of Llandinam (1818-90), founder of the Barry Railway Company, was a self-made industrialist, Liberal and fervent Calvinistic Methodist.

76. Penrhyn Castle, near Bangor, Gwynedd.
Thomas Hopper, 1827-40.
77. Clytha House, near Raglan, Gwent.
Edward Haycock, 1830.

78. Gate Lodge at Kinmel Park, Abergele,
Clwyd. W. E. Nesfield, c.1870.
79. Cardiff Castle, The West Wing seen from
Bute Park. William Burges, 1867-90.

80. Castell Coch, near Cardiff. William Burges, 1871-89.

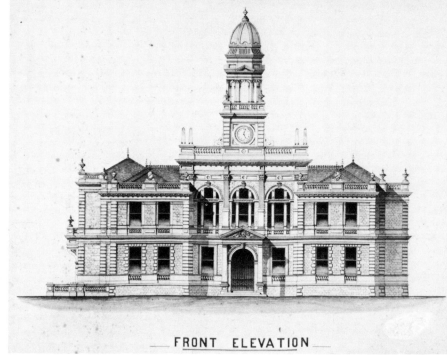

FRONT ELEVATION

81. Royal Institution of South Wales, Swansea, Glamorgan. Frederick Long, 1841.
82. Town Hall, Llanelli, Dyfed. Competition drawing of Front Elevation. William Griffiths, 1885.

83. University College, Aberystwyth, Dyfed.
Watercolour view of proposed building
(as a hotel). J. P. Seddon. Started 1864; reconstructed (after fire) 1885.

84. Mounton House, near Chepstow, Gwent.
H. A. Tipping, c.1910.

Chapter 11 **Early Twentieth Century**

'Arts and Crafts' and the 'Art Nouveau'

One of the chief benefactors of Welsh scholarship in the eighteenth century was Owen Jones (Owain Myfyr), born in Llanfihangel Glyn Myfyr, Clwyd, in 1741. Founder of the Gwyneddigion Society in London, this remarkable man spent many thousands of pounds publishing the work of the Welsh medieval poets, but when he died in 1814 he little knew that his five year old son — also named Owen Jones — was to become one of Britain's most famous architects in Victoria's reign. In 1851 the younger Jones became the Superintendent of the Works of the Great Exhibition in London and in 1852 joint Director of Decoration in Paxton's Crystal Palace[1]. Today he is probably best known for his original use of colour in new ways and for his monumental encyclopaedia *The Grammar of Ornament* published in 1856. He should be mentioned here because — as a forerunner of William Morris — the full significance of Jones's own pioneering in the improvement of wallpaper and textile design and furniture has only recently been recognized[2]. However, if Morris owed some debt to Owen Jones, as well as to others, the debt that our century owes to Morris himself as creator of the 'Arts and Crafts' movement is in no way lessened[3].

William Morris's immediate impact was in the 'decorative arts', including fabrics and furniture design, and not specifically in the field of domestic architecture. Imbued with fervour for good rural craftsmanship, which he associated with the pre-machine days of medieval Britain, there were thus medieval undertones (even Gothic Revival links) in his prints and artefacts. It was Morris's disciples — men such as Charles Voysey and George Walton — who carried the cleansing flame of the 'Arts and Crafts' movement into English and Welsh domestic architecture at the end of the nineteenth century and during the early years of the twentieth century.

While the 'Arts and Crafts' movement campaigned for a revival of good craftsmanship to combat the outpouring of tasteless factory–made goods produced almost everywhere, a genuine craft tradition still existed in many parts of Wales and survived at least until the First World War. The age-old masonry tradition — particularly in Gwynedd — was so powerful (even into the twenties) as to mean the continued use of indigenous materials as a matter of course, and not as the result of an introduced 'Arts and Crafts' style. In this context the style of the architect Herbert L. North in his housing estate (1910) at Llanfairfechan is of particular interest because his aim there was to exploit the character of *genuine* Welsh arts

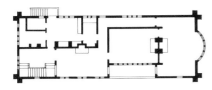

and crafts traditions by the sensitive use of indigenous materials such as the local small thick slates for roofing and also slate for fencing[4]. In his public buildings, e.g. the Hospital at Dolgellau (1928), North showed the same kind of sensitivity and ingenuity as he had done in his earlier domestic work.

In contrast to Herbert North in northern Wales, we have in southern Wales at Tybronna (in the suburbs of Cardiff) an excellent example of the work of Charles Voysey, direct heir to the 19th century 'Arts and Crafts' movement of William Morris. Although Voysey sprang from a Gothic Revival background his mature work was based on vernacular English domestic building and on the use of traditional materials. He introduced a fresh simplicity and functional naturalness which had more in common with the twentieth century than the nineteenth. Tybronna (1903) is his only important work in Wales but the feeling of unaffected charm given to it by the use of battered walls, steep roofs and tall chimneys is typical of Voysey's work at its best (fig. 115). Hundreds of suburban houses built throughout Wales in the early part of the century owe their inspiration to country houses by Voysey such as the one at Cardiff. Indeed, in a vestigial sense the 'Arts and Crafts' design language spoken by him had a profound influence on followers such as T. Alwyn Lloyd and S. Colwyn Foulkes who until the middle of this century were speaking a Welsh dialect of the language at (in the former case) Machynlleth Garden Village, Acton Park (Wrexham), Rhiwbina Garden Village (Cardiff) and Barry Garden Suburb, and (in the latter case) at Abergele, Beaumaris and Llanrwst. Generally, buildings in Wales influenced by the 'Arts and Crafts' movement were small in scale, but Mounton House, near Chepstow, is a splendid exception. Designed by H. Avary Tipping at the beginning of the century it is mansion-like in scale (plate 85). Yet, despite its size and somewhat formal symmetry, it still seems to reflect the vernacular tradition — partly as a result of its construction in stone and half-timbering and partly as a result of its carefully restrained detailing[5]. Another exception is George Walton's Coleg Harlech (1910) in Meirionnydd, an appropriate legacy of the 'Arts and Crafts' movement and the Workers Educational movement both of which were inspired by the teachings of William Morris.

The brief movement known as *Art Nouveau* was mainly concerned with decoration but was also, tenuously, derived from the Gothic Revival. The main features of this phenomenon were attenuated lines and flowing, often bizarre, forms. Buildings designed within the spirit of the "new art", or at least with traces of sinuous *Art Nouveau* decoration, range from a number of public houses to church halls at the turn of the century. One of the earliest examples is Henry Wilson's church at Brithdir (1896), Meirionnydd, mentioned on page 172, but the chief Welsh exponent appears to have been John Coates Carter, at one time in practice with John Prichard of Llandaf. Carter's own 'Red House' at Penarth is vaguely in the

115. Tybronna, Cardiff: plan and elevation

'Arts and Crafts' tradition with a hall-type living room complete with screen and inglenooks, but its main interest springs from the generally *Art Nouveau* flavour of the interior decoration. All Saints' Parish Hall (1906) by Carter, also in Penarth, has a curiously 'expressionist' appearance resulting from the sculptural relationship of its circular tower to the rest of the building, and its odd semi-circular windows and wide overhanging roof eaves. Coates Carter was indeed an enigmatic designer. His work reflects a highly personal and idiosyncratic tendency to search for solutions outside the mainstream of the architectural tides of his day.

While the *Art Nouveau* movement was only a transient episode in the story of Welsh architecture, as elswhere in Britain, revivalism of various sorts continued to be potent over a longer period[6]. To all intents and purposes commercial buildings often became little more than the architect's period claddings disguising the engineer's structural steel frames. Until well into the century, also, churches, schools and local libraries — such as the Carnegie libraries — were generally built in some form of 'Gothic'. Pointed windows and vaulted roofs were not, however, very satisfactory for educational buildings, and at Bangor R. T. Hare used the transitional rectangular Jacobean style for the new University College there in 1911. Nevertheless, this design was still very much in the romantic spirit of the Gothic Revival and the completed building with its soaring castellated central tower rising majestically above the roofs of the adjoining wings, looks (from a distance at least) more like a large monastic cathedral than a college.

Civic Grandeur

As the new century dawned neo-Classicism remained the favourite mode for civic and commercial buildings. Outstanding in this connection is Cardiff's justifiably famous civic centre in Cathays Park — justifiably famous, that is, as a monumental and permanent exhibition of neo-Classical buildings in all their various shades and categories (plate 86). But that is not all, for viewed in a certain light it is much more than that. Indeed, the creation of Cathays Park and its subsequent development to include some of the nation's principal buildings — however un-Welsh they might appear architecturally — is a singular reflection of the growing importance of Càrdiff and to a large extent validates the town's claim to city status and national capital. These buildings have been described elsewhere and it is sufficient here just to mention briefly the more important structures[7]. The vigorously modelled City Hall (by Lanchester, Stewart and Rickards, 1901–4), is a statement of amazing *bravura*. Heavily influenced by the Austrian Baroque, with overtones of French Baroque, it occupies with great self assurance the dominant position in the main front of the civic centre (fig. 116). Next to the City Hall on one side are the Law

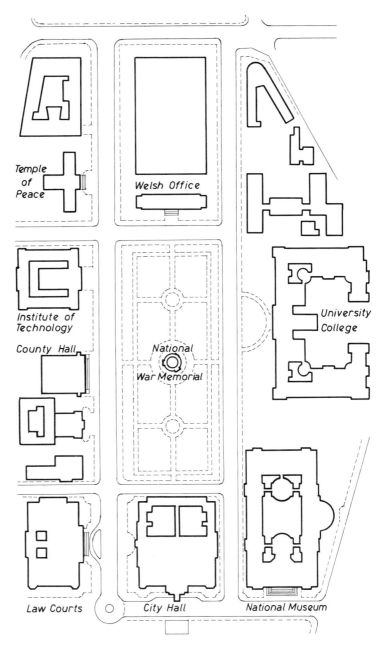

Temple
of
Peace

Welsh Office

Institute of
Technology

County Hall

University
College

National
War Memorial

Law Courts

City Hall

National Museum

116. Cathays Park, Cardiff: plan

195

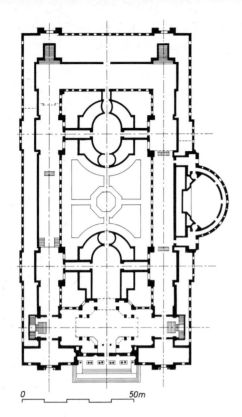

0   50m

Courts (by the same architects, but in a more restrained but closely related manner) and on the other side is the exceptionally fine neo–Grec style National Museum planned by D. Smith and C. Brewer in 1910 to a very formal, but as yet incomplete, axial layout (plate 87 and fig. 117). Behind these buildings are the University College of South Wales (W. D. Caroe, 1903–9) — a somewhat quizical composition in 'Early Renaissance' dress — and the County Hall (Vincent Harris, 1908–12) with its superbly detailed main facade in Greco–Roman style, a building of quite outstanding scholarship (plate 88). The Welsh National War Memorial (Sir J. Ninian Comper, 1924), an elegant temple–like structure with a circular colonnade of Corinthian columns, lies at the heart of the civic centre in the middle of the delightful Alexandra Gardens.

At Aberystwyth the National Library (by S. Greenslade), financed mostly by the voluntary contributions of ordinary Welsh people, was built between 1911 and 1937. As an architectural monument to a nation devoted to literature and poetry it is sadly disappointing and inappropriate in its inharmonious relation to its dramatic site, and unhappy also in its unsympathetic use of materials. These neither reflect the Wales of the past nor the possibilities of the age in which it was built. It has an officious–looking 'front' in white ashlared stone, as if it were facing a street, and nondescript sides and rear in sharply contrasted purple–red bricks. What might have looked reasonable in the close urban setting of a large city appears absurdly incongruous exposed amongst the hills above Aberystwyth[8].

The inter–war period is almost devoid of significantly progressive buildings. An obvious reason for this lacuna is the comparatively small amount of building of any sort that was carried out at this time. There was small chance for architectural innovation or development during an era of crippling economic depression. Advances in architectural thought and building methods were taking place elsewhere (cf. small nations like Finland and Czechoslovakia which were given a new lease of life after the First World War), but these advances found little room for expression in Wales. The very few public buildings that were erected here during this austere period are marked by a sterile watering–down of classical motifs, resulting in cold and stark neo–Classical monuments. Their superficial modernism is reminiscent of the international authoritarian architecture exemplified by Albert Speer's Zeppelinfeld at Nurnberg in Germany and by the arcaded 'Palace of Italian Civilisations' for Mussolini's 'Third Rome'.

This abstract neo–Classicism is typified in Wales by the smooth unemotional lines of Swansea's Guildhall erected in 1934 (plate 89), and by the angular stone columns of the Temple of Peace and Health (1938) in Cardiff's Cathays Park, both designed by Sir Percy Thomas. Ironically the Temple of Peace, intended as a monument to

117. National Museum of Wales, Cardiff: plan at ground level. The northern and central galleries have not been built

the visionary illusion of the League of Nations and to the ideals of Henry Richard (the Welsh "Apostle of Peace"), was opened on the eve of the Second World War by one of the war–bereaved mothers of the First World War.

Of all the later pre–1939 public buildings only the Newport Civic Centre (Cecil Howitt, 1937) has any colour and warmth (plate 90). But this is a 'revivalist' building. The monumentality of its Italianate conception and the symmetry of its plan are fortunately off–set by the staggered forms of the office blocks, with their low–pitched tiled roofs, and also by its hill–side setting. The result is a building which can claim to be the last in a well-defined series stylistically evolved from John Nash's Italianate houses which, in turn, had been inspired by the seventeenth–century paintings of Poussin and Claude Lorrain.

[1] Coincidently another Welsh architect — John Jones of Llanfairtalhaearn (better known as a poet by his bardic name of 'Talhaiarn') — was one of the Superintendents of Works for the original construction of the Crystal Palace in 1851.

[2] As Philip Henderson has pointed out in his book on William Morris 'the exhibition of Victorian and Edwardian decorative arts (of 1952) . . . finally exploded the myth that the Morris movement was alone responsible for the regeneration of Victorian design'. Nikolaus Pevsner has also noted (in *Pioneers of Modern Design)* that William Morris's early designs are crisper, lighter, and more daintily stylized, under some influence no doubt from the teachings . . . of Owen Jones whose *Grammar of Ornament* he possessed'.

[3] William Morris was partly Welsh by descent. On 25th March 1875 he wrote 'I am going . . . to look at my fatherland. We are going to Shrewsbury, and thence . . . to a farm on the very head waters of Severn and Wye, where we are to have ponies and go over the hills and far away . . .'

[4] Herbert North, with Harold Hughes, was the author of *The Old Cottages of Snowdonia* (1908). Note the significance of his words: 'We would draw the reader's attention to the *simplicity* of the old cottages . . . they were planned to be absolutely suitable to the requirements of the time. We must do the same, using to the full the additional real advantages we now possess, but *observing always the same simplicity.* Our building, besides being thoroughly practical, should have in it (the) element of beauty and poetry which gives it an individuality . . . the relations of window to wall, of chimney to roof, of mass to contour — a beauty for which many of the old cottages are so conspicuous. Further than that we cannot go'.

[5] H. A. Tipping was also responsible for some of the houses at Rhiwbina Garden Village, near Cardiff.

[6] Llangoed Castle, near Talgarth, for instance, was designed by Sir Clough Williams-Ellis as late as 1918 in a grand Tudor manner.

[7] See *Cardiff's Civic Centre* (by Edgar L. Chapell, 1946) and Chapter 9 of *Cardiff and the Valleys* (by the author, 1973).

[8] The development of the University campus (by Sir Percy Thomas, and others) at Penglais on the hill behind the National Library has now moderated the incongruity to a certain extent, but the campus had not been envisaged at the time when the National Library was designed. The first scheme (by H. V. Lanchester) for the Penglais campus was prepared in 1932 but was not approved. The first approved scheme for the campus was designed by Sir Percy Thomas in 1935.

85. Cathays Park, Cardiff. Aerial view from
the south.

86. National Museum of Wales, Cardiff. D.
     Smith and C. Brewer, 1910-27.
87. Old Glamorgan County Hall, Cardiff. V.
     Harris and T. A. Moodie, 1912.

88.   Guildhall, Swansea, Glamorgan. Sir Percy
        Thomas, 1934.
89.   Civic Centre, Newport, Gwent. Cecil
        Howitt, 1937.

Appendices

Appendix A: Some stones used locally in buildings

Geological System	Building Stone	Colour of Stone	Buildings where stone used
CAMBRIAN	Caerbwdy Grit	grey-purple	St. David's Cathedral
	Harlech Grit	grey-green	Harlech Castle
	Slate	green-purple	Castell Dolbadarn
INGNEOUS (VOLCANIC)	Felsite	cream-pink	Cricieth Castle
	Upper Tuff	dark-grey	Castell Dolwyddelan and Houses etc. at Dolgellau
	Criggion Granite	green	National School, Welshpool
ORDOVICIAN	Llandeilo Grit	buff	Whitland Abbey
	Preselau Slate	grey-green	Cilgerran Castle
	Aberllefeni Slate	blue-grey	Trawsfynydd Nuclear Power Station
SILURIAN	Grits	grey	Conwy Castle
OLD RED SANDSTONE	Red Sandstone	red-brown	Brecon Cathedral
	Brownstone	red-brown	Gwynfe Church (1899)
	Barbadoes	red-brown	Tintern Abbey
LOWER CARBONIFEROUS (LIMESTONE)	Cwrt yr Ala	white	Cardiff Castle (C19 restoration)
	Halkin Marble	polished	Interior of Halkin Church
	Llysfaen	white	Bodelwyddan Church
	Penmon	light-grey	Beaumaris Castle and Caernarfon Castle
UPPER CARBONIFEROUS	Millstone Grit	buff-brown	Dry-stone walling on edges of coalfield
	Cefn y Fedw Sandstone	buff	Ruabon Church and Wrexham Church
	Gwespyr Sandstone	buff-grey	Talacre Abbey (1824)
	Coal Measures Sandstone	yellowish	Flint Castle and Basingwerk Abbey
	Blue Pennant Sandstone	rusty-brown	Claerwen Dam
TRIASSIC (NEW RED SANDSTONE)	Bunter Sandstone	red	Holt Castle & Ruthin Castle
	Cil-Owen	red	St.Asaph Cathedral
	Radyr Stone	red	St. Michael's College, Llandaf
JURASSIC	Quarella Sandstone	white to pale green	Various churches in Glamorgan
	Sutton Stone	white	Llandaf Cathedral and Neath Abbey
	Blue Lias	grey	Cardiff Castle (Roman Walls)

204

Appendix B: Chronological Table

	Historical Events	Buildings and Architects
Roman	**43AD.** Romans invade Britain **74-78.** Roman conquest of Wales **383.** Roman departure from Wales	**c.80-100.** Caerleon Amphitheatre
Early Christian	**Early 5th cent.** Cunedda conquers N. Wales **5th to 6th cents.** Age of Saints **589(?).** Dewi Sant (St.David) died **616.** Battle of Chester — Wales isolated from rest of Britain **768.** Bangor accepts supremacy of Rome **878.** Rhodri Mawr died **Late 9th cent. or early 10th cent.** St.Davids accepts supremacy of Rome **950.** Hywel Dda died	**c.470.** Dinas Powys and Dinas Emrys **c.500.** Llanilltud Fawr monastery **c.784.** Clawdd Offa (Offa's Dyke) **9th to 11th cents.** Carved stone crosses
Medieval	**1067-87.** Norman invasion of Wales **1094.** Normans repelled from Gwynedd and Dyfed **1188.** Archbishop Baldwin (accompanied by Giraldus Cambrensis) preaches Crusades **1240.** Llywelyn I died **1276-7.** First War of Welsh Independence **1282-3.** Second War of Welsh Independence **1380(?).** Dafydd ap Gwilym died **1400-12.** Third War of Welsh Independence **1416.** Owain Glyndŵr died **1429.** Owain Tudor of Penmynydd m.Catherine widow of Henry V of England **1485.** Accession of Henry Tudor to English throne as Henry VII	**1067.** Chepstow Castle started **1090.** First Norman castle at Cardiff **1140-51.** Hendy-gwyn (Whitland) Abbey **1180-1193.** St. Davids Cathedral **1270-1320.** Tintern Abbey **1277.** Aberystwyth, Flint and Rhuddlan castles started **1283.** Caernarfon Castle started **1327-47.** Bishop's Palace (Great Hall), St.Davids **1430.** Raglan Castle started **1463.** St. Giles Church, Wrexham

	Historical Events	Building and Architects
Tudor	1536. Union of Wales and England; Suppression of Monasteries 1588. Translation of Bible into Welsh	1560-80. St. Fagans Castle 1567. Brick re-introduced by Sir Richard Clough at Bachegraig 1573-1652. Inigo Jones, architect
Renaissance	1646. Harlech and Raglan besieged during First Civil War 1648. Battle of St. Fagans (Second Civil War)	1609. Market Hall, Llanidloes 1636. Pont Fawr, Llanrwst 1670. Tredegar Park, Newport 1696/7. Capel Maes-yr-onen
Eighteenth Century	1743. Establishment of Welsh Calvinistic Methodist Church 1759. Dowlais Ironworks started 1794. *Essay on the Picturesque* by Uvedale Price	1719-89. William Edwards, engineer and architect 1724. Shire Hall, Monmouth 1756. Pont-y-tŷ-pridd, Pontypridd 1752-1835. John Nash, architect 1786-93. Hafod Uchtryd
Nineteenth Century	1804. Penydarren Tramroad 1839-43. Rebecca Riots 1841. Taff Vale Railway 1893. Establishment of University of Wales	1800-11. Tremadog new town 1810-69. John Jones (Talhaiarn), architect 1814. Gwrych Castle 1817-86. John Prichard, architect 1845-50. Britannia Tubular Bridge 1843-67. Llandaf Cathedral rebuilt c.1870. Concrete cottages at Tregynon 1845-85. University College, Abrystwyth
Twentieth Century	1914. Diestablishment of Church of England in Wales 1914-18. First World War 1929-34. Great Depression	1901-04. City Hall, Cardiff 1910. National Museum, Cardiff 1934. Guildhall, Swansea

Appendix C: Glossary of Welsh Architectural and Building terms

Abaty — abbey

Bangor — wattle
Beudy — cow shed
Bwa — arch
Bwthyn — one or two-roomed cottage

Capan — lintel
Capel — chapel
Carnedd — neolithic chamber-tomb (2500BC to 1500BC)
Carreg — stone
Castell — castle (L: castellum)
Cegin — kitchen (L: culina)
Cerrig diddos — crow-steps (on side of chimney or gable to carry water drips down from chimney)
Clas — cloister
Croglen — rood screen
Croglofft — small loft in roof of house
Cromen — dome, vault
Cromlech — burial chamber comprising tall upright stones supporting a massive capstone
Cwpwl — truss
Cwpwl bongam — cruck-truss

Drws — door

Eglwys — church
Eglwys gadeiriol — cathedral

Ffenestr — window (L: fenestra)

Grisiau — stairs (L: gressus = step)

Hafod — summer (farm) house; often of a temporary nature only
Hendref — winter (or main) farmhouse

Lintal — sill or cill (l: limen)
Llan — churchyard
Llech — slate
Llys — court (mansion)

Maen — stone
Maen clo — keystone
Maen hir — standing stone (menhir)
Maerdref — royal village
Melin — mill
Melin wynt — windmill
Mur — wall (L: murus)
Mynachdy — monastery

Nenbren — roof beam, ridge-piece
Neuadd — hall

Oriel — balcony, gallery

Pandy — fulling-mill
Penllawr — passage between upper and lower ends of a long-house
Pen-isaf — lower end of a long-house
Pen-uchaf — upper end of a long-house
Pont — bridge (L: pons)
Porth — doorway or gateway (L: porta)

Taflod — loft
Talcen grisiog — crow-stepped gable
Talcen tŷ — gable-end or pine-end
To — roof (L: tego)
To gwellt — thatch
Tomen — motte (L: tumulus)
Twmpath — motte
Tŵr — tower (L: turris)
Tŷ-clom — clay (or clod) house
Tŷ cyfrifol — gentry house (house of account)
Tyddyn — smallholding or croft
Tŷ-hir — long-house
Tŷ-unnos — one-night house, i.e. house erected between sunset and sunrise

Ysgubor — barn
Ystafell — room (L: stabellum)

Appendix D: Churches with Celtic-Romanesque features

Clwyd

Glyn-y-groes (Valle Crucis) Abbey, early C13

Llansilan, C14

Dyfed

Cellan

Llanbadarn Fawr, c.1200

Llandysul

Ystrad Fflur (Strata Florida) Abbey, 1164

Gwynedd

Aberconwy, 1190

Aberffraw, C12

Bangor, C12

Beddgelert, early C13

Clynnog Fawr, (pre-C15 church)

Cymer, 1199 and C13

Llanaber, early C13

Llanbabo, C12

Llanbeulan, C12

Llandrillo-yn-Rhos

Llaneugad, early C13

Llanfair-yng-Nghornwy

Llanfechell

Llangadwaladr, C12

Llangristiolus, C13

Llanrhwydrys, C12

Penmon, C12 and C13

Tywyn, C12

Ynys Seiriol

Powys

Llan-ddew, C13

Llanfair Caereinion, C13 (largely rebuilt 1868)

Llanfihangel-yng-Ngwynfa, (rebuilt C19)

Meifod

Source: 'The Native Ecclesiastical Architecture of Wales 1100-1285' by C. A. R. Radford, in *Culture and Environment* (1963)

Appendix E: The Greater Monastic Houses in Wales — 1071 to 1536

Note: Monastic order denoted thus,
(A) Augustinian Canons; (B) Benedictine;
(BN) Benedictine Nunnery; (C) Cistercian;
(CN) Cistercian Nunnery; (CL) Cluniac;
(P) Premonstratensian Canons; (T) Tironian.
Dates refer to earliest foundation of House.
Cistercian Houses derived from Whitland
(Hendy-gwyn) are shown in italics.

Clwyd

Basingwerk (C), 1131

Glyn-y-groes (Valle Crucis) (C), 1201

Dyfed

Caldy (T), after 1113

Cardigan (B), c. 1110-15

Carmarthen (A), by 1148

Haverfordwest (A), by 1200

Kidwelly (B), by 1115

Llanllyr (CN), c.1180

Pembroke (B), c. 1098

Pill (T), after 1113

St. Dogmaels (T), by 1120

Talyllychau (Talley) (P), by 1197; originally
Celtic monastery

Whitland (Hendy-gwyn) (C), c.1157

Ystrad Fflur (Strata Florida) (C), 1164

Glamorgan

Ewenni (B), 1141

Margam (C), 1147

Neath (C), 1130

Gwent

Abergavenny (B), 1087-1100

Chepstow (B), by 1071

Grace Dieu (C), 1226

Llantarnam (C), 1179

Llanthony (A), 1103

Malpas (CL), by 1122

Monmouth (B), by 1086

St. Kynemark (P), by 1291; site uncertain —
possibly Risca

Tintern (C), 1131

Usk (BN), 1236

Gwynedd

Aberconwy (C), 1190; transferred to Maenan in
1283

Beddgelert (A), c.1200; originally Celtic
monastery

Cymer (C), 1199

Penmon (A), after 1237; originally Celtic
monastery

Ynys Enlli (Bardsey) (A), 13th cent.; originally
Celtic monastery

Powys

Brecon (B), c.1110

Llanllugan (CN), by 1236

Ystrad Marchell (Strata Marcella) (C), 1170

Source: *The Welsh Church from Conquest to Reformation* by Glanmor Williams (1962)

Appendix F: Medieval Churches with Saddleback Towers

Dyfed

Llannon, Llanelli. (saddleback assumed — tower later reconstructed)

Llanrhian

St. Ishmaels. (saddleback assumed — tower later reconstructed)

Uzmaston

Walton West

Glamorgan

Cadoxton-juxta-Barry

Caerau, Cardiff

Cheriton

Ilston

Lisvane, Cardiff

Llanddewi

Llandow

Llanfrynach

Llangenydd (Llangennith)

Llanmadoc

Llanmihangel

Llansannor

Llantriddyd (Llantrithyd)

Marcross

Michaelston-le-pit, Cardiff

Michaelston-super-Ely, Cardiff

Newton Nottage, Porthcawl

Penarth. (demolished 1865)

Rhossili

Rudry

St. Brides-super-Ely

St. Georges-super-Ely

St. Lythans

Wick

Vaynor (Old Church), Merthyr Tydfil

Gwent

Llanfaches

Penallt

Wolvesnewton

Gwynedd

Llanfor, Bala. (reconstructed 1874)

Powys

Michaelchurch-on-Arrow

Sources:
(1) Author's notes supplemented by
(2) *A History of the Diocese of St. Asaph* (1874) by Rev. D. R. Thomas
(3) 'Notes on the Older Churches in the Four Welsh Dioceses' by Sir Stephen R. Glynne, in *Archaeologia Cambrensis* (various numbers)
(4) *Glamorgan* (1946), and *Monmouthshire* (1953) both by C. J. O. Evans

Appendix G: Medieval Churches with Timber Lantern-belfries

Note: position of lantern-belfry denoted thus, (N) over roof of nave; (T) above tower

Gwent

Llanddewi Rhydderch (T)

Llangiwa (Llangua), (N)

Skenfrith, (T)

Gwynedd

Mallwyd, (T)

Powys

Berriew, (N) demolished 1802

Betws Cedewain, (T)

Bleddfa, (N)

Buttington, (N)

Capel-y-ffin, (N)

Cascob, (T)

Ceri (Kerry), (t)

Discoed, (N) restored 1869

Glascwm, (N)

Llanbrynmair, (N) demolished 1868

Llandinam, (T) church rebuilt 1864

Llandrinio, (N)

Llandysilio, (N) demolished 1867

Llandysul (Llandyssil), (N) demolished 1866 ·

Llanfair Caereinion, (T) demolished 1868

Llanfihangel Helygen, (N)

Llanidloes, (T)

Llansanffraid-ym-Mechain, (N)

Llanwnog, (N) belfry rebuilt by 1866

Manafon, (N)

Newtown, (T)

Norton, (T) restored 1868

Pennant Melangell, (T)

Rhulen, (N)

Tregynon, (N)

Sources:

(1) Author's notes supplemented by

(2) *A History of the Diocese of St. Asaph* (1874) by Rev. D. R. Thomas

(3) *Notes on the Older Churches in the Four Welsh Dioceses* by Sir Stephen R. Glynne, in *Archaeologia Cambrensis* (various numbers)

Appendix H: Early Stone Castles in Wales — 1070 to c.1270

Note: Native castles shown in italics. Dates refer to probable earliest main building period in stone.

Clwyd

Caergwrle, c.1277
Dinas Brân, mid C13
Dyserth, 1241
Ewloe, mid C13
Pentrefoelas, C12
Prestatyn, C12

Dyfed

Cardigan, mid C13
Carew, C13
Carmarthen, early C13
Carreg Cennen, before 1277 (largely rebuilt in C14)
Cilgerran, early C13
Crychedd (Clydey), undated
Dinefwr, late C12 and C13
Dryslwyn, C13
Dyffryn Mawr, undated
Haverfordwest, C13
Llansteffan, late C12 or early C13
Llawhaden, C13
Manorbier, C12
Narberth, mid or late C13
Nevern (Nanhyfer), late C12
Newcastle (Castell Newydd) Emlyn, mid C13
Newport (Trefdraeth), C13
Pembroke, late C12
Tenby, early C13
Upton, mid or late C13
Wiston, late C12
Ystrad Meurig, C12

Glamorgan

Bovehill, (no remains)
Bridgend, late C12

Cardiff, c.1090 (early C13 keep)
Castleton, undated
Coity, late C12
Dinas Powys, C12
Fonmon, C13
Kenfig, C12
Llandough, (no remains)
Llangynwyd, C13
Llanmaes, undated
Llanquian, (no remains)
Llantrisant, mid C13
Morgraig, mid C13
Ogmore, 1120
Oxwich, undated
Penlline, early C12
Penrice, mid C13
Peterston, undated
Port Eynon, (no remains)
St. Fagans, C13
St. Georges, (no remains)
Tal-y-fan, undated
Trecastell (Llanharri), undated
Wenvoe, (no remains)
Weobley, C13
Whitchurch, undated
Wrinstone, (no remains)

Gwent

Abergavenny, C13
Caerleon, mid C13
Caldicot, early C13
Chepstow, c.1070
Dinham, C13
Grosmont, early C13
Langstone, undated
Llanfair Discoed, early or mid C13
Llanfaches, (no remains)
Machen, early C13
Monmouth, C12
Newport, C13 (only C14 remains)
Pencoed, C13

212

Appendix H— *continued*

Penhow, early C13

Skenfrith, early C13

Usk, late C12

White (Llantilio), late C12

Gwynedd

Aber Ia, late C12

Bere, 1221

Carndochan, mid C13

Cricieth, early and mid C13

Deganwy, early and mid C13

Dinas Emrys, late C12 or early C13

Dolbadarn, mid C13

Dolwyddelan, mid C13

Garn Fadryn, late C12

Prysor, C13(?)

Tomen Castell, C12

Powys

Blaen-llyfni, undated

Bleddfa, C12

Boughrood, undated

Brecon, C12

Builth (Buellt), mid C13 (rebuilt 1277)

Bwlch y ddinas, C12

Camlais, mid C13

Clyro, undated

Dolforwyn, C13

Einon Sais, (no remains)

Hyssington, undated

Knuckles, mid C13

Llan-ddew, undated

Llangattwg, (no remains)

Montgomery, C13

Nantcribba, undated

New Radnor, (no remains)

Painscastle, C12

Pencelli, undated

Pont-senni (Sennybridge), C13

Powys (Castell Coch), undated (largely rebuilt late C13)

Tretower, mid C12

Ystradfellte, undated

Source: 'Masonry Castles in Wales and the Marches' by A. H. A. Hogg and D. J. C. King in *Archaeologia Cambrensis* (vols. CXVI and CXIX)

Appendix I: Edwardian and Later Stone Castles — c.1270 to 1430

Clwyd

Caergwrle (Hope), repaired by Edward I c.1282
Chirk, late C13 or early C14
Denbigh, 1282
Flint, built by Edward I 1277
Harwarden, late C13
Holt, late C13 or early C14
Rhuddlan, built by Edward I 1277-82
Rhuthun, 1277

Dyfed

Aberystwyth, built by Edward I 1277-80
Carreg Cennen, largely rebuilt early C14
Dinefwr, repaired by Edward I
Dryslwyn, repaired by Edward I
Kidwelly, late C13
Laugharne, late C13
Llandovery, late C13
Llawhaden, largely rebuilt early C14
Picton, late C13 or early C14
Roch, late C13

Glamorgan

Barry, C14
Caerphilly, 1270 and early C14
Candleston, C14
Coch, late C13 or early C14
Llanbleddian, early C14
Llandaf, early C14
Llwchwr, late C13
Morlais, late C13
Neath, late C13 or early C14
Oystermouth, late C13
Pennard, late C13
Penlle'r Castell, late C13
Penmark, C14
St. Donats, late C13
St. Donats, late C13
Swansea, late C13 or early C14

Gwent

Llangibby, early C14
Llanhilleth, late C13
Raglan, 1430-70
Troggy, early C14

Gwynedd

Beaumaris, built by Edward I 1295-1300
Bere, repaired by Edward I
Caernarfon, built by Edward I 1283-6
Conwy, built by Edward I 1282
Cricieth, repaired by Edward I
Dolwyddelan, repaired by Edward I
Harlech, built by Edward I 1285-90

Powys

Aberedw, 1284
Bronllys, early C14
Builth (Buellt), rebuilt by Edward I 1277
Cefnllys, 1273
Crickhowell, late C13 or early C14
Hay, late C13
Powys, largely rebuilt late C13

Source: 'Masonry Castles in Wales and the Marches' by A. H. A. Hogg and D. J. C. King in *Archaeologia Cabrensis* (vols. CXVI and CXIX)

Appendix J: Medieval Planted Towns in Wales

Note 1: Towns founded by Welsh princes and bishops are shown in italics. Other early urban centres that may have been founded (or fostered) by native princes, etc. are:— Abergele, Hope and Old Denbigh in Clwyd; Cilgerran, St. Clears and Trefilan in Dyfed; Llanfaes (Old Beaumaris), Llanrwst, Nefyn, Pwllheli, Old Caernarfon and Tywyn in Gwynedd; Machynlleth, Presteign and Old Welshpool in Powys.

Note 2: The number of burgage plots in each town (where known) is shown in brackets, after the date of the town's foundation.

Clwyd
Caerwys, 1290
Denbigh, 1283-90 (120); walled late C13
Dyserth, 1248
Flint, 1277; walled 1277
Holt, 1282-1311 (204)
Overton, 1292
Rhuddlan, 1278; embanked defence
Rhuthun, 1282

Dyfed
Abergwili, by 1326 (25)
Aberystwyth, 1277 (157); walled 1277-80
Adpar, 1326 (96)
Cardigan, c.1165 (172); walled late C13 or early C14
Carmarthen, 1109 (281); walled 1233
Dryslwyn, c.1271 (48)
Dinefwr, 1276-80 (11+44)
Haverfordwest, 1110 (360); walled
Kidwelly, 1106-15; walled late C13
Lampeter, 1271-7 (26)
Laugharne, by 1278; walled
Llandeilo, by 1326 (41)
Llandovery, c.1276 (81)
Llanelli, undated
Llawhaden, 1290-92 (174)
Narberth, c.1150
Newcastle Emlyn, 1303 (62)

New Moat, by 1219 (89)
Newport, c.1197 (46)
Pembroke, 1110 (227); walled
Templeton, by 1283
Tenby, early C12 (247); walled mid C13
Wiston, 1135

Glamorgan
Aberafon, c.1147
Bridgend, by 1197
Caerphilly, 1271 (116)
Cardiff, 1081-93 (421); walled in timber by 1184, in stone by 1349
Cowbridge, 1090-1262 (279); walled
Kenfig, 1140-47 (142); embanked defence
Llantrisant, by 1262 (198)
Llwchwr, after 1100
Neath, 1100-30 (128)
Swansea, 1116; walled early C14

Gwent
Abergavenny, 1087-1100 (239); walled
Chepstow, 1072-75 (308); walled 1272-78
Grosmont, 1154-89
Monmouth, 1070-72; walled late C13
Newport, by 1188 (256); walled
Skenfrith, after 1190
Trellech, c.1150 (271)
Usk, by 1131 (300)
Whitecastle, after 1185

Gwynedd
Bala, c.1310 (53)
Beaumaris, 1295 (154); walled
Bere, 1284
Caernarfon, 1283 (63); walled 1283-95
Conwy, 1283 (124); walled 1283-87
Cricieth, 1284 (26)
Deganwy, 1284
Harlech, 1283 (29)
Newborough, 1303

Powys

Brecon, 1087-1100; walled

Builth, 1095-1102

Caersws, undated

Cefnllys, 1240-46 (20)

Dolforwyn, 1273

Hay, c.1237 (184); walled

Knighton, by 1260 (162)

Llanfyllin, c.1293 (30)

Llanidloes, 1280-93 (66); embanked defence

Montgomery, 1223; walled in timber early C13, in stone late C13

New Radnor, 1257 (262); walled

Newtown, 1280-1321

Paincastle, 1231 (50)

Old Radnor, 1095-1100

Rhaeadr, c.1304

Talgarth, by 1309 (73)

Trefnant, 1278

Welshpool, 1247-52 (225)

Source: *New Towns of the Middle Ages* by Maurice Beresford (1967)

Appendix K: Tower-houses in Wales

Clwyd
The Tower, near Mold
Bodidris, Llandegla

Dyfed*
Eastington, Rhoscrowther
Old Rectory, Angle
Priory Farm, Pembroke
Roch Castle, Roch
Upton Castle, near Carew
West Tarr Farm, near Tenby

Glamorgan
Candleston Castle, near Bridgend
Oxwich Castle, Gower
Weobley Castle, Gower

Gwent
Kemys House, near Newport
Penhow Castle, Penhow

Gwynedd*
Pen-y-bryn, Aber (early C17)
Gwydir Castle, Llanrwst

Powys
The Tower, Sgethrog, near Brecon
The Tower, Talgarth

Sources:*Houses in the Welsh Countryside* by Peter Smith (1975) and Volume One of *Caernarvonshire: A Survey and Inventory* by The Royal Commission on Ancient and Historical Monuments in Wales (1956).

*Note:There is literary evidence for other Tower-houses at Barmouth, Meirionnydd (Gwynedd) and Bonville's Castle, near Saundersfoot (Dyfed). Both of these have been demolished.

Appendix L: Select Bibliography

Only works dealing specifically with Wales or works which refer to Welsh buildings in detail are included in this list. For individual buildings before the nineteenth century the most valuable source, apart from the Department of the Environment's official guidebooks, is to be found in articles in *Archaeologia Cambrensis* (published by the Cambrian Archaeological Association). Other articles of interest are published from time to time in the year books of the various county historical societies. For nineteenth-century buildings the most important source is the contemporary numbers of *The Builder*.

1. General

Beazley, E. and Brett, L.	*Shell Guide to North Wales* (London, 1971)
Beazley, E. and Howell, P.	*The Companion Guide to North Wales,* (London, 1975)
Bell, D.	*The Artist in Wales* (London, 1957)
Breconshire Education Committee.	*Atlas Brycheiniog — Breconshire Atlas* (Brecon, 1960
Department of Environment	*Ancient Monuments in Wales* (London, 1973)
Evans, C.J.O.	*Glamorgan* (Cardiff, 1946)
Evans, C.J.O.	*Monmouthshire* (Cardiff, 1953)
Foster, I.Ll. and Alcock, L.	*Culture and Environment* (London, 1963)
Fox, Sir Cyril	*Ancient Monuments — South Wales* (London, 1954)
Harlech, Lord	*Ancient Monuments — North Wales* (London, 1954)
Henderson, Philip	*William Morris: His Life, Work and Friends* (London, 1967)
Hilling, John B.	*Cardiff and the Valleys — Architecture and Townscape* London, (1973)
Hilling, John B.	*Plans and Prospects — Architecture in Wales 1780-1914,* catalogue of Welsh Arts Council Exhibition 1975 (Cardiff, 1975)
Hitchcock, Henry-Russell	*Architecture: Nineteenth and Twentieth Centuries* (Harmondsworth, 3rd. edit. 1969)
Jordon, R.F.	*Victorian Architecture* (Harmondsworth, 1966)
Lewis, W.J.	*Atlas Hanesyddol Ceredigion — Cardiganshire Historical Atlas* (Aberystwyth, 1969)

Moore, D. (edit.) — *The Land of Dyfed in Early Times* (Cardiff, 1954)

Moore, D. (edit.) — *The Irish Sea Province in Archaeology and History* (Cardiff, 1970)

Nash-Williams, V.E. (edit.) — *A Hundred Years of Welsh Archaeology* (Gloucester, 1946)

Pevsner, Nikolaus — *Pioneers of Modern Design* (London, 3rd. edit., 1960)

Rees, Vyvyan — *Shell Guide to Mid-Western Wales* (London, 1971)

Rees, Vyvyan — *Shell Guide to South-West Wales* (London, 1963)

Royal Commission on Ancient and Historical Monuments — *Anglesey* (London, 1937)

Royal Commission on Ancient and Historical Monuments — *Caernarvonshire*, 3 vols. (London, 1956-64)

Thomas, Dewi-Prys. — 'The Architecture of Merioneth' in *Atlas Meirionnydd* (Bala, 1974)

Williams, A.H. — *An Introduction to the History of Wales*, 2 vols. (Cardiff, 1941 and 1948)

Williams, D. — *A History of Modern Wales* (London, 1950)

Verey, David — *Shell Guide to Mid-Wales* (London, 1960

2. Physical Environment

Bowen, E.G. (edit.) — *Wales, a Physical, Historical and Regional Geography* (London, 2nd. edit., 1967)

Davies, Margaret — *Wales in Maps* (Cardiff, 1951)

Emery, F.V. — *The World's Landscapes No. 2 — Wales* (London, 1969)

Thomas, T.M. — *The Mineral Wealth of Wales and its Exploitation* (Edinburgh, 1961)

3. Early Remains

Ashe, Geoffrey (edit.) — *The Quest for Arthur's Britain* London, 1968)

Bowen, E.G. — *The Settlements of the Celtic Saints in Wales* (Cardiff, 2nd. edit., 1956)

Chadwick, N.K. and Dillon, M. — *Celtic Realms* (London, 1967)

Chadwick, N.K. — *The Celts* (London, 1970)

Daniel, G.E. and Foster, I.Ll. — *Prehistoric and Early Wales* (London, 1965)

Fox, Sir Cyril — *The Personality of Britain* (Cardiff, 1959)

Grimes, W.F. — *The Prehistory of Wales* (Cardiff, 1951)

Houlder, C. and Manning, W.H. — *South Wales Regional Archaeology* (London, 1966)

Nash-Williams, V.E.	*Early Christian Monuments of Wales* (Cardiff, 1950)
Watson, K.	*North Wales Regional Archaeology* (London, 1965)
Wheeler, R.E.M.	*Prehistoric and Roman Wales* (Oxford, 1925)

4. **Churches and Chapels**

Clarke, B.F.L.	*Church Builders of the Nineteenth Century* (London, 1938; reprinted Newton Abbot, 1969)
Davies, E.T.	*Religion in the Industrial Revolution in South Wales* (Cardiff, 1965)
Gilyard-Beer, R.	*Abbeys* (London, 1958)
Gresham, Colin A.	*Medieval Stone Carving in North Wales* (Cardiff, 1968)
Hughes, H.	*The Old Churches of Snowdonia* (Bangor, 1924)
King, R.J.	*Handbook to the Welsh Cathedrals* (London, 1887)
Lindley, Kenneth	*Chapels and Meeting Houses* (London, 1969)
Radford, C.A.R.	'The Native Ecclesiastical Architecture in Wales (1100-1285)' in *Culture and Environment* (London, 1963)
Thomas, Rev. D.R.	*A History of the Diocese of St. Asaph* (Oswestry, 1874)
Tyrell-Green, E.	'The Church Architecture of Wales' in *Transactions of the Honourable Society of Cymmrodorian* (1916-7)
Williams, Glanmor	*The Welsh Church from Conquest to Reformation* (Cardiff, 1962)

5. **Castles**

Colvin, H.M. (edit.)	*The History of the King's Works,* vol.I 'The Middle Ages', (London, 1963) n.b. Chapter VI was republished in 1974 as 'The King's Works in Wales 1277-1330'
Hogg, A.H.A. and King, D.J.C.	'Early Castles in Wales and the Marches' in *Archaeologia Cambrensis*, vol. CXI (Cardiff, 1963)
Hogg, A.H.A. and King, D.J.C.	'Masonry Castles in Wales and the Marches' in *Archaeologia Cambrensis*, vol. CXVI (Cardiff, 1967)

Hogg, A.H.A. and King D.J.C.	'Castles in Wales and the Marches — Additions and Corrections' in *Archaeologia Cambrensis,* vol. CXIX (Cardiff, 1970)
Morris, John E.	*The Welsh Wars of Edward I* (Oxford, 1901; reprinted 1968)
Neaverson, E.	*Medieval Castles in North Wales — A Study of sites, water supply and building stones* (Liverpool, 1947)
O'Neil, B.H.St.J.	*Castles* (London, 1960)
Simpson, W.D.	*Castles in England and Wales* (London, 1969)
Taylor, A.J.	*The King's Works in Wales 1277-1330,* (London, 1974)
Wales Tourist Board	*Castles and Historic Places in Wales* (Cardiff, 1975)

6. Houses

Bevan-Evans, M. and Jones, W.H.	*Farmhouse and Cottages in Flintshire* (Hawarden, 1964)
Davis, Terence	*John Nash* (London, 1966)
Fox, Sir Cyril, and Raglan, Lord	*Monmouthshire Houses,* in 3 vols. (Cardiff, 1951, 1953 and 1954)
Gwyndaf, Robin	'Sir Richard Clough of Denbigh' (Part 3) in *Transactions of the Denbighshire Historical Society,* vol. 22 (Denbigh, 1973)
Jones, S.R. and Smith, J.T.	'Breconshire Houses' in *Brycheiniog,* vols. IX, X, XI, XII, XIII and XVI (Brecon, 1963--1972)
Lowe, J.B. and Anderson, D.N.	*Iron Industry Housing Papers,* nos. 1 to 7 (Cardiff, 1971-1974)
Peate, I.C.	*The Welsh House* (Liverpool, 3rd. edit. 1946)
Smith, P.	'Rural Housing in Wales' in *The Agrarian History of England and Wales,* vol. IV, edit. J. Thirsk (Cambridge, 1966)
Smith, P.	*Houses in the Welsh Countryside* (London, 1975

7. Town Planning

Beazley, E.	*Madocks and the Wonder of Wales* (London, 1967)
Bell, Colin and Rose	*City Fathers* (London, 1969)
Beresford, Maurice	*New Towns of the Middle Ages* (London, 1967)
Carter, Harold	*The Towns of Wales* (Cardiff, 1965)
Johns, Ewart	*British Townscapes* (London, 1965)
Jones, J.S.	*Hanes Rhymni a Phontlottyn* (1904)

Lewis, E.H.	*Penodau yn Hanes Aberaeron a'r Cylch* (Llandysul, 1970)
Rees, J.F.	*The Story of Milford* (Cardiff, 1954)

8.   **Engineering and Industrial**

Beckett, D.	*Bridges* (London, 1969)
de Mare, Eric	*Bridges of Britain* (London, 1975)
Jervoise, E.	*The Ancient Bridges of Wales and Western England* (London, 1936)
Jones, D.G.	*Rhamant y Pontydd* (Llandybie, 1969)
Klingender, F.D.	*Art and the Industrial Revolution* (London, 2nd. edit. 1968)
Lloyd, J.	*The Early History of the Old South Wales Ironworks* (London, 1906)
Rees, M.	*Mines, Mills and Furnaces* (London, 1969)
Wilkins, C.	*History of the Iron, Steel and Tinplate Trades of Wales* (Merthyr Tydfil, 1903)

Index of Architects, Designers and Engineers

Index of Architects Engineers and Designers working in Wales and their Buildings

Note: Only buildings mentioned in the text (and notes) are included in this list. Generally, where only one date is shown it refers to the completion of the building. An asterisk before the name of a building indicates that the attribution is not certain. (D) after the name of a building indicates that the building has been demolished.

General Index

DATE

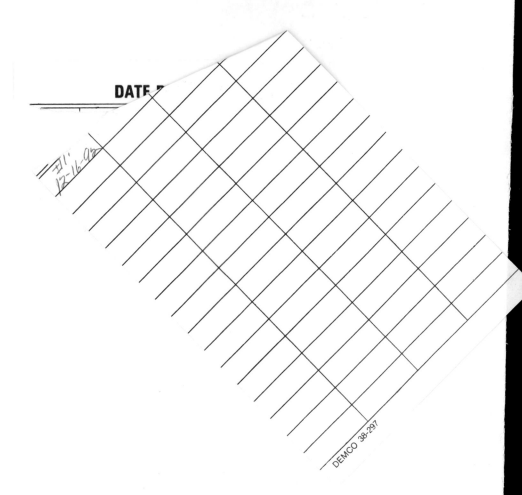

#1
12-16-92

DEMCO 38-297